A
SYSTEM

OF

UNIVERSAL GEOGRAPHY,

FOR

COMMON SCHOOLS:

IN WHICH EUROPE IS DIVIDED ACCORDING TO

THE LATE ACT OF THE

CONGRESS OF VIENNA.

———

" Geography and Chronology are the two Eyes of History."
                                        LORD CHESTERFIELD.

" Geography informs you where events happened, and Chronology at
what time. Without these helps your reading would be a confused
mass, without order, light or perspicuity."—BENNETT.

BY THE REV. NATHANIEL DWIGHT, A. M.

ALBANY:

PRINTED BY WEBSTERS AND SKINNERS,
At their Bookstore, corner of State and Pearl-streets.

1817.

District of Connecticut, ss.

BE IT REMEMBERED, that on the twenty-first day of October, in the fortieth year of the Independence of the United States of America, *Nathaniel Dwight*, of the said district, hath deposited in this office the title of a book, the right whereof he claims as author, in the words following, viz.

A System of Universal Geography, for common schools : in which Europe is divided according to the late Act of the Congress at Vienna. " Geography and Chronology are the two Eyes of History."—LORD CHESTERFIELD.

"Geography informs you where events happened, and Chronology at what time. Without these helps your reading would be a confused mass, without order, light or perspicuity."—BENNETT.

By the Rev. Nathaniel Dwight, A M.

In conformity to the Act of Congress of the United States, entitled " An act for the encouragement of learning, by securing the copies of maps, charts and books, to the authors and proprietors of such copies, during the times therein mentioned."

(Signed) HENRY W. EDWARDS,
Clerk of the district of Connecticut.

A true copy of record, examined and sealed by me,

(Signed) HENRY W. EDWARDS,
Clerk of the district of Connecticut.

PREFACE TO THE FIRST EDITION

DURING an employment of several years
school keeping, I observed that the science of G
graphy was but little attended to in the early ye
of childhood. There are various reasons for
inattention to so important a branch of educat
One of these is, the great expense of procur
books proper for it: an other is, the plan of bo
which have been intended for that purpose is s
as cannot be easily comprehended by children,
remembered by them. I think that both these
jections are obviated in this treatise. The expe
of this book is so small that it may be easily affo
ed, and the form of a catechism admits of its be
much more comprehensive, and more easily und
stood by children, than any of the small Geog
phies which have been heretofore designed for th
It will enable them usefully to improve many ho
of their early years, which for want of someth
of this kind, are entirely lost:—And should the
edition meet with suitable encouragement, the fut
editions will be enlarged and amended, as the
thor finds means and time for the purpose.

Hartford, May 12, 1795.

RECOMMENDATIONS.

WE the subscribers have perused "*A short but comprehensive System of the Geography of the World by way of Question and Answer : principally designed for Children and Common Schools, by* NATHANIEL DWIGHT,"—and are of opinion that the compilation is judicious, and better calculated to impress the facts which it contains on the minds of Children, than any other heretofore published. We with pleasure recommend it to the use of Instructors, as being well calculated to lessen their own labors, and to facilitate the means of improvement in the minds of their young pupils.

> JOHN TRUMBULL,
> NATHAN STRONG,
> ABEL FLINT,
> CHAUNCEY GOODRICH,
> JOHN PORTER,
> ANDREW KINGSBURY,
> JONATHAN BRACE,
> TAPPING REEVE,
> JOHN ALLEN.

Letter to the Editor of the Edition printed in Boston.

ROXBURY, December 4, 1795.

SIR,

HAVING attentively perused Mr. DWIGHT's "*System of the Geography of the World ;*" and also considered most of the works of this kind already extant ; I cannot but view it, for method, style, perspicuity and plainness of expression, as one of the best performances of the kind that I have ever seen. Indeed, the plan of managing the subject by question and answer, which modern experience has sufficiently evinced to be the most useful and impressive upon the young and tender mind, gives it a decided preference, in my opinion, to every other. I wish you success in the publication of it ; and assure you, I shall give it all the aid in my power, to its introduction into the several schools in this town, and its vicinity.

Yours, &c.   THOMAS CLARK.

Mr. David West.

INTRODUCTION.

Q. What is GEOGRAPHY ?

A. It is a description of the EARTH.

Q What is the EARTH ?

A. It is a planet, and one of the bodies of the SOLAR SYSTEM.

Q. Of what bodies does the SOLAR SYSTEM consist ?

A. Of the sun, the planets, the satellites or moons, the asteroids, and the comets.

Q. What is the SUN ?

A. It is the centre of the system, and larger than all the other bodies which compose it. It is the great source of light and warmth and comfort. All the other bodies of the system revolve around it.

Q. Describe the Sun.

A. It is an immense globe, 883,246 miles in diameter, and 1,380,000 times as large as the Earth. It revolves on its axis, from west to east in 25 days, 14 hours and 8 min. Through a telescope, numerous large spots are seen on its surface.

Q. How many PLANETS are there ?

A. *Seven.* Their names, arranged according to their distances from the Sun, and beginning with the nearest, are Mercury, Venus, the Earth, Mars, Jupiter, Saturn and Herschell.

Q. Arrange the planets according to their size.

A. Jupiter is the largest, then Saturn, Herschell, the Earth, Venus, Mars, and Mercury.

Q. What is the axis of a planet ?

A. It is that diameter of a planet, around which it revolves.

Q. How many ROTATIONS have the planets ?

A. Two : a *Diurnal Rotation* on their axes ; and an *Annual Revolution* in their orbits or paths round the Sun. Both are from west to east.

Q. Describe MERCURY.

A. It is 3,224 miles in diameter, and 36,583,825 miles from the Sun. Its bulk is nearly $\frac{1}{15}$th part of the Earth. Its year, or time of annual revolution round the Sun, is 87 days and 23 hours. It rolls in its orbit 110,000 miles in an hour.

Q. Describe VENUS.

A. It is 7,687 miles in diameter, and 68,368,000 miles from the Sun. In bulk it is almost $\frac{8}{9}$ths of the Earth. Its day, or time of rotation on its axis, is 23 hrs. 22 min. ; and its year, or time of annual revolution, 224 days 17 hours. It rolls in its orbit 87,000 miles in an hour. Venus can be seen in the day-time, once in eight years ; and is, to us, the nearest and brightest of the planets.

A 2

Q. Why are Mercury and Venus called INFERIOR PLANETS ?

A. Because their orbits are within the orbit of the Earth. They are always on the same side of the Earth with the Sun, and apparently at no great distance from it. Sometimes they are seen by the help of a telescope, to pass over the face of the Sun : when they appear like small round black spots.

Q. Describe the EARTH.

A. It is 7,928 miles in its mean diameter, and 24,917 in circumference. The axis or shortest diameter, is 7,911 miles ; and the equatorial, or longest diameter, is 7,945 miles. The difference between them is 34 miles. The surface of the Earth contains 197,459,101 square miles ; and the solid globe of the Earth 260,909,292,265 cubical or solid miles. Its day, or time of rotation on its axis, is 24 hours ; and its year, or time of revolution in its orbit, is 365 days, 5 hours, 48 minutes and 48 seconds. Its mean distance from the sun is 94,507,428 miles. It rolls in its orbit 75,222 miles in an hour, which is 140 times faster than a cannon ball.

Q. What is the ATMOSPHERE ?

. A. It is an immense body of air, about 45 miles high, surrounding the earth.

Q. Describe MARS.

A. The diameter of Mars, is 4,189 miles ; and its mean distance from the Sun, is 144,000,023 miles. Its bulk is about $\frac{7}{24}$ths of the Earth. Its day or time of rotation on its axis, is 24 hours, 39 minutes, and 22 seconds long ; and its year, or revolution in its orbit, 1 year, 321 days, 23 hours, and 31 minutes. It moves 50,000 miles an hour in its orbit.

Q. Describe JUPITER.

A. Jupiter, the largest of the planets, is 89,170 miles in diameter, and 491,702,301 miles from the Sun. The length of its day is 9 hours, 55 minutes ; and of its year 11 years, 314 days, 13 hours and 45 minutes. It is about 1,400 times as large as the Earth. It is encircled by faint substances called *belts.* It moves in its orbit about 30,000 miles an hour.

Q. Describe SATURN.

A. Saturn is 79,042 miles in diameter ; and 901,668,908 miles from the Sun. It is about 1000 times as large as the Earth. The length of its day is 10 hours, 16 minutes and 2 seconds ; and of its year, 29 years, 166 days, 15 hours and 25 minutes. It moves about 22,000 miles an hour in its orbit.

Q. What is there remarkable in the appearance of Saturn ?

A. A large *Ring* which encircles it. The outer diameter of this ring is 204,883 miles, and its inner diameter 146,345 ; so that its breadth is 29,269 miles ; and the distance from the inner part of it to the surface of the planet is 33,651 miles.

The thickness of the ring does not probably exceed 1000 miles. The ring has a common axis with the planet, and revolves on it in 10 hours, 32 minutes and 15 seconds.

Q. Describe HERSCHELL.

A. Herschell is 35,112 miles in diameter, and 1,803,534,392 miles from the Sun. It is nearly 90 times as large as the Earth. It rolls 15,000 miles an hour in its orbit. It is not yet determined whether it revolves on its axis. Its year, or the time of its annual revolution is 83 years, 150 days and 18 hours.

Q. Why are Mars, Jupiter, Saturn, and Herschell, called, SUPERIOR PLANETS?

A. Because their orbits are without, or larger than the orbit of the Earth. The Sun is sometimes directly between the Earth and each of the Superior Planets ; but this is never true of an Inferior Planet.

Q. How many SATELLITES are there in the system ?

A. There are 18 : the Earth has 1 : Jupiter 4 : Saturn 7 ; and Herschell 6. They revolve around their primaries ; and in company with them around the Sun.

Q. Describe the Satellites of the Earth.

A. The Earth's satellite, or the Moon, is 2,180 miles in diameter and about $\frac{1}{49}$th part as large as the Earth. Its mean distance from the earth is 239,029 miles. It revolves on its axis in 27 days, 7 hours and 43 minutes ; and in the same time around the Earth. The same side of the Moon is always turned towards the Earth. An eclipse of the Moon takes place when the Earth is directly between it and the Sun ; and an eclipse of the Sun, when the Moon is directly between the Sun and the Earth. By the aid of a telescope, Dr. Herschell has discovered mountains and volcanoes in the Moon.

Q. Describe the ASTEROIDS.

A. They are small celestial bodies, whose orbits are between those of Mars and Jupiter. They are four in number : Vesta 120 miles in diameter ; Ceres 160 ; Pallas 110 ; and Juno 119. They are between 200 and 300 millions of miles from the Sun.

Q. What are the COMETS ?

A. They are bodies moving in very eccentric orbits round the Sun, and are usually followed by a long train of light called a tail. The great comet of 1680, when nearest the Sun, was only 122,000 miles from its surface ; and then moved 880,000 miles in an hour. When farthest it was more than 12,000 million miles from the Sun. The times of only two of them are known, and their number probably will not be ascertained.

Q. Exclusive of the comets, how many bodies are there in the solar system.

A. There are 30; of which eight were known to the antients, viz: the Sun, Mercury, Venus, the Earth, Mars, Jupiter, and Saturn. Jupiter's Moons and five of Saturn's were discovered in the 17th century; the Planet Herschell, his six moons, and two of Saturn's in the 18th; and the four asteriods in the 19th.

Q. What are the FIXED STARS?

A. They are those stars, which always keep at the same apparent distance from each other. They are easily distinguished from the planets by their twinkling. The number visible to the naked eye, throughout the whole firmament, is 3,130. Astronomers have arranged them into groupes, called *Constellations;* the number of which is 90. Their whole number is supposed to be about 75,000,000. The distance of the nearest fixed star is supposed to exceed 5 billions of miles. A cannon ball would not reach the nearest of them in a million of years. It is not now doubted that each one of the fixed stars is a Sun; surrounded by systems of planets; each of which is inhabited by many millions of inhabitants: All these, except the inhabitants of this fallen world, are with the best reason, believed to be virtuous beings. United, they form the immense empire of JEHOVAH.

Q. What is the *Figure* of the Earth?

A. It is a ball or globe.

Q. What is a CIRCLE?

A. It is a plane figure, bounded by a line, which is every where equally distant from the centre. The line which thus bounds it is called the *circumference;* and a strait line, passing through the centre and touching the circumference at each end, is called a *diameter.*

Q. How many kinds of circles are drawn on the surface of the Earth?

A. Two: *Great Circles*, which divide the Earth into equal parts; and *Small Circles*, which divide it into unequal parts.

Q. What are the *Degrees* of a Circle?

A. The circumference of every circle is supposed to be divided into 360 equal parts called degrees; each degree into 60 equal parts called minutes; and each minute into 60 seconds.

Q. What is the EQUATOR?

A. It is the circumference of a great circle passing from E. to W. round the Earth, 90 degrees distant from either pole, and dividing the Earth into northern and southern hemispheres.

Q. What is a MERIDIAN ?

A. It is a great circle cutting the Equator at right angles, and passing through the two poles. The number of meridians is unlimited. Each one divides the earth into eastern and western hemispheres.

Q. What is the HORIZON ?

A. It is a great circle, dividing the Earth into upper and lower hemispheres. Every place has its own horizon, and is 90 degrees distant from it.

Q. What are the TROPICS ?

A. Two small circles parallel with the Equator : one, the *Tropic of Cancer*, is drawn 23° 28′ N. of the Equator ; and the other, the *Tropic of Capricorn*, is drawn at the same distance South of it. The belt between them is called the *Torrid Zone*, and is about 47 degrees broad.

Q. What are the POLAR CIRCLES ?

A. They are two small circles parallel with the Equator : one (the *Arctic Circle*,) drawn 23° 28′ from the north pole ; and the other, the *Antarctic Circle*, drawn at the same distance from the south pole. The belts between the Tropics and Polar Circles are called the *Temperate Zones*, and are each about 43 degrees broad ; the spaces within the Polar Circles are called the *Frigid Zones*.

Q. What is LATITUDE ?

A. It is distance from the Equator measured on a meridian, either north or south. There are 90 degrees of N. latitude, and 90 degrees of S. latitude.

Q. What is LONGITUDE ?

A. It is distance from a meridian, either E. or W. measured on the Equator. There are 180 degrees of East longitude, and as many of West longitude. The longitudes of the following work are measured from the royal observatory at Greenwich, 5 miles east of London.

Q. Why are there not as many degrees of latitude as of longitude ?

A. Longitude is reckoned from a meridian half round the Earth, to the opposite part of the same meridian ; but latitude is reckoned only from the Equator to the poles or a quarter round the Earth.

Q. Wherein do the degrees of longitude and latitude differ?

A. The degrees of latitude are all nearly equal. The degrees of longitude decrease from the equator to the poles. At the poles a degree of longitude is nothing. In latitude 60 it is half what it is on the Equator.

Q. What is the length of a degree of longitude at the Equator and of a degree of latitude every where ?

A. It is 60 geographical miles, or 69½ English miles.

Q. What are Parallels of Latitude ?

A. They are small circles, parallel to the Equator ; and on artificial globes are usually drawn at the distance of every 5 or 10 degrees.

Q. What places are in the same latitude ?

A. Those that are under the same parallel.

Q. What places are in the same longitude ?

A. Those that are under the same meridian.

OF THE EARTH.

Q. What is the number of square miles on the surface of the Earth ?

A. About 197 millions.

Q. How is the Earth divided ?

A. Into *Land* and *Water.*

Q. What is the number of square miles of each ?

A. There are about 45 million square miles of land, and about 152 millions of water.

Q. What are the Divisions of the Land ?

A. The Land is divided into Continents, Peninsulas, Isthmuses, Promontories, Islands and Mountains.

Q. What are the Divisions of the Water ?

A. The Water is divided into Oceans, Seas, Straits, Bays or Gulfs, Lakes and Rivers.

Q. What is a CONTINENT ?

A. It is the largest division of the Land, and is entirely surrounded by water. There are two continents : the *Eastern Continent*, and *America.* The Eastern Continent contains about 27,000,000 square miles ; and America 14,000,000.

Q. What is a PENINSULA ?

A. It is a tract of land surrounded by water, except at one narrow neck, which connects it with another tract. Africa, South America, Scandinavia and Spain, are large peninsulas.

Q. What is an ISTHMUS ?

A. It is a neck of land, connecting a peninsula with the main. The two most remarkable isthmuses are that of Darien, 34 miles wide, uniting North and South America ; and that of Suez, 60 miles wide, uniting Africa and Asia.

Q. What is a PROMONTORY ?

A. It is a broad tract of land running out into the Sea, and terminating in a point called a *Cape.* Hindoston, Corea, Alaska and California, are large promontories.

Q. What is a MOUNTAIN ?

A. It is a tract of land elevated to a great height above the surrounding country. Mountains are usually found in long ranges; but sometimes in single solitary summits. The most considerable ranges are the *Rocky mountains*, the *Cordillera of Mexico*, and the *Andes*, all constituting one range; the *Altaian Mountains*, the *Uralian Mountains*, the *Mountains of the Moon*, the *Range of Mount Atlas* and the *Alps*.

Q. What is an OCEAN?

A. It is the largest division of water; corresponding to a continent. There are five Oceans: the *Pacific*, E. of Asia and New-Holland and W. of America, 10,000 miles wide; the *Atlantic*, E. of America and W. of Europe and Africa, 3,000 miles wide; the *Indian*, E. of Africa, S. of Asia and W. of New-Holland, 3,000 miles wide; the *Northern*, N. of America, Asia and Europe, 3,500 miles wide; and the *Southern*, S. of America, Africa and New-Holland, 7,500 miles wide. They all really form one immense Ocean, embosoming the various divisions of the land.

Q. What is a SEA?

A. A sea is a mass of water surrounded by land except at one narrow pass, connecting it with the ocean or another sea. It corresponds to a *peninsula*. The Mediterranean, 2,000 miles long, is the largest sea in the world, bordering Europe, Asia and Africa. The other large seas are the Baltic, the Black Sea, the Red Sea, and Hudson's Sea.

Q. What is a STRAIT?

A. It is a narrow pass connecting a Sea with the Ocean.— The most noted straits are the Straits of Gibraltar 15 miles wide; and the Straits of Babelmandel 18 miles wide. It corresponds to an *Isthmus*.

What is a BAY or GULF?

A. It is a body of water partly inclosed by the land, and corresponds to a promontory. The most considerable bays are the Gulf of Mexico, Baffin's Bay, the Bay of Biscay, the Arabian Sea and the Bay of Bengal.

Q. What is a LAKE?

A. It is a body of water, usually fresh, entirely surrounded by land, and corresponds to an island. The largest lake in the world is the Caspian, whose waters are salt. It is 650 miles long, and contains 150,000 square miles. The other large lakes are Superior, Michigan, Huron, Slave Lake, and the Aral in Asia.

Q. What is a RIVER?

A. It is a stream of fresh water, originating in numerous springs, and flowing in a narrow channel to the Sea. It corresponds to a range of mountains. The most considerable rivers are the Amazon, Missouri, Niger and Nile, the Kiang and the Hoango.

Q. What is supposed to be the population of the globe ?

A. About 765,000,000. They are all descended from a common origin ; but, owing to difference of climate and mode of life, are endlessly various in their features, stature and complexion. Those of the Frigid Zone are of a yellowish tawny ; the savages of temperate regions are of a red or copper complexion ; the civilized men of the same regions are fair ; those near the tropics are swarthy ; those near the equator are of a dark tawny. Those of Africa are universally darker than the inhabitants of corresponding latitudes elsewhere ; and, near the equator, are of a shining jet black.

Q. What GOVERNMENTS are found on the globe ?

A. Monarchies and Republics.

Q. What RELIGIONS prevail on the globe ?

A. The Christian, Jewish, Mahometan and Heathen.— About 475 millions of mankind are supposed to be heathens ; about 215 millions are called Christians ; about 72 millions Mahometans ; and about 3 millions of Jews. A generation of men lasts about 30 years. Of course, every 30 years, these immense multitudes of our race descend into the grave, and appear before the last tribunal.

Q. What parts of the world are hitherto little known ?

A. The north, the west, and the central parts of N. America ; the middle and the south of S. America ; the great body of Africa ; the north and central parts of Asia ; almost the whole of New-Holland ; and the great islands in its neighbourhood.

Of the EASTERN CONTINENT.

Q. What is the situation of the Eastern continent ?

A. It lies between 77° N. latitude, and 34° 50′ S ; and between 17° 31′ W. and 190° E. or 170° W. Thus, it stretches through 112 degrees of latitude, and through 207 of longitude.

Q. What are its remote limits ?

A. In the North, Cape Taimoura, and in the east, East Cape, both in Asia ; in the South, Cape L'Aguillas, a little farther S. than the Cape of Good Hope, and in the West, Cape Verd, both in Africa.

Q. What is its extent ?

A. The greatest length, from E. Cape in the N. E. to Cape L' Aguillas in the S. W, is about 11,000 miles ; and the breadth from S. E. to N. W. is about 4,500. It contains about 27,000,000 square miles.

Q. What are the divisions of the Eastern Continent ?

A. It is divided into Europe, Asia and Africa.

Q. What is its population?
A. About 730 millions.
Q. What large seas are embosomed by the Eastern Continent?
A. The Mediterranean, having Europe and Asia on the north, Asia on the east, and Africa on the south, is 2000 miles long, and contains 800,000 square miles. The Red Sea 1450 miles long is between Asia and Africa. The Euxine or Black Sea, between Europe and Asia, is 800 miles long and 400 broad. The Baltic, in the N. of Europe, is, from its mouth in a winding direction to its head, about 1350 miles long and 150 broad.

OF EUROPE.

Q. What is the situation of Europe?
A. It lies in the N. W. part of the Eastern Continent, between 36° 6' 30" and 71° 10' north latitude; and between 9° 35' 30" west, and 63° east longitude.
Q. What are the remote limits?
A. North Cape, in Norway, is the most northern; the Rock of Gibraltar, in Spain, is the most southern; the Rock of Lisbon, in Portugal, is the most western; and the mouth of the river Cara, on the Frozen Ocean, the most eastern.
Q. What is the extent of Europe?
A. It is 3300 miles long from N. to S.; and 2500 broad; containing 3,000,000 square miles.
Q. How is Europe bounded?
A. On the N. by the Frozen Ocean; on the E. by Asia; on the S. by the Mediterranean Sea; and on the W. by the Atlantic.
Q. How is Europe divided?
A. Europe is now divided into the following territories; Norway, Sweden, Russia, Denmark, Prussia, Great Britain, the Netherlands, Germany, Austria, France, Switzerland, Spain, Portugal, Italy, and Turkey.
Q. What are the great rivers of Europe?
A. The Wolga, the Danube, and the Rhine.
Q. What are the mountains of Europe?
A. The Uralian, the Carpathian, the Alps, and the Pyrenees.
Q. What religions prevail in Europe?
A. The Christian universally, except in Turkey, which is a Mahometan country, although the majority of its population is Christian. Jews are scattered thinly over every European

B

country. The three great divisions of the Christian are, the Protestant Church, the Catholic Church, and the Greek Church.

Q. What is the population of Europe?

A. It amounts to 179,874,000 ; or, in round numbers, to 180,000,000. Of these, about 90,000,000 are Catholics ; about 37,000,000 of the Greek Church ; about 48,000,000 Protestants ; 2,000,000 Jews ; and 3,000,000 Mahometans.

Q. What *governments* are found in Europe?

A. Russia, Prussia, Denmark, Austria, Spain, Portugal, Naples, and Turkey, are absolute monarchies ; Norway, Sweden, Great Britain, the Netherlands, and France, are limited monarchies ; and Switzerland is a republic.

Q. What are the great *islands* of Europe?

A. In the S. Sicily, Sardinia, and Corsica ; in the W. Great Britain and Ireland ; and in the N. Nova Zembla, and perhaps Spitsbergen and Iceland ; although the two latter are properly American Islands, being much nearer to Greenland than to Norway.

OF THE SWEDISH DOMINIONS.

Q. What countries are under the dominion of the king of Sweden?

A. Norway and Sweden in Europe, constituting together the peninsula of Scandinavia ; and the island of St. Bartholomews in the West Indies.

Q. What is the population of all these territories?

A. About 3,292,000 ; of which 3,262,000, are in Europe.

OF NORWAY.

Q. What is the situation of Norway?

A. It is the N. W. country of Europe, lying between 58° and 71° 10' north latitude ; and between 6 and 27 east longitude. The Atlantic, between Norway and Greenland, is about 375 miles wide ; and the German Ocean between Norway and Scotland is 280.

Q. What is the extent of Norway?

A. It is 1050 miles long from N. to S ; and its greatest breadth is 235 ; but, N. of lat. 64, it is not on an average more than 60. It contains about 125,000 square miles.

Q. How is it bounded?

A On the N. by the Frozen Ocean ; E. by Sweden, from which it is separated by lofty mountains ; S. by the Scaggerac or mouth of the Baltic ; and W. by the Atlantic.

Q How is it divided?

A. Into four governments ; Christiansand, Aggerhuys, Bergen, and Drontheim.

Q. What is the climate?

A. On the southern coast, it is moderate. In the interior, and in the N. it is very severe; but every where healthy.

Q. What is the face of the country?

A. It is chiefly mountainous, and to a great extent incapable of cultivation.

Q. What is the principal river?

A. The Glomme, which runs S. 300 miles, and falls into the Staggerac.

Q. What lake is there in Norway?

A. Lake Mioss, in lat. 63° 30' is 60 miles long and 15 broad.

Q. What mountains are there?

A. The Norwegian range, separates Norway from Sweden, and winds about 1100 miles.

Q. What are the productions?

A. The country is too cold for grain. The pastures are excellent. Cattle and horses are raised in great numbers.— The Norway pine, fir, birch, and oak, are the common forest trees.

Q. What are the animals?

A. The reindeer, elk, bear, wolf, lynx, fox, hare, beaver, and Norwegian mouse: the eagle and falcon.

Q. What are the minerals?

A. The silver mines of Kongsberg are the richest in Europe, and yield annually 54,000l. sterling. Gold is found in small quantities. Copper is abundant.

Q. What is the religion of Norway?

A. The Lutheran. The country is divided into 4 dioceses.

Q. What is the government?

A. Norway is a distinct kingdom, allied to Sweden; but governed by its own laws. The king of Sweden is its king. His representative has the title of viceroy. The power of making laws is vested in the king and the diet. The form of government is a limited monarchy.

Q. What is the population?

A. It amounted in 1802, to 910,074. As the births are to the deaths as 47 to 35, it is now probably about 960,000.

Q. What is the revenue?

A. It is about 700,000 dollars.

Q. What is the military strength?

A. The army consisted in 1802, of 32,053 infantry, and 10,478 cavalry: in all 42,531: besides a well trained militia of 40,000.

Q. What are the manners and customs of the Norwegians?

A. The houses are of wood. Those of the peasants have an opening in the top instead of a chimney. Their food is milk, cheese, salt fish, and oat-bread. They are tall, well made, robust, brave, honest, and hospitable ; yet ferocious and litigious.

Q. What is the language ?

A. It is a dialect of the Gothic. The inhabitants are universally taught to read and write.

Q. What is the capital ?

A. Bergen, on the W. coast, in lat. 60, 23. It has a noble harbour, and 19,000 inhabitants. Christiana, in lat. 59, 7, at the head of the Scaggerac, has 10,000. Drontheim, in 63, 26, has 9000. The other towns are Christiansand, Christiansund, Kongsberg, and Frederickshall.

Q. What is the commerce of Norway ?

A. The exports are fish, lumber, furs, horses, cattle, fish-oil, tallow, butter, copper, hides, marble, millstones, and a few other articles.

Q. What natural curiosity is near the coast of Norway ?

A. The Malstrom, a remarkable whirlpool near the Loffoden isles, in lat. 68° N. Its roar is heard many leagues ; and its force is so great, as to draw in ships at the distance of th ree miles, and swallow them up.

Q. To what kingdom did Norway lately belong ?

A. To Denmark until the year 1813.

Q. How is Norway situated with respect to the other countries of Europe ?

A. It lies W. of Sweden and Russia ; N. of Denmark, Holland, Netherlands, France, Switzerland, and Germany ; N. E. of Spain, Portugal, England, Ireland, and Scotland ; N. W. of Italy, Turkey in Europe, Bohemia, Hungary, Poland, and Prussia.

OF SWEDEN.

Q. What is the situation of Sweden ?

A. It lies in the north of Europe, between 55° 20' and 71° N. latitude ; and between 11° and 30° east longitude. It is 1200 miles long from N. to S. and about 220 broad ; containing about 190,000 square miles.

Q. How is it bounded ?

A. On the W. by the Cattegat and Norway ; on the N. by the Northern Ocean ; on the E. by Russia and the Gulf of Bothnia ; and on the S. by the Baltic. A few years since, Sweden ceded to Russia the extensive country of Finland, E. of the Gulf of Bothnia, and about two-fifths as large as the present kingdom.

Q. What are the divisions ?

A. Sweden is divided into 4 governments ; Gothland, Sweden Proper, Norland and Lapland. These are subdivided into 25 provinces.

Q. What is the climate?

A. It is every where cold. The Baltic is frozen over every winter.

Q. What is the face of the country?

A. It is diversified with numerous lakes and rivers, rocks and vallies, forests and fields.

Q. What are the rivers?

A. The Dahl runs S. E. 260 miles, and falls into the Gulf of Bothnia : also the Clara, the Gotha, and the Motala.

Q. What are the lakes?

A. Lake Wener is 80 miles long and 50 broad. Lake Wetter is 80 by 12. Lake Meler is 60 by 18. Lake Enara in the north is 70 by 30.

Q. What are the mountains?

A. The long chain which divides Sweden from Norway.

Q. What are the forest trees?

A. The Norway pine, the fir, ash, alder, birch, willow, lime, elm, and oak... The Swedish forests are very numerous and extensive.

Q. What are the animals?

A. The bear, lynx, wolf, beaver, otter, and glutton.

Q. What are the minerals?

A. Gold, silver, copper, and iron. The copper mine of Fahlun has been wrought about 1000 years.

Q. What is the religion?

A. The Lutheran. Sweden is divided into 14 dioceses, and 2537 parishes.

Q. What is the government?

A. It is a limited hereditary monarchy. The supreme power is in the diet, which is composed of the king and the states.

Q. What is the population?

A. In 1800, it was 2,347,301. If it has increased as fast since, as it did in the preceding 10 years, it is now (1815) about 2,700,000. Probably it exceeds that amount.

Q. What is the military strength?

A. It consists of 18,424 regulars, and 34,611 national troops : in all 53,035.

Q. What is the naval strength?

A. In 1808, it consisted of 20 ships of the line, 16 frigates, and 22 smaller vessels, in all 58 : besides 200 gallies.

Q. What is the Swedish revenue?

A. It amounted, in 1809, to £6,000,000. In 1807, the national debt amounted to $13,233,632.

Q. What are the manners and customs ?

A. In vivacity and address, the Swedes resemble the French. They are fair, robust, and well formed, hardy and brave. The peasants have been distinguished for their probity and good morals.

Q. What is the state of literature ?

A. Schools are established in every parish. There are two universities : at Upsala and at Lund.

Q. What is the language ?

A. A dialect of the Gothic.

Q. What is the capital ?

A. Stockholm, in lat. 59° 20' 31" N.; and long. 18° 9' 30" E. It is built on an isthmus, between lake Meler and an inlet of the Baltic. Most of the houses are of stone. The harbour is deep, not easy of access, and well defended. The population, in 1800, was 75,517 ; and the number of houses 4137.

Q. What are the other towns ?

A. Carlscrona, in the S. in lat. 56° 11' is the chief road of the royal navy, and has a population of 13,800. Gottenburg, on the Cattegat in 57° 42' N. has a fine harbour, and 13,218 inhabitants, and is a place of extensive trade. Nordkoping, a little S. of Stockholm, has 8629. Upsala, N. of the capital, is a town of great antiquity.

Q. What are the manufactures ?

A. They are of copper, iron, and steel, cloths, hats, watches, sail-cloths, and shipbuilding ; also of wool, silk, and cotton.

Q. What is the state of trade ?

A. The chief exports are iron, timber, pitch, tar, hemp, copper, herrings, and train-oil. The chief imports are corn, tobacco, sugar, coffee, drugs, silk, and wines. In 1781, the exports amounted to 1,368,830l. 13s. 5d. : and the imports to 1,008,392l. 19s. 6½d.—2290 ships entered, and 2485 cleared out.

Q. What islands in the Baltic belong to Sweden ?

A. Oland, 70 miles long by 6, with a population of 8000 ; Gothland, 70 miles by 24, having Wisbay for its capital : and the Isles of Aland in the Gulf of Bothnia, 80 in number ; of which Aland, the largest, is 40 miles by 16, and has 11,260 inhabitants.

OF LAPLAND.

Q. Where is the country called Lapland ?

A. It comprehends the northern parts of Norway and Sweden, and the N. W. of Russia in Europe ; or the country W. of the White Sea, and N. of about lat. 65.

Q. What is the climate ?

A. Almost all the country lies within the Arctic circle, and is very mountainous.

Q. What are the rivers?

A. The Tana, the Kemi, the Torrea, the Halix, the Lulea, the Pelea, and the Skelestea.

Q. What are the lakes?

A. Lake Enara.

Q. What are the mountains?

A. The mountains of Olonetz in the E. and those of Kolen in the W.

Q. What are the trees?

A. The fir, the pine, and the birch.

Q. What are the animals?

A. The reindeer is the most common domestic animal; bears, foxes, martens, and beavers.

Q. What is the religion?

A. The Lapps or Laplanders now profess Christianity. About 100 years since, they were heathens.

Q. What is the population?

A. The whole number of Lapps is estimated at 60,000. They are about 4½ feet high, of a yellowish tawny, with short black hair, dark eyes, large heads, high cheek bones, wide mouths and thick lips. They live partly in huts and partly in tents.

Q. What is the language?

A. The *Laponic*, a distinct and peculiar dialect.

Q. What are the towns?

A. Kola in Russian, and Tornea in Swedish Lapland. The inhabitants manufacture their own domestic utensils.

OF THE RUSSIAN EMPIRE.

Q. What is the situation of the Russian empire?

A. It is in the north of Europe and Asia; lying between 42° and 77° north latitude, and between 21° and 190° east longitude. Russia also claims the western coast of America, as far S. as Portlock harbour, in lat. 59.

Q. What is its extent?

A. Its length, in Europe and Asia, from west to east, is about 5000 miles. Its breadth is about 1750 miles; although, in the widest part, it is not less than 2150. The whole territory contains about 7,500,000 square miles.

Q. How is it bounded?

A. On the N. by the Frozen Ocean; on the E. by Behring's Straits, the Sea of Kamtschatka, Sea of Ochotsk and Channel of Tartary; on the S. by Chinese Tartary, Independent Tartary, Persia, Turkey in Asia, the Black Sea, and

Turkey in Europe; and on the W. by Austria, Prussia, the Baltic, and Sweden.

Q. What extensive territories have been added to the Russian empire.

. A. In Europe, the province of Finland taken from Sweden; and a large tract of Polish territory called the duchy of Warsaw; and in Asia, all that part of Persia, which lay west of the Caspian.

Q. What are the divisions of the Russian empire?

A. It is divided into Russia in Europe, and Asiatic Russia.

Q. What is the population of the whole empire?

A. Without the late additions, from the census of 1796 and the registers of births and deaths kept since that period, it is found to have been in 1808, 41,403,197. If we suppose a proportional increase since that period the number in 1815 will be about 44,300,000. Russia received in Finland a population of 834,828. Including this and the other additions, it must exceed 60 millions..

OF RUSSIA IN EUROPE.

Q. What is the situation of Russia in Europe?

A. It lies between 44 and 70 north latitude, and between 21 and 63 east longitude.

Q. What is the extent?

A. It is 1800 miles long from N. to S. and about 1200 broad: containing 1,500,000 square miles.

Q. How is it bounded?

A. On the N. by the Frozen Ocean; on the E. by Russia in Asia; on the S. by the Black Sea and Turkey; and on the W. by Austria, Prussia, the Baltic and Sweden.

Q. How is it divided?

A. Before the late additions, it was divided into 38 governments.

Q. What is the climate?

A. In the south, it is the fine temperate climate of Italy; and in the north, the wintry climate of Lapland.

Q. What is the face of the country?

. A. Russia is chiefly a plain country. Some of the plains extend several hundred miles.

Q. What is the soil?

A. The middle and south of Russia are generally fertile. The harvests are abundant, although the agriculture is much neglected. Rye is cultivated in the north; wheat in the middle and south; and barley, oats, and millet every where. Rice and maize are attempted. Tobacco, hemp, and flax are abundant. Apples, pears, plums, and cherries are among the fruits.

Q. Describe the river *Wolga ?*

A. It rises in the Valday mountains, in lat. 57, and pursues a S. E. course of 3200 miles, to the N. W. corner of the Caspian.

Q. Describe the *Dneiper ?*

A. It rises north of Smolensk, and runs a southerly course of 1200 miles, to the northern angle of the Black Sea.

Q. Describe the *Don ?*

A. It rises near Donskop, and runs S. E. and S. W. about 800 miles, to the head of the Sea of Azof.

Q. What are the other rivers ?

A. The *Dneister*, the *Dwina*, the *Northern Dwina* and the *Neva*.

Q. What are the lakes ?

A. *Ladoga* lake is 140 miles long from N. to S. and 80 broad. The *Onega* lake is 150 miles long and 50 broad, and N. E. of the Ladoga. Lake *Peipus*, and lake *Seimen*.

Q. What are the mountains ?

A. The Uralian mountains, and the mountains of Olonetz.

Q. What are the forest trees ?

A. The fir, pine, larch, elm, lime, birch, alder, aspen, maple, and sycamore, the oak, poplar, ash, and hornbeam.

Q. What are the animals ?

A. The white bear, the souslik, the wolf, lynx, elk, and the other wild animals of Europe. The Russian horses are often excellent. In the S. cattle and sheep are in astonishing abundance.

Q. What are the minerals ?

A. The metals are found chiefly in Asiatic Russia. The annual value of the gold mines is about 1,200,000 roubles ; of the silver 30,000,000 ; of the copper 2,000,000 ; of the iron 8,000,000. Lead, arsenic, antimony and zinc, are abundant.

Q. What is the religion ?

A. That of the Greek church. It is under the government of the *Sacred Synod*, of which the emperor is president. There were, in 1805, 36 bishoprics, of which 4 are metropolitan ; 26,598 parish churches, chiefly of brick ; 483 cathedrals ; 44,487 of the regular clergy ; 54,239 readers and sacristants ; and 58 spiritual schools.

Q. What is the government ?

A. The monarch has the title of czar, and is absolute. Each province has a governor general, and an executive council.

Q. What is the population ?

A. From the census of 1808, and the registers of births and deaths kept since that period, it is found to have been in 1808, without the late additions, 36,356,028. If we suppose the increase, since to have been proportional, it is now (1815) about 38,900,000, and including the addition from Finland, about 39,800,000. If the duchy of Warsaw be included, it will amount to 41,800,000.

Q. What are the nations occupying Russia in Europe?

A. The *Slavonians* are the body of the population, and occupy the western and southern parts of the kingdom. The Cossacks in the south are Slavonians. The *Finns* are chiefly in the north and northeast, and are divided into 12 tribes.

Q. What is the military strength of Russia?

A. In 1805, it consisted of 659,054 men. There is also a national militia of 612,000. There are no better officers or soldiers than the Russian.

Q. What is the naval strength?

A. The Russian navy in 1805, consisted of 32 ships of the line, 18 frigates, 59 smaller vessels, and 226 galleys, carrying 4428 guns, and manned by 45,769 men.

Q. What is the revenue?

A. In 1809, it amounted to 115,000,000 roubles, and the national debt to 100,000,000.

Q. What are the characteristics of the inhabitants?

A. The Finns are short, have flat faces, deep cheeks, dark grey eyes, thin beards, yellow hair, and sallow complexions. The Slavonians are large, well made, have small eyes, noses and mouths, white teeth, low foreheads, bushy beards, reddish hair, and fair complexions.

Q. What languages are spoken?

A. Various dialects of the Finnic and Slavonian. The Russian, a dialect of the latter, is rich and harmonious, and has 36 letters.

Q. What are the capitals?

A. Petersburgh and Moscow.

Q. Describe Petersburgh?

A. It is built on the Neva, close to its mouth, in 59° 56′ 23″ N. and 30° 25′ 15″ E. The houses are of wood or brick.—— The population, in 1805, amounted to 271,137. The exports as early as 1797, amounted to 32,450,911 roubles.

Q. Describe Moscow?

A. It is on the Moskva, a tributary of the Wolga, in 55° 45′ 45″ N. and 37° 38′ 30″ E; and is 26 miles in circumference. Before the burning of Moscow, in 1812, it contained 300,000 inhabitants of almost all nations. It had 484 churches. A bell in the Kremlin, the great national cathedral, weighs 432,000 lbs.

Q. Describe Cronstadt?

A. It is on the island of Retusari, 20 miles W. of Petersburgh, and has a noble harbour, and a population of 40,000.

Q. What are the other towns?

A. Kiow, on the Dneiper, with 40,000 inhabitants; Riga, at the mouth of the Dwina, with 30,000; Tula, on the Upa, with 30,000; Wilna, on the Willa; and Jareslaw, on the Wolga, each with 20,000.

Q. What are the manufactures?

A. Salt, coarse wines, brandy, potash, salt-petre, dying colours, medicines, tobacco, sail-cloth, cordage, coarse linens and cottons, silks, carpets, hats, leather, glass, wax, powder, and iron, copper and brass utensils.

Q. What is the state of commerce?

A. The exports by water, amount to about 40,000,000 roubles. They are iron, flax, tobacco, hemp, cordage, lumber, soap, tar, hemp-oil, sail-cloth, coarse linens, furs, salt-petre, grain, brandy, and various other articles. An important overland commerce is carried on with China.

OF THE GRAND DUCHY OF WARSAW.

Q. What is the grand duchy of Warsaw?

A. In 1772, Austria, Prussia and Russia, with a profligacy unexampled, except in the annals of the French revolution, agreed to dismember the kingdom of Poland. In that year, their plan was in part accomplished. In 1793, they completed the nefarious project. Since that period, each of these countries has been desolated, their capitals plundered, and that of one of them burnt. The division which fell to Prussia, in 1793, except the territory of Posen, now constitutes the grand duchy of Warsaw. In 1807, it was taken from Prussia and annexed to Saxony; and in 1815, it was taken from Saxony, enlarged by a considerable addition from Gallicia, and annexed to Russia, as a distinct territory, of which the emperor of Russia is king.

Q. What is the situation of this duchy?

A. It has Prussia Proper, N; Silesia, W; Gallicia, S; and Russian Poland, E.

Q. What is the population?

A. Before *Posen* was taken from it, and a part of Gallicia added, it amounted to 2,277,000. Probably it now amounts to 2,000,000.

Q. Who are the inhabitants?

A. *Poles*: a people distinguished for bravery and intelligence; for personal strength and symmetry; and for beauty both of features and expression. No braver or more high spirited nation is known in Europe. They were ruined by the corruption of their nobles, and their deplorable form of government.

Q. What is the capital ?
A. Warsaw, on the Vistula, with a population of 64,421.
Q. What is the government ?
A. The emperor of Russia has not yet decided this question.

OF THE RUSSIAN ISLES.

Q. What islands belong to Russia in Europe ?
A. *Nova Zembla*, and *Kalgueva* ; and near the coast of Greenland, *Spitzbergen*.
Q. Describe Nova Zembla ?
A. Nova Zembla is separated from the continent by the Straits of Weggatz, is between 69° and 77° N. lat. and 52° and 70° E. long. and contains about 125,000 square miles. It is uninhabited. The Russian hunters and whalers resort thither in the summer. It is rocky and destitute of verdure. Reindeer, white bears, and white and blue foxes are found here. Russia claims it. Kalgueva is a much smaller island, a little E. of the mouth of the White Sea.
Q. What is the situation of Spitzbergen ?
A. Spitzbergen is really an American Island, lying only 150 miles E. of Greenland, and 320 from Norway. It is between 76° and 80° 7' N. latitude, and between 9° and 20° E. longitude. It is 300 miles long, and 140 broad. The climate is so severe that the island is rendered uninhabitable. The country is covered chiefly with rocks and mountains of ice. The reindeer and the arctic fox are the only animals. The Dutch whalers visit it every summer.

OF THE DANISH DOMINIONS.

Q. What territories belong to Denmark ?
A. In Europe, the peninsula of Jutland, and the islands in the Baltic, Zealand, Funen, Lapland, Folster, and some others, constituting Denmark Proper ; Iceland, and the Ferro Isles ; and in the West Indies, St. Croix, St. Thomas, and St. John. In North America, the large peninsula or island of Greenland.
Q. What large territory has Denmark lately lost ?
A. Norway, ceded to Sweden.

OF DENMARK.

Q. What is the situation of Denmark ?
A. The peninsula lies between 53° 35' and 57° 45' N. latitude ; and between 7° 55'. and 11° 5' East. Its northern extremity is 70 miles S. from Norway. It is 290 miles long, and from 35 to 195 broad ; and contains 15,948 square miles ;

the island of Zealand is 80 by 50, and contains 2884. Fupen is 50 by 30, and contains 1938.

Q. What are the divisions?

A. It is divided into 8 provinces, Aalburg, Aarhuus, Riperhuus, Wiborg, Schelswick, Holstein, Zealand, and Funen.

Q. How is the peninsula bounded?

A. On the N. by the Scaggerac; on the E. by the Cattegat, the Little Belt, and the Baltic; on the S. by Germany and the Elbe; and on the W. by the German Ocean.

Q. What is the climate?

A. It is humid, but mainly temperate. The soil of the island is very fertile; that of the peninsula is much less so. The agriculture is superior. Hops, tobacco, turnips, madder, rye, barley, wheat, and oats, are every where cultivated. Wheat is the great staple. The number of sheep, in 1780, was 847,000.

Q. What are the rivers?

A. The *Eyder* and the *Gulden*. The *Lymfiord* is a long narrow bay, in the peninsula.

Q. What is the religion?

A. The Lutheran. There are six bishoprics.

Q. What is the constitution?

A. It is an absolute monarchy.

Q. What is the population?

A. In 1796, it was 1,490,384; and in 1808, by accurate estimate, 1,548,000. Of which 1,030,000 are in the peninsula. These estimates include the duchy of Holstein.

Q. What is the military strength?

A. It amounts to 38,776 regular troops, and a militia of 59,000.

Q. What is the naval strength?

A. In 1809, it consisted of 2 frigates, and 17 smaller vessels.

Q. What is the revenue?

A. It amounts to $3,600,000.

Q. What is the language?

A. A dialect of the Gothic, and similar to the Swedish, Norwegian and Icelandic.

Q. What is the state of literature?

A. Each parish has a school, and all the inhabitants are taught to read and write. There are also numerous Latin schools, and two universities, at Copenhagen and Kiel.

Q. What is the capital?

A. Copenhagen, in 55° 41′ 4″ N. and 12° 35′ 15″ E. It is on the E. shore of Zealand, 25 miles S. of the Sound, is admirably built, has a fine harbour, and in 1806, had 97,438 inhabitants. Its commerce is extensive.

C

Q. Describe Altona?

A. It is on the Elbe below Hamburgh, and has 30,000 inhabitants. The other towns are Kiel, Schleswick, Odensee, and Aalburg.

Q. What are the manufactures?

A. Leather, earthen ware, calicoes, cottons, muskets, sabres, cannon, saltpetre, silks, course linens and woollens, and thread-lace.

Q. What is the state of trade?

A. The exports are corn, horses, oxen, hogs, bacon, beef, butter and cheese.

OF THE DANISH ISLANDS.

Q. What islands in the Baltic belong to Denmark?

A. Zealand, Funen, Lapland, Falster, Moen, Langeland, Aeroe, Alsen, Femeren, Hindsholm, Samsoe, and farther eastward, Bornholm.

OF THE FERRO ISLANDS.

Q. What is the situation of the Ferro Islands?

A. They lie between 61° 15' and 62° 20' N. lat.; one third of the distance from the Shetland Islands to Iceland: about 240 miles N. W. of Scotland; and 360 W. of Norway. They are 22 in number, and consist of a group of steep high rocks separated by narrow channels. They have a thin soil. Only 17 are inhabited. In 1801, the population was 5265. They yield a revenue of 640l. ster. They compose 7 parishes and 39 congregations, with each its church. Each parish has a clergyman. The religion is Lutheran. The inhabitants can all read and write; and are a moral and religious people.

OF ICELAND.

Q. What is the situation of Iceland?

A. Iceland is properly an American island; being only 120 miles E. of Greenland, while it is 600 N. W. of Scotland, and 700 W. of Norway. It lies between 63° and 67° N.; and 13° and 28° W. It is 400 miles long, and 270 broad.

Q. What is the climate?

A. It is intensely cold in winter, and often very hot in summer. The country is chiefly mountainous. Corn will not grow. Cattle and sheep are the chief objects of husbandry. The vallies form fine meadows.

Q. What are the rivers and mountains?

A. The Skalfanda, Oxarfird and Brua, all run from S. to N. The mountains are broken ridges. Snaefeld is 6861 feet

high. Heckla, 25 miles from the S. coast, and 5000 feet
high, is a celebrated volcano.

Q. How are the inhabitants supplied with fuel ?

A. The fuel is chiefly *drift-wood*, floated on the coast.

Q. What is the religion ?

A. The Lutheran. The see of Skalholt has 127 parishes,
and the see of Hoolum 62. The clergy have from 400 to
500 dollars salary.

Q. What is the government?

A. Iceland is a colony of Denmark. The population is
60,000. The revenue is $30,000. The Icelanders are of
a middle size, moral, faithful and hospitable. Their houses are made of drift-wood, or lava.

Q. What is the language ?

A. It is the purest dialect of the ancient Gothic, and is remarkably rich in poetical expressions. All the inhabitants
are taught to read and write, and are well instructed in the
doctrines of religion. The Icelanders have long been distinguished for their attention to letters. The number of
their poets is very great. *Sturleson*, the author of the *Edda*,
died in 1241.

Q. What are the towns ?

A. Skalholt in the S ; Hoolum in the N ; and Besested
in the S. W.

Q. What are the manufactures and commerce ?

A. Leather and coarse woollens. The exports are cider,
down, fish, flesh, butter, oil, skins and wool.

OF PRUSSIA.

Q. What is the situation of the Prussian territories?

A. The eastern, and much the largest division of the
Prussian territories, lies N. of Bohemia, Moravia, and the
duchy of Warsaw, between 51o and 569 N. latitude and between 28° and 40° 40′ east longitude. The principal western division lies on the Rhine, between the Netherlands
on the N. W. and Hanover on the N. E.

Q. What is its extent ?

A. The eastern division is 630 miles long, from S. W. to
N. E. and 350 miles broad.

Q. How is Prussia bounded ?

A. Prussia is bounded on the N. by the Baltic and Russia ; E. by Russia and Poland ; S. by Austria and Saxony ;
and W. by Germany.

Q. How is Prussia divided ?

A. Prussia is now divided into the following 10 provinces, and 25 circles : viz.

Provinces.	Circles.	Capitals.
1. East Prussia	Koningsberg Gumbinnen	Koningsberg
2. West Prussia	Dantzic Marienwerder	Dantzic
3. Posen	Posen Bromberg	Posen
4. Silesia	Breslaw Buntzlau Reichenbeck Oppeln	Breslaw
5. Brandenberg	Berlin Potsdam Frankfort	Berlin
6. Pomerania	Stettin Coslin	Stettin
7. Saxony	Magdeburg Weisenfels Erfurt	Magdeburg
8. Munster	Munster Bielefield Hamm	Munster
9. Duchy of the Lower Rhine	Cologne Coblentz	Cologne
10. Cleves and Berg	Dusseldorf Cleves	Dusseldorf.

Q. What territories has Prussia lately gained?

A. At the peace of Tilsit, Prussia lost large territories. These, except the duchy of Warsaw, have been restored to her; and with them large tracts on the Rhine, and about half of the kingdom of Saxony.

Q. What is the climate?

A. It is on the whole cold and moist. The southern provinces are the most healthy.

Q. What is the face of the country?

A. Prussian Poland is an immense plain, having a soil of superior fertility. Silesia is still more fertile, and is a succession of hills and vallies. Brandenberg is a barren sandy country. Saxony is one of the richest countries in Europe, and in its surface resembles Silesia. The large territory on the Rhine is extensively productive.

Q. What is the state of agriculture?

A. In the Polish provinces, in Silesia, Saxony, and the territory on the Rhine, every variety of grain and vegetables, is raised in abundance; also hops, flax, hemp, tobacco, saffron, and madder. In Brandenberg, they raise buckwheat, turnips, and a little rye.

Q. What are the rivers ?

A. The *Memel* is the N. E. boundary, about 200 miles. The *Vistula* rises in the Carpathian mountains, and winds northward about 500 miles to the Baltic. The *Oder* rises in the same mountains, and pursues a northwestern course of 400 miles to the same. The Elbe is now a Prussian river for many miles. The Weser and the Ems water the territory on the Rhine ?

Q. What lakes are there ?

A. The *Spelding See,* in the E. is about 20 miles every way, and supplies the river Pregel. .

Q. What bays are there on the coast ?

A. The *Curisch-Haff* is the estuary of the Memel, and is about 70 miles long, and 30 broad. The *Frisch-Haff* is the estuary of the Vistula, and is 70 miles long and narrow. The *Grass-Haff* is that of the Oder. These bays are separated from the main sea by long sand-bars.

Q. What is the extent of the Prussian seacoast ?

A. About 600 miles.

Q. What are the mountains ?

A. The mountains of Silesia are a branch from the Carpathian chain.

Q. What are the minerals ?

A. Amber is a peculiar product of Prussia, found on the neck of sand inclosing the Frisch-Haff.

Q. What is the religion of Prussia ?

A. The Lutheran is established. Calvinism is also prevalent.

Q. What is the government ?

A. An absolute monarchy. No vestige of a senate, or delegates from the people, is known.

Q. What is the military strength ?

A. In 1806, the Prussian army amounted to 239,667 men.

Q. What is the revenue ?

A. The Prussian revenue will now fluctuate between 30 and 35 millions of dollars.

Q. What is the population ?

A. In Prussia Proper and Polish Prussia, 2,210,606 ; and in the German possessions 8,990,804 : in all 11,101,510.

Q. What is the character of the people ?

A. The proper Prussians are dull and gloomy. The Saxons are gay and lively. The Poles are high spirited and full of enthusiasm. They are the handsomest race in Europe.

C 2

Q. What languages are spoken here ?

A. In the Polish provinces the *Slavenian ;* and elsewhere the *German.* The German of the Saxons is distinguished for its purity.

Q. What is the state of literature ?

A. Saxony is the only part of this country, which has been distinguished for its attention to literature. It has given birth to many celebrated writers. Common education is sadly neglected in the Prussian territories.

Q. What is the capital ?

A. Berlin, the Prussian capital, lies on the N. bank of the Spree, a branch of the Elbe, in 52° 31' 44!' N. and 13° 28'' E ; on a barren sandy plain. It is admirably built, and has 14 Lutheran churches, 10 Calvinistic, and 4 Catholic. It is 4⅝ miles on the river, and 3 broad: containing 156,664 inhabitants.

Q. Describe the other towns ?

A. Breslaw in Silesia is a very extensive and beautiful city, on the S. bank of the Oder, in 51° 3' N ; and has 62,923 inhabitants. Koningsberg is on the Pregle, near its entrance into the Frisch-Haff, has an extensive commerce, and 56,410 inhabitants. Dantzic, on the Vistula, 4 miles from its mouth, has a very extensive commerce and 42,273 inhabitants. Coblentz, Treves and Cologne, are large towns on the Rhine.

Q. What are the manufactures?

A. Thread, linens, laces, ribbands, velvets, carpets, paper, glass, porcelain, iron and brass utensils, and woollens.

Q. What is the state of commerce ?

A. Corn, timber, wax, honey, hemp, flax, yarn and potash, are exported. Under the fostering care of the present king the Prussian commerce bids fair to be very extensive.

OF THE BRITISH DOMINIONS.

Q. What territories belong to the British empire ?

A. The territories belonging to Great Britain are found in the four quarters of the globe.

Q. What territories belong to it in Europe ?

A. Great Britain and Ireland and the adjacent isles: Heiligeland, Gibraltar and Malta.

Q. What territories in Asia, and in the adjacent isles ?

A. British India, British Ceylon, British Sumatra, British New-Holland, New South Wales, and Norfolk island.

Q. What territories in Africa and its islands ?

A. Isle of France, colony of Good Hope, and colony of Sierra Leona.

Q. What territories in America !

A. In N. America, New-Britain, the Canadas, New-Brunswick, Nova Scotia, Newfoundland; Cape Breton, and St. John's; in the West Indies, the Bahamas, Jamaica, and most of the Carribbean Islands; and, in S. America, Guiana.

Q. What is the situation of the *Island of Great Britain ?*

A. It lies in the Atlantic, off the W. coast of France, the Netherlands, Denmark and Norway, between 50° and 58° 45' N. and between 1° east and 6° 30' west. It is 588 miles long from N. to S; and in the S. 370 broad, containing 77,243 square miles.

Q. How far is it from the continent?

A. At the Straits of Dover it is 20 miles; and generally about 120 from France and Holland; about 350 from Denmark, and 280 from Norway.

Q. What countries does it include?

A. Scotland, England and Wales. The population, in 1811, was, exclusive of the army and navy, 11,956,303.; and including them, 12,552,144; to which if we add 4½ millions supposed to be the population of Ireland, it will make the population of the two islands about 17 millions. The number of dwelling houses in Great Britain was in 1801, 1,937,289; and in 1811, 2,163,946, making an increase of 226,457.

OF SCOTLAND.

Q. What is the situation of Scotland?

A. It is the northern part of Great Britain, between 54°, 44' and 58° 45' N; and between 1° and 6° 30' W. It is 280 miles long, and 180 broad; containing 27,794 square miles.

Q. How is it bounded?

A. On the N. by the Atlantic; on the E. by the German Ocean; on the S. by England; and on the W. by St. George's Channel and the Atlantic.

Q. How is it divided?

A. Naturally into *Highlands* and *Lowlands*; and politically into 33 counties or shires.

Q. What is the climate?

A. It is moist and chilly, but less cold than the opposite coast. The country is about two thirds mountainous. The S. E. is a beautiful succession of hills and valleys. Scotland is not distinguished for its fertility, or for the excellence of its agriculture.

Q. What are the rivers?

A. The *Clyde* in the W. the *Tweed*, the *Forth*, the *Dee* and the *Spey*.

Q. What are the lakes?

A. Scotland is full of lakes. Loch *Lomond*, the largest, is

30 miles by W. Loch *Linne*, Loch *Awe*, Loch *Shin*, and Loch *Erichi*, are also of considerable extent.

Q. What are the mountains?

A. The *Cheviot Hills*, in the S. and the *Grampian Hills*, running from S. W. to N. E. and separating the Highlands from the Lowlands. *Ben Nevis*, the highest summit is 4350 feet high.

Q. What are the minerals?

A. Lead, iron and coal.

Q. What is the religion of Scotland?

A. The Scotch Church is Calvinistic in its tenets, and has the presbyterian form of government. It is under the superintendence of a general assembly, 15 provincial synods, and 78 presbyteries. In 1803, there were 877 churches, and 936 ministers. The Seceders, Burghers, and Episcopalians are also numerous.

Q. What is the government?

A. Scotland sends 16 peers, and 45 members to the British parliament.

Q. What is the population?

A. In 1801, it was 1,599,068, and in 1811, 1,805,688 : making an increase of 206,620.

Q. What is the character of the people?

A. The Scotch are distinguished for their industry, sobriety, and good morals. All the inhabitants can read and write, and useful information is universally diffused. Their parish schools resemble those in Connecticut.

Q. What languages are spoken here?

A. In the Lowlands, it is the ancient *Scandinavian*, mixed with the English; both of *Gothic* origin. In the Highlands, it is the *Gaelic*, a dialect of the Celtic.

Q. What are the universities of Scotland?

A. There are four : St. Andrews, Aberdeen, and Edinburgh, on the eastern coast; and Glasgow on the western.

Q. What is the capital?

A. Edinburgh. It is built at a small distance from the Forth. Many of the houses in the old town are 13 and 14 stories high. The new town is regular and elegant. The population in 1801, was 82,560.

Q. Describe Glasgow?

A. It lies on the Clyde, and is the most commercial and populous city in Scotland. It is generally well built, and carries on many important manufactures. The number of inhabitants in 1801, was 77,385; and in 1811, 108,830. The other large towns are Perth, Dundee, Aberdeen, Greenock, and Paisley.

Q. What are the Scotch manufactures ?

A. Linens, the most important article, to the amount of 750,000l. sterling; Scotch carpets, woollens, caps, stockings, thread, ardent spirits, and manufactures of iron.

Q. What is the state of the Scotch commerce ?

A. Scotland carries on an extensive trade with the West Indies and the United States, as well as with Europe. The exports in 1809, amounted to 4,383,100l. sterling.

Q. In what important fisheries do the Scotch engage ?

A. In the herring and salmon fishery, on the coast; the whale fishery in Baffin's Bay, and the eastern coast of Greenland; and the cod fishery on the Banks of Newfoundland.

OF THE SCOTTISH ISLES.

Q. What are the Scottish Islands ?

A. The Shetland Isles, the Orkneys, and the Hebrides.

Q. What is the situation of the *Shetland* Isles ?

A. They are 90 miles N. E. of Scotland, 250 W. from Norway, and 150 S. E. of the Ferro Isles; between 60° and 61° N. and between 0° 51' and 20° 30' W. They are 86 in number, of which 20 are inhabited. The population of the whole groupe was, in 1801, 22,379.

Q. Which are the largest islands of the groupe ?

A. Mainland, 60 miles long and 12 broad, has 15,593 inhabitants. Yell, N. E. of Mainland, 20 miles long and 12 broad, has 2965. Unst, E. of Yell, 12 miles long and 4 broad, has 2359.

Q. What is the situation of the *Orkneys* ?

A. They lie N. of Scotland, being separated by Pentland Frith 12 miles over; between 58° 50' and 59° 30' N. and between 2° 30' and 3° 30' W. Their number is 30, of which 26 are inhabited. The whole population is 24,478.

Q. Which is the largest of the Orkneys ?

A. Mainland, 30 miles long and 13 broad, containing 13,176 inhabitants. Kirkwall, its capital, has 2,621.

Q. What is the situation of the *Hebrides* ?

A. They lie off the W. coast of Scotland, between 55° 30' and 599 N; and between 5 and 9 W. They are about 70 in number, and have 80,080 inhabitants.

Q. Which are the largest isles of the Hebrides ?

A. Skey, 50 miles long and 40 broad, with a popualtion of 17,091: and Lewis, 60 miles long and 20 broad, with 12,164. The other large islands, are North and South Vist, Mull Jura, Illa, Arran, and Bute. Rothsay, in Bute, containing 5231 inhabitants, is the chief town.

OF ENGLAND.

Q. What is the situation of England ?

A. England may be said to lie between Scotland and France on the N. and S., and between Ireland and the Netherlands on the W. and E. It is between 50° and 55° 45' N. latitude ; and between 1° E. and 60° W. longitude.

Q. What is the extent ?

A. It is 380 miles long, and 330 broad : containing 42,439 square miles, exclusive of Wales ; and, with Wales, 49,450.

Q. How is it bounded ?

A. On the N. by Scotland ; on the E. by the German Ocean ; on the S. by the English Channel ; and on the W. by St. George's Channel.

Q. How is England divided ?

A. Into 40 counties ; and, including Wales, into 12 more.

Q. What is the climate of England ?

A. It is a variable climate and humid, compared with that of France. Winter commences in October, and lasts till April. The face of the country is generally a succession of hills and valleys. In the W. it is extensively mountainous.

Q. What is the soil ?

A. It is generally very fertile. The English agriculture is superior to that of any other country. The cultivated acres in England and Wales amount to 30,620,000, and the uncultivated to 7,380,000. Almost all the grain consumed by the inhabitants is raised here.

Q. What are the rivers ?

A. The Severn runs S. W. about 150 miles, to St. George's Channel. The Thames runs S. E. 140 miles, to the German Ocean. The other rivers are the Great Ouse, the Trent, the Ouse, the Humber and the Tweed.

Q. What are the minerals of England ?

A. The tin mines of Cornwall are the richest in the world. Lead and iron are abundant. Coal abounds to an astonishing degree at Newcastle, in the N. E.

Q. What is the established religion ?

A. The Episcopalian. The king is the head of the national church. England and Wales are divided for ecclesiastical purposes, into 2 provinces and 25 bishoprics. The number of Episcopal parishes is 11,164. These, in 1811, had 10,532 incumbents, of whom 6120 were non-residents and 4412 residents in their parishes, and 632 were vacant. The number of licensed dissenting churches, at that time, was 12,160 ; occupied by Congregationalists, Baptists, Methodists, and Catholics. There are many dissenting churches which are not licensed. Probably a considerable majority of the population are dissenters.

Q. What is the government of the British empire?

A. It is a limited hereditary monarchy. The supreme power is vested in the parliament, consisting of the king, the house of lords, and the house of commons. The latter consists of 489 members for England, 24 for Wales, 100 for Ireland, and 45 for Scotland : in all 658.

Q. What is the population of England?

A. In 1801, it contained, exclusive of Wales, 8,331,434; and in 1811, 9,543,235 : including Wales, it contained in the former period, 8,872,980; and in the latter 10,150,615 : making an increase of 1,277,635 in 10 years. If to these be added the army and navy, the population of England and Wales in 1801, was 9,344,488 ; and in 1811, was 10,746,856.

Q. What is the amount of the national debt?

A. On the 1st of Feb. 1813, it amounted to 706,394,209l. sterling, drawing an interest of 22,680,872l. sterling, annually ; or about 3½ per cent.

Q. What is the amount of the British revenue?

A. In 1812, it amounted to 105,718,000l. sterling.

Q. What is the military strength?

A. In 1811, it consisted of 532,660 of all descriptions, and scattered over the whole empire.

Q. What is the British naval strength?

A. In 1813, it amounted to 255 ships of the line, 22 fifties, 208 frigates, 262 sloops and brigs, and 161 smaller vessels : in all 908, manned by 138,324 seamen and marines.

Q. What is the language of England?

A. It is a mixture of the Saxon, French, Greek and Latin; all of Gothic origin. Saxon is the basis of the English, both as to its construction, and as to the number of words derived from it.

Q. What is the state of English literature?

A. It is more flourishing than that of any other country, at any period. Here learning, science and the arts are fostered both by the nation and the government also.

Q. What are the universities?

A. There are two : Oxford, which has 17 colleges ; and Cambridge, which has 16.

Q. What is the capital of England?

A. London, the largest city of Europe, and of the eastern continent W. of China. It stands on the Thames, in lat. 51° 32' N. and long. 0° 5' W. of Greenwich ; is 6 miles long, 3 broad, and 16 in circuit. The houses, 126,414 in number, are of brick, and the streets are excellently paved. This city is the mart of the world; greatly surpassing every other in its commerce. Its population, in 1801, was 864,845 ; and in 1811, it exceeded *eleven hundred thousand*.

Q. Mention the other large towns ?

A. *Manchester*, on the Mersey, has 84,020 inhabitants ; *Liverpool*, at the mouth of the Mersey, has 77,653, and a most extensive commerce ; *Birmingham*, in the centre of England, has 73,670 ; *Bristol*, near the mouth of the Avon, has 63,645 ; *Leeds*, on the Aire, has 53,162 ; *Norwich*, in the E. on the Wensum, has 36,850 ; *Sheffield*, on the Don, has 31,314 ; *Portsmouth*, on the S. coast, the grand naval arsenal of England, has 32,166 ; *Hull*, on the Humber, has 29,516 ; and *Newcastle*, on the Tyne, has 28,366.

Q. What is the state of English manufactures ?

A. Every variety of manufactures flourishes in this country ; and most of them to an extent and perfection totally unrivalled. Those of woollen, cotton, iron, copper, silk, tin, glass, wood and the precious metals, are the most important. The value of the manufactures in 1812, was estimated at 140,000,000*l.* sterling ; and the number of persons employed by them, including their families, 3,000,000.

Q. What is the state of English commerce ?

A. The commerce of England is carried on with every country on the globe. The exports are of every variety of manufacture and produce. In 1812, they amounted to 73,-725,602*l.* ster. ; and the imports to 60,424,876*l.* The number of vessels engaged in foreign commerce, in 1812, was 28,061 ; their tonnage 3,160,293 tons ; and the men employed in them 184,352. In the same year the number of coasting vessels was 3,070 ; and their estimated tonnage 307,000.

OF THE ENGLISH ISLANDS.

Q. Which are the English islands ?

A. Isle of Man, Scilly Isles, Isle of Wight, Guernsey, Jersey, Alderney and Sark.

Q. Describe the Isle of Man ?

A. It is midway between England, Scotland, Ireland and Wales, in St. George's Channel ; is 30 miles by 15 ; and has a population of 30,000. It is divided into 17 parishes, and has a bishop.

Q. Describe the Scilly Isles ?

A. They lie off the Land's End about 66 miles, and are 145 in number. St. Mary's, the largest, is 9 miles in circuit, and has 700 inhabitants. The whole population is 1000. Shipwrecks are frequent in these seas.

Q. Describe the Isle of Wight ?

A. It is off the coast of Hampshire, is 23 miles long, 18 broad, and 60 in circuit; containing 100,000 acres. Newport is the capital. The island is very fertile and beautiful, and has 24,000 inhabitants.

Q. Describe Guernsey?

A. Guernsey is in the English Channel, 36 miles from the French coast; and is 14 miles by 13. It is hilly, healthy, and fertile; has a town called Port St. Pierre, and 21,500 inhabitants.

Q. Describe Jersey?

A. It is half way between Guernsey and the French coast, and 84 miles from England; is 12 miles long, 6 broad, and has 20,000 inhabitants. Sark is a little isle between Guernsey and Jersey; and Alderney is another, near Cape La Hogue.

OF WALES.

Q. What is the situation and extent of Wales?

A. It lies in the W. of England, between 51° 25′ and 53° 32′ N. latitude; and 2° 56′ and 5° 30′ W. longitude. It is 140 miles long, and 105 broad; containing 7011 square miles. It has St. George's Channel W. and N; England E. and Bristol Channel S.

Q. What is the population?

A. In 1801, it was 541,546; and, in 1811, 607,380. The Welsh are a hardy race of mountaineers, retaining the pure and simple manner of the ancient Celts. Their language is a dialect of the Celtic. The country is almost wholly mountainous.

Q. What islands are off the coast?

A. Anglesea is the largest. It contains 74 parishes, and 37,002 inhabitants.

OF IRELAND.

Q. What is the situation of Ireland?

A. It lies W. of Great Britain, between 51° 10′ and 55° 30′ N.; and between 5° 35′ and 10° 35′ W. Its least distance from Scotland is 12 miles, from Wales 40, and from England 75. It is 320 miles long, and 180 broad; containing 27.457 square miles.

Q. How is it bounded?

A. On the W. and N. W. by the Atlantic; on the N. E. by the Straits of Port Patrick; and on the E. and S. E. by St. George's Channel.

Q. How is Ireland divided?

A. Into 4 provinces: Ulster, Connaught, Leinster, and Munster; which are subdivided into 32 counties.

Q. What is the climate?

D

A. It is distinguished for its humidity, but is temperate. The country is mostly level, fertile, and abounding in pasturage.

Q. What are the rivers ?

A. The Shannon runs S. and S. W. 170 miles. The Barrow runs S. and empties near Waterford; and the Boyne at Drogheda.

Q. What are the lakes ?

A. Lough Earn, in the N. W. 30 miles by 12 : Lough Neagh, in the N. E. 22 by 12 : lakes Corrib, Ree and Derg.

Q. What is the religion ?

A. The Episcopalian is established ; but about three fourths of the people are Catholics; and about one eighth Presbyterians. Ireland is distributed into 4 archbishoprics : Armagh, Dublin, Chashel and Tuam. These are subdivided into 18 bishoprics.

Q. What is the population ?

A. It is now estimated at 5,000,000.

Q. What is the amount of the Irish revenue ?

A. In 1808, it amounted to 6,174,000l. sterling.

Q. What is the military strength ?

A. The regulars are incorporated with the other national troops. The militia, in 1808, amounted to 21,473.

Q. What are the manners of the Irish ?

A. They are impatient of injuries, quick in their resentments, and vehement in all their affections. They are of a quick apprehension, courteous and patient of fatigue. Their funeral howls and other barbarous ceremonies still remain in some parts of the country. The poorer classes are exceeddingly oppressed by the *middle men*, and live in a state of abject poverty. Their education is wholly neglected.

Q. What is the language of the Irish ?

A. It is the Erse, a dialect of the Celtic.* The Irish of the N. are descendants of a colony from Scotland. There is one university in the island, that of Dublin.

Q. What is the capital ?

A. Dublin, on the E. coast, at the mouth of the Liffy, in a delightful valley. It is about 10 miles in circuit. It had 167,899 inhabitants, in 1802, and is the second city in the two islands.

Q. Describe Cork ?

A. It is on the S. coast, on a marshy island, surrounded by the estuary of the Lee ; has one of the noblest harbours in Europe, and a population of 70,000. Its exportation exceeds that of any city in the island.

Q. What are the other towns ?

* Note—The English language is now generally spoken in Ireland.

A. Limerick, on the Shannon, with 50,000 inhabitants; Waterford, in the S. E. on the Suire, with 30,000 ; Belfast, in the N. E. with 18,000 ; and Kilkenny, an inland town, in the S. E. with 16,000.

Q. What are the manufactures of Ireland ?

A. Linen and linen yarn are the two important articles. The number of yards of linen exported, in 1808, was 44 millions.

Q. What is the state of commerce ?

A. Within a few years, the commerce of Ireland has experienced an unexampled increase. The amount of exports in 1808, was 12,577,517*l.* sterling; and, of imports, 8,860,325*l.*

OF THE NETHERLANDS.

Q. What is the situation of the Netherlands?

A. They lie on the western shore of Europe, directly E. of England ; between 49° 30' and 53° 30' north latitude, and between 2° 25' and 7° east longitude.

Q. Why are they so called ?

A. Because they are very low flat countries, not much elevated above the level of the sea, and lie near the mouths of the Rhine, the Moselle, and the Scheldt.

Q. What is their extent ?

A. They are 280 miles long, from north to south ; and, in the widest part, 200 broad : containing 28,915 square miles. On the coast they reach from about 15 miles N. E. of Dunkirk to the Dollart bay, or the mouth of the Ems.

Q. How are they bounded ?

A. On the W. and N. by the German Ocean ; on the E. by Germany ; and on the S. by France.

Q. What is their extent of seacoast ?

A. About 250 miles along the western coast, and about 80 on the northern.

Q. How are these countries divided ?

A. Into 14 provinces, viz. Groningen, Friesland, Overyssel, Holland, Utrecht, Guelders and Zealand, which formerly constituted the republic of Holland ; and Brabant, Flanders, Hainault, Namur, Liege, Limburg, and Luxemburg, which were formerly Belgium, or the Netherlands.

Q. What are the inhabitants of these countries called ?

A. Those of the first seven are called the *Dutch ;* and those of the last seven the *Belgians,* and perhaps more frequently the *Flemings ;* although this latter name belongs appropriately to the inhabitants of Flanders.

Q. What is the climate ?

A. It is moist, and in the north cold. The natives are healthy and vigorous. In the S. E. the vine is cultivated without difficulty.

Q. What is the face of the country?

A. It is almost every where an uniform flat. In the southeast, however, there is a pleasant succession of hills and vallies. The coast is dyked to an immense extent, to prevent inundation from the sea.

Q. What are the rivers of the Netherlands?

A. The Rhine, the Maas or Meuse, the Scheldt, the Moselle, and the Vecht.

Q. Describe the Rhine?

A. It rises in the S. E. of Switzerland, and pursues a northwest course to the German Ocean. Its whole length is about 800 miles.

Q. What are the vegetable productions?

A. Holland is chiefly devoted to pasturage. Madder and tobacco are cultivated to some extent. The soil of the Netherlands is highly productive, and the agriculture superior. Flax is every where cultivated. The butter and cheese of all the Low Countries is excellent.

Q. What number of inhabitants are there in the Netherlands?

A. Holland, in 1809, contained 1,864,416, or 158 to the square mile; and the Netherlands Proper, in 1808, 4,140,255, or 236 to the square mile: making a total of 6,008,671, or 203 to the square mile.

Q. What is the character of the people?

A. The Dutch are phlegmatic, honest, industrious, avaricious, and unsociable. Smoking tobacco prevails throughout all classes, and both sexes. The Flemings in the north resemble the Dutch; those in the south are more like the French borderers.

Q. What languages are spoken in the Netherlands?

A. The *Low-Dutch* throughout Holland, and the *Flemish* in Belgium. A corrupt mixture of Flemish and French, called the *Walloon*, is spoken near the French frontier.

Q. What is the religion of the Netherlands?

A. All religions are tolerated. The prevailing religion of Holland is *Calvinism*. The church is governed by a national synod and subordinate synods; and in 1803, it contained 1570 ministers. There are also 50 Walloon-Calvinist churches, and about 350 Catholic. The prevailing religion of the Netherlands Proper is the Catholic. There is one archbishopric, that of Malines, and 10 bishoprics.

Q. What is the state of learning and the arts?

A. Holland has heretofore produced some of the greatest physicians, divines and jurists. Common learning is universally diffused over that country. The Flemish also were formerly much celebrated for their cultivation of painting and sculpture.

Q. What is the seat of government?

A. The Hague. It lies in the province of Holland, not far from the coast, is very healthy, is admirably built on ground somewhat elevated, and in 1796, contained 38,433 inhabitants.

Q. Which is the largest city?

A. Amsterdam, also in the province of Holland. It is built on piles of wood in a low marshy soil, on an arm of the Zuyder Zee. The houses are neat and well made, but the streets are narrow. It contained in 1796, 217,024 inhabitants. It is, next to London, the most commercial city in Europe.

Q. What are the other towns?

A. Brussels, on the Senne, containing 66,297 inhabitants : Antwerp, on the Scheldt, has 56,318 : Ghent on the same river, has 55,161, and Rotterdam, on the Rhine, has 33,800.

Q. What universities are there in the Low Countries?

A. Those of Leyden, Utrecht, Groningen, Harderwicke and Franeker in Holland ; and those of Louvain, Tournay, Douay, and St. Omer in the Netherlands.

Q. What is the commerce of the Low Countries?

A. Formerly that of Holland yielded in its importance only to that of England. Under the present government it will probably revive. The valuable productions of the Netherlands will also furnish the foundation of a large domestic exportation.

Q. What is the form of government?

A. A limited hereditary monarchy. The reigning family is the illustrious *House of Orange.* The chief of the government takes the title of king of the Netherlands. The form of government resembles that of England.

Q. What is the amount of the revenue?

A. The commercial enterprize of the Dutch and the agricultural enterprize of the Belgians, promise an easy and abundant revenue. Its amount has not yet been ascertained.— That of Holland, in 1808, was $25,000,000. Probably that of the whole country will be $50,000,000.

Q. What is the military and marine strength?

A. A standing army of about 25,000 or 30,000 men is to be kept up in time of peace. The navy of Holland alone, in 1806, consisted of 16 ships of the line, 10 frigates, and 21 smaller vessels. In 1813, several of the French ships, at Antwerp, were given to this kingdom by the allies.

D 2

Q. What islands belong to the kingdom of the Netherlands?

A. Cadsand, South Beveland, Walcheren, Tholen and Schouwen, in the estuary of the Scheldt; Overflakee, Goeree, Voorn, Beierlandt, Dort and Isselmonde, in that of the Rhine; Texel, Vlieland and Ameland, off the mouth of the Zuyder Zee.

Q. What foreign dominions belong to this kingdom?

A. In Asia, Java, and the Spice Islands. In America, the islands of Eustatia, Curracoa and Saba.

OF GERMANY.

Q. What is the situation of Germany?

A. It lies between 44° 45' and 54° 45' N. lat.; and between 5° and 19° E. long.

Q. What is its extent?

A. It is 700 miles long from N. to S.; and in its greatest breadth, in lat. 51° about 610 miles broad.

Q. How is Germany bounded?

A. On the N. by Denmark and the Baltic: on the E. by Prussia Proper, Poland and Hungary; on the S. by the Adriatic, Italy and Switzerland; and on the W. by France, the kingdom of the Netherlands, and the German Ocean.

Q. What are the great rivers of Germany?

A. The *Danube*, the largest, is in the south of Germany, and is elsewhere described; as are the *Rhine* in the W; and the *Oder* in the E. The *Elbe* rises in the Sudetic mountains in Silesia, and pursues a N. W. course of 600 miles to the German Ocean. The *Weser* runs N. N. W. and falls into the German Ocean 70 miles S. W. of the Elbe. The *Ems* is a smaller river, W. of the Weser. The *Mayn* is a large tributary of the Rhine, flowing from E. to W. and dividing the states of Germany into those N. of the Mayn, and those S. of the Mayn.

Q. What is the climate of Germany?

A. Germany has generally a cold and healthy climate. Owing to the difference of elevation, there is no great difference in the temperature of the northern and southern regions.

Q. What is the face of the country?

A. North of the Mayn, Germany chiefly presents wide sandy plains, which appear in a former period to have been extensively overflowed. South of the Mayn, the country is chiefly mountainous. Germany contains many extensive forests, which consist almost wholly of varieties of the oak.

Q. What religions prevail in Germany?

A. Prostestants are most numerous. Almost all the Germans N. of the Mayn, including those under Prussia, are Lutherans or Calvinists. They are also numerous S. of that river. The Austrian territories are the strong hold of the Catholics in Germany ; but even in these Protestants are numerous, especially in Bohemia and Moravia.

Q. What is the language of Germany ?

A. The *German* is dialect of the Gothic, and is purest in Saxony and Hanover.

Q. What is the government of Germany ?

A. Germany is composed of numerous independent states, and of four free towns. Each of these is independent, and is governed by its own laws. For the maintenance of tranquility and independence, the separate states were united by the Congress of Vienna, under the GERMANIC CONFEDERATION. The members of this confederation are equal in their rights. The ordinary concerns of the confederation are confided to the *federative diet*. The making and alteration of its fundamental laws to the *general assembly*.

Q. Give an account of the federative diet ?

A. It consists of plenipotentiaries from the various states, or members of the confederation. Austria presides in the diet. All the members thus represented vote individually or collectively, in the following manner.

1 Austria	- - - - -	1 vote
2 Prussia	- - - - -	1
3 Bavaria	- - - - -	1
4 Saxony	- - - - -	1
5 Hanover	- - - -	1
6 Wurtemberg	- - - -	1
7 Baden	- - - -	1
8 Hesse Cassel	- - - -	1
9 Hesse Darmstadt	- - -	1
10 Denmark for Holstein	- -	1
11 Netherlands for Luxemburg	- -	1
12 House of Saxe	- - -	1
13 Brunswick and Nassau	- - -	1
14 House of Mecklinburgh	- - -	1
15 Holstein, Oldenburg, Anhalt and Schwartzburg		1
16 Hohenzollern, Lichtenstein, Reuss, Lippe, and Waldeck	- - -	1
17 Lubeck, Frankfort, Bremen, and Hamburg		1
	Total	17 votes

Q. What are the rights of the members of the confederation ?

A. Each state has a right to make propositions ; and the

presiding state is bound to bring them under deliberation in a given time.　Questions are decided by a simple majority. The states are bound to defend each other from all attack. When war has been declared, no member may enter on separate negociations.　Each member may form alliances with foreign states ; but may not contract engagements contrary to the security of the confederation.　The states may not make war upon each other ; but are bound to submit their differences to the diet.　The diet is a permanent body ; but may adjourn from time to time.

Q.　Give an account of the general assembly ?

A.　When fundamental laws are to be made or altered the diet resolves itself into the general assembly ; in which the distribution of the votes is as follows :

	Votes.	Inhab.		Votes.	Inhab.
Prussian States	4	8,990,000	Reufs-Greitz	1 }	
Saxony	4	1,185,000	Reufs-Loberftein	1 }	90,000
Hanover	4	1,201,009	Lippe-Schauenberg	1 }	
Heffe Caffel	3	575 000	Lippe-Detmold	1 }	95,000
Holftein (Denmark)	3	330,000	Lubeck	1	50,000
Luxemburg (Netherlands)	3	410,000	Hamburgh	1	150,000
Brunfwick Wolfenbuttle	2	250,000	Bremen	1	50,000
House of Naffau	2	272,000	Fraukfort	1	55,000
Mecklinhurgh-Schwerin	2 }				
Mecklinburgh-Strelitz	1 }	420,000	Germany N. of the Mayn	48	15,053,000
Saxe Weimar	1 }				
Saxe Gotha	1 }		Auftrian States	4	10,350,000
Saxe Coburg	1 }	450,000	Bavaria	4	3,250,000
Saxe-Meinangen	1 }		Wurtemberg	4	1,185,000
Saxe Hildburghausen	1 }		Baden	3	930,000
Holftein Oldenberg	1	150,000	Heffe-Darmstadt	3	275,000
Anhalt-Deffk	1 }		Hohenzollern-Heclingen	1 }	
Anhalt-Bernberg	1 }	130,000	Hohenzollern-Sigmaringen	1 }	75,000
Anhalt Kothen	1 }		Lichtenstein	1	55,000
Waldeck	1	80,000			
Schwartzburg-Sonderhaufen	1 }	120,000	Germany S. of the Mayn	21	16,120,000
Schwartzburg-Radolftadt	1 }		Total	69	31,173,000

Q.　Who presides in the general assembly ?

A.　The plenipotentiary of Austria.　A majority of two thirds is necessary to carry a vote.　The first meeting of the diet was on the first of September, 1815.　*Frankfort on the Mayn*, is the place of its sessions.

Q.　What foreign powers have possessions in Germany ?

A.　Prussia in the N. E. ; Austria in the S. E. ; Denmark and Great Britain in the N. W.; and the king of the Netherlands in the W.

Q.　What is the population of Germany ?

A.　If we include Bohemia, Moravia and Silesia within the limits of Germany, as is now customary, it will contain, according to the best estimates founded on the latest enumerations, 31,173,000 inhabitants.　Of these, as will be seen by the table, 20,080,000 are subject to the four crowns of Austria, Prussia, Denmark, and the Netherlands; and the remaining 11,093,000 to native German princes.

OF THE KINGDOM OF SAXONY.

Q. What is the situation and extent of the kingdom of Saxony?

A. It lies N. of Bohemia and S. of the Prussian territories. It is 130 miles long from E. to W.; and in the W. about 70 miles broad; containing about 6000 square miles. The Elbe runs through the heart of the kingdom.

Q. What are the productions?

A. The soil and climate are remarkably favorable to fertility. The country is uncommonly rich both in agricultural and mineral productions. The manufactures are numerous and valuable.

Q. What is the population?

A. Since the late losses, the population amounts to 1,182,744. The revenue amounts to about 4,000,000 dollars. The government is nearly absolute. The religion is the Protestant. Saxony is distinguished for the purity of its language and for the extent of its literature.

Q. What is the capital?

A. Dresden. It is a beautiful town on the Elbe, having 2644 houses and 49,094 inhabitants.

Q. Describe Leipsic?

A. It stands on the river Plisse, in a beautiful plain, and has 30,796 inhabitants. Its celebrated university was founded in 1409. Here is an annual fair of books for all Germany.

OF THE KINGDOM OF HANOVER.

Q. What is the situation and extent of the kingdom of Hanover?

A. It lies in the N. W. of Germany, having Holland on the W.; the German Ocean N. W.; the Elbe N. E.; Prussia E.; Hesse Cassel and the Prussian territories S. It is 200 miles long from E. to W.; and in its greatest breadth, 125: containing about 12,500 square miles.

Q. What are its great rivers?

A. The Elbe, the Weser, and the Ems. The whole coast, from the Elbe to the Ems, or about 200 miles, belongs to Hanover. Its commercial advantages are thus very great.

Q. What are the productions?

A. The agricultural productions are abundant; and the mineralogy is rich. Metals, linens, timber, peat, cattle and grain are exported.

Q. What territories belong to Hanover?

A.	Inhab.		Inhab.
East Friesland	150,000	Pt. of Lauenburg	20,000
Lower Munster	100,000	Luneburg	250,000
Part of Lingen	22,000	Calenburg	225,000
Bentheim	30,000	Hildesheim with Goslar	116,900
Osnaburgh	150,000	Grubenhagen	250,000
Diepbolz	12,000		
Hoya	60,000	Total	1,455,000
Verden	70,000		

Q. What is the religion ?

A. The Lutheran. The king of Great Britain is also king of Hanover. The revenue will now probably equal 3,000,000 dollars. The government is conducted by a council of regency. The literature of this country has been celebrated. The university of Gottingen is well known.

Q. What is the chief town ?

A, Hanover, on the Leine, with 2194 houses, and 21,360 inhabitants. Embden, near the mouth of the Ems, has a population of 15,000, and Luneburg of 12,100. Bremen, a free city on the Weser, has a population of 50,000.

OF THE HOUSE OF MECKLINBURGH.

Q. Where are the territories of Mecklinburgh ?

A. They have Danish Holstein W. ; the Baltic N.; Prussia E. and S. E.; and the Elbe S. W. They contain about 7800 square miles, and 420,000 inhabitants. The country is not very productive. It is divided into two duchies—Schwerin, and Strelitz. The former is much the largest and most powerful.

Q. What is the chief town ?

A. Rostock, on the mouth of the Warne. It has 2508 houses, and 13,756 inhabitants. Schwerin, on Schwerin Lake, has 9801.

OF THE HOUSE OF HESSE.

Q. Where are the territories of Hesse ?

A. Hesse-Cassel lies N. of the Mayn, and Hesse-Darmstadt S.; both in the Circle of the Upper Rhine. They contain 4380 square miles, and a population of 850,000. The revenue of the two landgraves exceeds $2,000,000. Darmstadt, the largest town, has a population of 11,350.

OF THE KINGDOM OF WURTEMBERG.

Q. Where is the kingdom of Wurtemberg ?

A. In the S. W. part of Germany. It contains 7220 square miles; and, in 1807, 1,181,372 inhabitants. The king has a revenue of about $5,000,000. The country is very rich and productive. Grain is extensively exported.

Q. What is the religion ?

A. The Lutheran is established. There are a considerable number of Calvinists and Waldenses. The people are generally educated.

Q. What is the capital ?

A. Stutgard. It stands near the Neckar, and has 29,680 inhabitants. Here are manufactories of stuffs, silk stockings and ribbands.

OF THE KINGDOM OF BAVARIA.

Q. Where is the kingdom of Bavaria ?

A. It comprehends almost all the circle of Bavaria, the S. E. part of Swabia, and large tracts in Franconia. Austria lies E. and S ; Switzerland S. W. ; and Wurtemberg partly on the N. W. It contains about 35,000 square miles.

Q. What is the appearance of the country ?

A. The S. and W. is mountainous. The eastern and largest division is a plain. The mountains abound with minerals. The country is extensively productive. The exports are wheat, cattle, wood, salt and iron.

Q. What are the manufactures ?

A. Coarse cloths, stuffs, stockings, velvet, carpets and clocks.

Q. What is the population ?

A. In 1807, it was 3,231,570. Since that time the population of the Tyrol, 620,854, has been transferred to Austria. But Saltzberg, Aschaffenberg and Wurtzburg have been added. The population is now probably about 3,250,000.— They are chiefly Catholics.

Q. What is the government ?

A. A monarchy nearly absolute. The revenue is about $9,000,000. The army, in 1807, was 35,894.

Q. What is the capital ?

A. Munich. It stands on the Iser, is a beautiful town, and has 48,740 inhabitants. Nuremberg on the Pignitz, has a population of 80,000 ; and Augsberg, near the Lech, of 28,534.

Q. Are there not many other principalities in Germany ?

A. There are, both N. and S. of the Mayn ; but they are too unimportant to deserve particular notice in so small a work. Their names and population have already been mentioned.

OF THE AUSTRIAN EMPIRE.

Q. What territories belong to Austria ?

A. Austria has dominions in Poland, Hungary, Germany, Italy and Turkey.

Q. What are the Austrian dominions in Poland ?

A. East Gallicia, West Gallicia, and the Buckovina, with a population of 5,051.000.

Q. What are the Hungarian states ?

A. Hungary, Slavonia, Croatia, and Transylvania, with a population of 9,859,000.

Q. Which are the German possessions ?

A. Bohemia, Moravia, Austrian Silesia, archduchy of Austria ; Interior Austria, including Stiria, Carinthia, Carniola, Friuli, Trieste, the Tyrol, and the countries of Trent and Brixen, and the electorates of Mentz and the Rhine, and the country of Isenberg: with a total population of 10,350,000.

Q. Which are the Italian possessions of Austria ?

A. The territory of Venice including Istria, the duchies of Milan and Mantua, and the counties of Bormio, Chiavenna, and the Valteline, with a population of 6,071,927.

Q. Which are the Austrian territories in Turkey ?

A. Morlachia, Dalmatia and Ragusa, together with the Seven Islands, with a population of 820,000.

Q. What is the situation of the Austrian empire ?

A. It lies between 42° and 53° N. lat. and between 8° and 27° E. long. The greatest length, from the eastern limit of Transylvania to the Tioino, the western boundary of Milan, in lat. 46°, is 840 miles. The common breadth about 520. The whole number of square miles is about 230,000.

Q. How is Austria bounded ?

A. On the N. by Saxony and Prussia ; on the N. E. by the duchy of Warsaw ; on the east by Russia and Turkey ; on the S. by Turkey, the Adriatic and the Po ; and on the W. by the Adriatic, the dominions of Sardinia, Switzerland and the kingdom of Bavaria.

Q. What is the climate of the Austrian dominions ?

A. It is generally mild and salubrious.

Q. What is the face of the country ?

A. It is every where variegated ; either mountainous, or a succession of hills and vallies. The only plains of any extent are the great plain in the West of Hungary, and the plains of Gallicia.

Q. What is the soil ?

A. It is extremely fertile and productive. The state of agriculture is flourishing, except in the Hungarian states. There we find prodigious tracts of forest.

Q What are the rivers ?

A. The Danube rises in the S. W. of Germany near Friborg, and pursues an eastern and southern course of 1500 miles to the Black Sea ; its great branches in Austria, are on

the S. the Inn, the Drave, and the Save ; and, on the N. the
Theisa. The Elbe and the Mulda are rivers of Bohemia ; the
Vistula, the Bug and the Dneister, of Gallicia, the Adige and
the Po, of the Italian territories. They are elsewhere described.

Q. What are the lakes ?

A. The two largest are in Hungary. Platen, 45 miles by
3 ; and Neusidler, 13 by 4.

Q. What are the mountains ?

A. The Carpathian mountains, between Hungary and
Gallicia ; the Sudetic chain, N. E. of Moravia and Bohemia ;
the Erzgeburg, on the W. of Bohemia ; and the Tyrolese
Alps, in the S. W.

Q. What forest trees are found here ?

A. The elm, wych-elm, lime-tree, birch, alder, oak, walnut, chesnut, beech, hornbeam, poplar, aspen, sycamore, maple, ash, pine, fir, and larch.

Q. What are the animals ?

A. The horses and cattle are very numerous and excellent. The latter are of a slaty blue. The wild animals are
the bison, bear, boar, wolf, chamois, marmot and beaver.

Q. What are the minerals ?

A. Austria is very rich in minerals. Mines of gold, silver,
tin, lead, copper, iron, salt, and coal, are extensively wrought.
The famous salt mines of Wielitska, near Cracow in Gallicia,
are well known.

Q. What is the religion ?

A. The Roman Catholic is established. All others are now
in a sense, tolerated. Protestants, of various sects, are found
in Bohemia, and Moravia. Lutherans are numerous in Austria. A majority of the Hungarians are Protestants and of
the Greek Church. The Transylvanians are a mixture of
Christians of every denomination, Jews and Mahometans.
The Italian States are Catholic.

Q. What is the government ?

A. Austria is an hereditary empire, with nearly absolute
power in the sovereign ; whose title is emperor of Austria,
king of Hungary, king of Bohemia and Moravia, &c. Hungary is a limited monarchy. The diet consists of the pre-
lates, barons, gentry and burghers. Bohemia is a limited
monarchy. The states have the sole power of laying taxes.
Transylvania has its states, who possess much of the sovereign power. Croatia and Sclavonia constitute a viceroyalty.
Milan and Mantua are duchies.

Q. What is the population ?

E

A. The population of the various parts of the Austrian dominions, in 1808, calculated chiefly from enumerations made within the present century, is 32,151,927.

Q. What is the military strength?

A. In 1809, it was 346,791 men.

Q. What is the naval strength?

A. Till lately, Austria had no harbor but that of Trieste. Now her sea coast extends, on the W. side of the Adriatic, to the Po; and on the E. side, to the Boiana, in lat. 41° 30′. As yet, she has no ships of war except on the Danube, and two or three frigates just built on the Adriatic.

Q. What are the manners and customs?

A. The higher as well as the lower classes are generally ignorant and uneducated throughout the empire; less so however in Bohemia and Moravia, than elsewhere. In these provinces, also, profligacy of manners is less general.— Crimes are not common, and capital punishments not frequent. The Hungarians are a high spirited people, partially civilized. They are a tribe of Finns. The Transylvanians, Croats, and Sclavonians are savage and lawless. In the eastern provinces of the empire, gypsies are very numerous. The Italians, in the Austrian empire, are proverbially licentious.

Q. What languages are spoken?

A. In the hereditary states, the German or High Dutch, a dialect of the Gothic; in Hungary, the Hungarian, a dialect of the Finnic; in the Polish provinces, as well as extensively in Hungary, and universally in the other Hungarian states, different dialects of the Sclavonian; and in the Italian provinces the Italian.

Q. What is the capital?

A. Vienna, on the S. bank of the Danube, in a fertile plain in lat. 48° 15′; long. 16° 30′ E. The houses are of brick, covered with stucco. The population, in 1801, was 232,049.

Q. What other large cities are there in the hereditary states?

A. Prague, the capital of Bohemia, on the Mulda, with 80,317 inhabitants; Gratz, in Stiria, on a branch of the Drave, with 40,000 inhabitants; Brunn, the capital of Moravia, on a branch of the Danube, with 23,598; and Trieste, on the Adriatic, with 23,633.

Q. What large towns are in the Polish provinces?

A. Leopold, or Lemburg, in Gallicia, on the head waters of the Bug, with 50,000 inhabitants; * Cracow, in Lodomiria,

* N. B. Cracow is now a free city under the protection of Austria.

the head of the Vistula, with 25,000 ; and Brody, on t
Bug, with 25,000.

Q. What are the large towns in the Hungarian states ?

A. Pesth and Buda, on opposite sides of the Danul
with a united population of 61,000 ; Debritzin, on a bran
of the Theisa, with 35,000 ; Presburg, the seat of gove
ment, on the Danube, 35 miles from Vienna, with 32,00
Theresienstadt, on a branch of the Theisa, with 28,000 ;
Szegelin, at the confluence of the Marosh and Theisa, w.
25,347 ; all in Hungary. Cronstadt, in the S. E. part
Transylvania, with 18,118.

Q. What are the cities in the Italian provinces ?

A. Venice, built on a multitude of islands in the Adria
with 137,240 inhabitants ; Milan, on the Adda, a branch
the Po, with 128,862 ; Verona, on the Adige, with 55,88
Padua, on the Brenta, with 34,000 ; and Mantua, the bi
place of Virgil, on the Mincio, 20,343.

Q. What are the manufactures of Austria ?

A. Linens, woollens, stockings, silks, gold and silver la
glass, paper, porcelain and mirrors.

Q. What is the state of commerce ?

A. The most important part of the Austrian commerce
internal, carried on between the various provinces. T
chief exports are horses, cattle, sheep, grain, flax, saffr
hemp, quicksilver and other metals ; and various wines,
pecially the Tokay from Hungary.

OF THE AUSTRIAN ISLANDS.

Q. What islands belong to Austria?

A. In consequence of the late annexation of Istria, D
matia and Venice, Austria is become possessed of the Isle
Quarnaro, and the Dalmatian Isles, near the E. coast of
Adriatic ; and of the Seven Islands not far from its mou

Q. Describe the Isles of Quarnaro ?

A. They lie in the Gulf of Fiume. The largest are Ch
so, Veglia, Arbo, Pago and Melada. The population
36,000. Cherso, the largest, is about 150 miles in circt
Its capital, Cherso, has 3000 inhabitants. They are rou
and mountainous, but productive.

Q. Describe the Dalmatian Isles ?

A. They lie along the coast of Dalmatia, and are num
ous. The largest are Grossa, Brazza, Lesina, Curzola,
leda, Lagosta, Cazzola, Cazza, and Lissa. They are a
rough and mountainous, but very productive. They hav
population of 59,000, and contain, in all, about 1550 squ
miles. Lesina and Curzola are considerable towns.

Q. What is the situation of the *Seven Islands?*

A. They lie in the Ionian Sea, below the mouth of the Adriatic, not far from the coast of Turkey.

Q. What is their number?

A. Including all the islets, they are very numerous, but only seven are worthy of note.

Q. Give an account of those seven?

A. Their names, extent and population are as follows:

	Sq. miles.	Inhab.	Towns.
Corfu	219	65,000	Corfu
Paxos	34	6,000	Paxos
St. Maura	110	16,000	Amaxichi
Cephalonia	428	55,000	Argostol
Ithaca	66	7,000	Theaki
Zante	120	30,000	Zante
Cerigo	98	8,000	
	1075	187,000	

Q. Which are the chief towns?

A. Corfu and Zante, have each about 12,000 inhabitants, and Argostol has 6000. A part of the inhabitants are Greeks and a part Catholics. Their trade is considerable. Fruits, wines and oil are exported.

OF THE FRENCH EMPIRE.

Q. What territories belong to the French empire?

A. France and Corsica, in Europe; the Isle of Bourbon, in Africa; Cayenne, in S. America; and Martinique, Guadaloupe, and St. Lucia, in the West Indies. France also claims, but has not yet possessed herself of the large island of St. Domingo.

OF FRANCE.

Q. What is the situation of France?

A. It lies in the W. of Europe, between 42° 10' and 51° N.; and between 4° 40' W. and 7° 30' E. Its northern limit is three degrees S. of the middle latitude of Europe.

Q. What is its extent?

A. The length, from Dunkirk to the Pyrenees, is 630 miles; and the greatest breadth from Cape St. Mahe to the Rhine, is 560. The contents are 161,810 square miles.

Q. How is it bounded?

A. On the N. W. by the English channel; on the N. E. by the Netherlands; on the E. by Germany, Switzerland and Italy; on the S. E. by the Mediterranean; on the S. W. by the Pyrenees; and on the W. by the Bay of Biscay.

Q. How is France divided?

A. France is now divided into 83 departments.

Q. What is the climate?

A. It is temperate and dry. The eastern frontier is much colder than the western. The olive flourishes in the S. and the vine generally throughout the kingdom.

Q. What is the face of the country?

A. It is generally uneven, but rarely mountainous. Large fertile plains are found on many of the rivers.

Q. What is the soil?

A. The country, in the N.W. and S. W. has an indifferent soil. The rest of the kingdom is eminently fertile. The vine, maize, wheat, millet, and the olive, are the most important crops.

Q. What are the rivers?

A. The Loire, rises in the Cevennes, and runs N. W. and W. 500 miles, to the Bay of Biscay. The Garonne, rises in the Pyrenees, and runs N. W. 300 miles to the same bay. The Rhone, rises in Switzerland, and runs W. and S. 400 miles to the Gulf of Lyons. The Seine runs about 300 miles to the English channel.

Q. What are the mountains of France?

A. The Pyrenees are on the southern frontier. The chain of the Cevennes runs from N. to S. Mount Jura is on the borders of Switzerland.

Q. What are the minerals?

A. Silver, quicksilver, copper, lead and iron; coal, freestone, gypsum and alum.

Q. What is the religion of France?

A. The Roman Catholic. By the new constitution all religions are tolerated.

Q. What is the government?

A. A limited hereditary monarchy. The legislative power is vested in the king, a house of peers, and a house of delegates chosen by the people.

Q. What is the population?

A. In 1812, the population of the present limits of France was 28,397,215 : making 175 to a square mile.

Q. What is the military strength?

A. A standing army is now maintained of about 200,000 men. At the present time France has but a very small number of veteran troops. Her old army was wholly destroyed in Russia, in Germany, and at Waterloo.

Q. What is the naval strength of France?

A. In 1809, it amounted to 40 sail of the line and 30 frigates. A considerable part of it has since been captured.

Q. What is the revenue?

E 2

A. It amounts to about 600,000,000 francs, or nearly 120,000,000 dollars. The national debt, in 1807, was about 2000 millions of francs. The arrears since that period are stated at 1305 millions : making a total of more than 3300 millions.

Q. What is the national character ?

A. The French are remarkable for quickness of apprehension, vivacity and gaiety ; and for taste in dress and in equipage. They are inferior to no nation in courage and activity, are polite and complaisant to strangers. The ladies are sensible and handsome, are singularly easy in their behaviour, and distinguished for their wit and sprightliness.

Q. What is the language ?

A. The French is a corruption of the Latin, intermixed with the Gothic. On the coast, between the Seine and the Loire, remains of the Celtic are obvious in the vernacular tongue.

Q. What is the state of literature ?

A. Since the revolution the French have been distinguished for their progress in mathematics and physical science. Learning, properly so called, can hardly be said to exist in France at the present time.

Q. What is the capital ?

A. Paris, on both sides of the Seine, 150 miles from its mouth, in 48° 52' N. latitude. It is 11 miles in circuit, has 32,000 houses, of from four to seven stories high, and had, in 1807, 547,756 inhabitants. The streets are generally without sidewalks and filthy, and too often narrow. There are 12 bridges across the Seine, and 26 quays on its banks. It contains 83 churches, 40 chapels, 10 abbeys, 28 priories, and 103 convents.

Q. Describe Marseilles ?

A. It is at the foot of a rocky mountain, on a noble harbour in the Mediterranean ; and has a fine arsenal and armory, and 96,413 inhabitants.

Q. Describe Bordeaux ?

A. It is 70 miles up the Garonne, on the N. W. bank ; and has an ample and well fortified port, and has 90,992 inhabitants.

Q. Describe Lyons ?

A. It is at the conflux of the Rhone and Saone, is the seat of very extensive manufactures, and has 88,919 inhabitants.

Q. What are the other large towns ?

A. Rouen, N.E. of Paris, on the Seine, with 84,283 inhabitants ; Nantes, on the Loire, with 77,162 ; Toulouse, on the Garonne, with 50,171 ; Orleans on the Loire, with 1,937 ; and Amiens, on the Somme, with 41,299.

Q. What are the other important seaports ?

A. Toulon, on the Mediterranean ; Brest, Boulogne, and Rochefort, on the Atlantic.

Q. What are the manufactures ?

A. They have been greatly depressed by the late government, but are beginning again to flourish. The most important are silks, woollens, cottons, linens, laces, articles of iron, glass and porcelain. The French manufactures are excellent.

Q. What is the state of the French commerce ?

A. The French commerce is just beginning to revive. In 1784, the exports and imports amounted, each, to about 20 millions sterling. The chief exports were woollens, cottons, claret, and other wines, brandy, cattle, wheat and leather.

OF THE FRENCH ISLANDS.

Q. What are the French islands ?

A. Corsica, and a few small isles on the French coast.

Q. What is the situation of Corsica ?

A. It is in the Mediterranean, N. of Sardinia, between 41° 51′ and 42° 54′ N. and between 8° and 10° E. It is 106 miles long, and from 40 to 50 broad ; containing about 4000 square miles. The climate is mild and moderately healthy ; the country mountainous and fertile ; the produce flax, wheat, rye, barley and millet.

Q. What is the population ?

A. In 1807, it was 185,695. They are Catholics. Bastia, the capital, in the N. E. has 11,366 inhabitants.

Q. What islands are near the coast of France ?

A. The Hyeres Isles, in the Mediterranean, near Toulon ; Oleron, Re, Yeu, Noirmoutier, Belleisle, Ushant and St. Marcou, in the Atlantic.

OF SWITZERLAND.

Q. What is the situation and extent of Switzerland ?

A. It lies between 45° 40′ and 48° N. latitude, and between 6° and 10° 45′ E. longitude. It is 200 miles long from E. to W. and 160 broad ; containing about 18,000 square miles.

Q. How is it bounded ?

A. On the N. by Alsace and the kingdom of Bavaria ; on the E. by Austria ; on the S. E. and S. by the Austrian possessions in Italy, and by the kingdom of Sardinia ; and on the W. by France.

Q. How is Switzerland divided ?

A. Into the following 22 cantons. Of these, the two first, Argow and Berne, constituted the old canton of Berne.

Counting those two as one, the first thirteen are the old
thirteen cantons; and the last eight are new cantons:

Argow	134,444	Uri	17,500
Berne	232,508	Glarus	24,000
Basil	42,193	Neufchatel	47,000
Soleure	43,610	* Pays de Vaud	145,215
Schaffhausen	27,590	† Geneva	215,844
Zurich	200,000	‡ The Vallais	120,000
Appenzel	60,000	§ Tessino	161,000
Friburg	89,610	The Grisons	100,000
Lucern	110,000	St. Gall	162,000
Underwald	21,200	Thurgau	75,000
Zug	14,735		
Schweitz	31,400	Total	2,073,889

Q. What is the face of the country?

A. Switzerland consists almost wholly of high mountains
and deep vallies. Many of the mountains are covered with
eternal snows.

Q. What is the climate?

A. The cold of winter is very severe. In summer, the
harvests are often injured by frosts. The climate is generally healthy. The inhabitants are extensively subject to a
disease called the *goitere*.

Q. What is the soil?

A. It is usually fertile in the vallies, and extensively so
on the sides of the smaller hills. Sufficient grain is raised
to supply the inhabitants.

Q. What are the rivers?!

A. The Rhine, the Rhone, and the Inn, rise in Switzerland. The Aar, runs northward 150 miles, and joins the
Rhine at Waldshut. The Adda, in the S. E. runs through
the Valteline.

Q. What are the lakes?

A. The Lake of Constance, in the N. E. is 45 miles long
and 15 broad. The Rhine passes through it. The Lake of
Geneva, in the S. W. is 40 miles by 9. The Rhone runs
through it. The lakes of Neufchatel, Zuric, Thun, and
Lucerne, are all tributaries to the Rhine. Lakes Maggiore
and Como, are on the S. frontier.

Q. What are the mountains?

A. In the S. and S. E. different ranges of the Alps. In the
W. the range of Mount Jura. Mount Blanc, now on the confines of Savoy, is 15,662 feet above the ocean, and surpasses

* Called also *Waadt.*

† This was the population of the territory of Geneva in 1808. A
considerable tract was ceded to it from Savoy, in 1815.

‡ The population of this beautiful territory is undoubtedly underrated.

§ Called also the *Italian Bailliages.*

in height all the mountains of the Eastern continent.

Q. What are the vegetable productions?

A. All the plants of a cold climate are found on the mountains, and those of more temperate regions occur in the plains and vallies. The oak, elm, beech, ash, lime, and hornbeam are the most common forest trees.

Q. What are the animals?

A. The horses and cattle of Switzerland are large and vigorous. The ibex, chamois, marmot, rabbit and hare, are among the wild animals.

Q. What are the minerals?

A. Iron, sulphur, crystal, rock salt, granite, porphyry, asbestos, jasper and agate.

Q. What are the natural curiosities?

A. The Glaciers of the Alps. They are immense masses of ice near the summits of those mountains, presenting almost every variety of surface.

Q. What is the religion of the Swiss?

A. Calvinism is the prevailing religion. From one third to two fifths of the inhabitants are, however, Catholics. The Swiss are distinguished for their information, their good morals and their attachment to religion.

Q. What is the government?

A. Each canton constitutes a distinct republic governed by its own laws. For the common security, the cantons are also united in a confederated republic, governed by the general diet. To this body each canton sends two members, but has only one vote.

Q. What is the population?

A. The population of the several districts, according to the latest enumerations and estimates, may be seen in the preceding table; according to which that of the whole country amounts to 2,073,889. At the present time it is not probably less than 2¼ millions.

Q. What is the military strength?

A. It amounted, in 1809, to 15,023; beside a considerable number of soldiers in foreign service. In 1815, the cantons raised an army of 30,000 men. The Swiss are excellent soldiers.

Q. What is the revenue?

A. It amounted, at the same period to about $550,000 dollars. The national debt is very small. The cantons of Zurich and Berne, have a large sum in the English funds.

Q. What are the manners and customs?

A. Next to the Scotch, the Swiss are the most moral and virtuous nation in Europe. They are industrious, frugal, unostentatious in their dress, dwellings, and mode of living, and unusually frank and simple in their manners. The state of society is remarkably happy.

Q. What is the language?

A. The Swiss is a distinct language, and a dialect of the Gothic.

Q. What is the state of literature?

A. Switzerland has heretofore produced many men of distinguished learning and science. The inhabitants, as a body, are unusually well informed.

Q. What is the state of education among the Swiss?

A. The inhabitants, like those of New England, are universally taught reading, writing and arithmetic. There are colleges at Basil, Berne, Zurich, Lucerne and Schaffhausen.

Q. What are the large towns?

A. Basil is the largest town within the old limits of Switzerland. It stands on the Rhine, a small distance S. of the German frontier, and has 15,060 inhabitants. Berne the capital, is on the Aar, between lakes Thun and Neufchatel, and has a population of 13,339.

Q. What are the other towns?

A. Zurich, on the mouth of lake Zurich, has 10,153 inhabitants; and Lausanne, on the lake of Geneva, has 9,965.

Q. Where is Geneva?

A. It is on the Rhone, at the mouth of Geneva lake; and will ever be remembered as the residence of Calvin, the greatest of the reformers. Its population, in 1802, was 23,309. It is the largest and most flourishing city in the whole country.

Q. What are the manufactures?

A. The Swiss manufacture linens, cottons, woollens, muslin, silk handkerchiefs, and ribbands. They can hardly be said to carry on commerce except among themselves. A part of the produce of the country is carried overland to Genoa in Italy.

OF THE SPANISH EMPIRE.

Q. What territories belong to the Spanish empire in Europe?

A. Spain, and the islands Majorca, Minorca and Ivica.

Q. What territories in Africa?

A. Ceuta, Melilla, and a few other towns, on the N. coast of Morocco; the Canary Islands; the isle of Fernando Po; and Prince's Island.

Q. What territories in Asia?

A. Several clusters of islands in the Pacific Ocean, viz. the

Philippines, the Ladrones, the Carolinas, and Magindanao.

Q. What territories in America?

A Florida, Mexico, and Guatemala, in North America; Cuba, the eastern division of St. Domingo, Porto Rico, and Margarita, in the West Indies; New Grenada, Venezuela, Peru, Chili and Buenos Ayres, in South America.

OF SPAIN.

Q. What is the situation of Spain?

A. Spain and Portugal constitute a peninsula, which lies in the S. W. of Europe. Spain lies between 9° 18' west and 3° 45' east longitude; and between 36° 6' and 43° 46' north latitude.

Q. What is the extent of Spain?

A. Its greatest length, from west to east, is 650 miles. Its breadth is 550. The number of square miles is 191,510.

Q. How is Spain bounded?

A. On the N. by the Bay of Biscay; on the N. E. by the Pyrenees, which divide it from France; on the E. by the Mediterranean; on the S. by the Mediterranean, the Straits of Gibraltar, and the Atlantic; and on the W. by Portugal and the Atlantic.

Q. What extent of seacoast has Spain?

A. On the Mediterranean about 840 miles; in the S. W. 180; in the N. W. 180; on the Bay of Biscay 350; in all 1550.

Q. How is Spain divided?

A. Into 16 kingdoms or provinces.

Q. What is the climate of Spain?

A. In the summer, the air is hot, damp and unhealthy. Malignant fevers originate and prevail in the seaports. Several of the highest mountains are covered with snow throughout the year.

Q. What is the soil of Spain?

A. That of the northern and central kingdoms is indifferent. That of the eastern and southern kingdoms, except Andalusia, is rich, fertile, and in a high state of cultivation.

Q. Are there any mineral waters in Spain?

A. Those of Seville, Cordova, and Grenada, are in high repute.

Q. What is the face of the country?

A. Generally, Spain is a broken mountainous country.

Q. What are the mountains of Spain?

A. The Pyrenees, between France and Spain, wind about 300 miles. The highest summit, Mount Perdu, is about 11,000 feet high. The Cantabrian Mountains, the Sierra Morena, and Sierra Nivada, run through Spain from east to west. Montserrat, is a single mountain, in a plain north of Barcelona, and is more than 11,000 feet high. It is 16 miles in circumference; and is inhabited by numerous monks who retire to it for devotion and live in hermitages.

Q. What are the rivers of Spain?

A. The Ebro, runs S. E. 400 miles to the Mediterranean. The Guadalquivir, runs S. W. about 300 miles, and the Guadiana, about 450 to the Atlantic. The Tagus, runs S. W. about 520 miles through Spain and Portugal to the Atlantic, emptying at Lisbon. The Douro and the Minho are farther north.

Q. What is the number of inhabitants in Spain?

A. Spain is not thickly inhabited; it has about ten millions and five hundred thousand inhabitants.

Q. What are the characteristics of the Spaniards?

A. In their persons they are generally tall, with swarthy complexions, but their countenances are very expressive. They are grave, proud, jealous, and indolent; but sensible, brave, faithful, and possessed of a high sense of honor. The Spanish ladies are celebrated for their wit and vivacity. The Spanish factors have ever been remarkably faithful to the foreigners who have employed them.

Q. What are the customs of the Spanish?

A. The ladies paint themselves very much. Both sexes live very temperately, drinking but little wine. They usually drink coffee and chocolate, morning and evening, and eat flesh at noon. Both men and women commonly sleep after eating.

Q. What are their diversions?

A. They consist chiefly in dancing, serenading and bull-baiting, which last is a very barbarous practice.

Q. What is the religion of Spain?

A. The established religion is Roman Catholic, and no other sects are tolerated. The kings of Spain have been so uniform in their professions of this religion that they are styled " Most Catholic."

Q. What is the language of Spain?

A. It is a majestic and expressive language, and the foundation of it is Latin.

Q. What is the state of learning in Spain?

A. There is very little encouragement given to education, and consequently very little attention paid to learning in Spain. The despotism of their government damps all useful improvement.

Q. What is the number of archbishoprics and bishoprics?

A. There are 8 archbishoprics and 48 bishoprics. The whole number of clergy, in 1787, was 188,625. The number of cathedrals is 117 ; of parishes 18,537 ; of monasteries, 2146 ; and of nunneries 1023.

Q. What is the capital of Spain ?

A. Madrid, the capital lies on the Manzanares, a tributary of the Tagus, in 40° 25' N. and 30° 12' W. ; and is surrounded by a wall, with 15 gates. The streets are straight, clean and well paved. The number of houses are 14,100, and of inhabitants 156,672. The houses are chiefly of brick.

Q. What are the other large towns ?

A. Barcelona, has 111,410 inhabitants ; Valentia, 105,000 ; Seville, 80,268 ; Cadiz, 57,387 ; and Grenada, 52,345.

Q. What is the commerce of Spain ?

A. Spain carries on considerable commerce with her American and Asiatic colonies, and with the ports of the Mediterranean. The exports are wool, silks, wine, raisins, brandy, fruits, salt, tobacco, &c. ; and the imports are fish, hardware, corn, butter and cheese, linen, flax, sugar and spices.

Q. What are the manufactures of Spain ?

A. Tobacco, soap, silks, woollens, leather, paper, salt-petre and powder.

Q. What is the government ?

A. A despotic monarchy.

Q. What is the revenue ?

A. About 35 millions of dollars. The national debt is about 311 millions.

Q. What is the military strength of Spain ?

A. In time of peace, the standing army is 70,000. In 1806, it amounted to 153,840.

Q. What is the naval strength of Spain ?

A. In 1808, the Spanish navy amounted to 218 vessels of war; of which 42 were of the line, 30 frigates, and 146 smaller vessels.

OF THE SPANISH ISLANDS.

Q. What islands lie off the coast of Spain ?

A. Majorca, Minorca, Ivica and Fromentera, in the Mediterranean ; and the isle of Leon in the Atlantic.

Q. Describe Majorca ?

A. It is 55 miles long and 46 broad, with an extent of 1300 square miles, and a population of 135,900. It is fertile, and produces corn, wine, oil, honey, and fruits. It is about 90 miles S. S. E. from Barcelona. The capital, Palma, has an university, 23 churches, and 29,259 inhabitants.

Q. Describe Minorca ?

F

A. It lies 23 miles N. E. from Majorca, is 37 miles long by 14 broad, and has a population of 33,000. Port Mahon is the capital. It contains about 450 square miles.

Q. Describe Ivica?

A. It is 40 miles S. W. from Majorca, and about the same distance east from Cape Nao. It is 15 miles long by 12 wide, and contains about 140 square miles and 10,000 inhabitants. Ivica the capital is in the S. E.

Q. Describe Fromentera?

A. It is a little island S. of Ivica, now uninhabited.

Q. What was the ancient name of these islands?

A. The Balearic islands.

OF THE FORTRESS OF GIBRALTAR.

Q. Where is this fortress situated?

A. At the southern extremity of Spain, within the Straits of Gibraltar, in lat. 36° 6' N. and long. 5° W.

Q. Describe it?

A. It is an immense rock, rising out of the Mediterranean, about 1400 feet high, two miles long and one broad. On the W. side, is the bay or harbor. The town on the western declivity of the rock, contains 500 houses and 8500 inhabitants. The garrison contains about 5000 men and 300 cannon. It is supposed to be impregnable.

OF THE PORTUGUESE EMPIRE.

Q. What territories belong to the king of Portugal?

A. In Europe, Portugal; in Asia, Goa, and the Islands of Timor and Macao; in Africa, the Madeiras, the Azores, the Cape Verd Islands, and some territories in Congo, and on the southeastern coast; and in America, Brazil.

OF PORTUGAL.

Q. What is the situation of Portugal?

A. It is the westernmost country of Europe, lying between 36° 56' and 42° 7' N. latitude; and between 6° and 9° 35' 30'' W.

Q. What is the extent of Portugal?

A. It is 360 miles long, and 150 broad; containing 35,998 square miles.

Q. How is Portugal bounded?

A. On the N. and E. by Spain, on the S. and W. by the Atlantic Ocean.

Q. How is Portugal divided?

A. Into 6 provinces: Entre-Duero-é-Minho, Tras-os-Montes, Beira, Estremadura, Alentejo and Algarve.

Q. What are the mountains of Portugal?

A. The Serra Monchique and the Serra d'Estrella. The Rock of Lisbon is about 3000 feet high.

Q. What are the rivers of Portugal?

A. The Gaudiana, the Tagus, the Douro, and the Minho, have been described in the account of Spain. The Mondego is the largest river running wholly in Portugal. Its course is more than 100 miles.

Q. What is the population of Portugal?

A. In 1780, it was 3,556,712; or 99 on a square mile.

Q. What are the characteristics of the Portuguese?

A. They are generally of a small stature, and swarthy complexion, are well-formed, and have regular features and black eyes. They are bigoted, revengeful, and extravagantly fond of parade, music, dancing and bull-fights. The peasants are mere slaves. The Portuguese of the north, are industrious, rough and hospitable: those of the south are polished and indolent.

Q. What is the religion of the Portuguese?

A. The Roman Catholic. No other is tolerated.

Q. Give an account of the Portuguese clergy?

A. They consist of a patriarch, two archbishops, fifteen bishops, and an immense host of inferior clergy. The revenue of the patriarch is 109,124l. sterling. There are 418 monasteries, and 108 nunneries.

Q. What is the language of Portugal?

A. It resembles the Latin more than it does any other European language. It likewise has a close affinity to the Spanish, but is more melodious.

Q. Describe Lisbon?

A. It is on the northern bank of the Tagus, several miles from its mouth. It contains 44,057 houses, and 350,000 inhabitants. In point of commerce, Lisbon is the third city in Europe.

Q. Describe Oporto?

A. It stands on the north side of the Douro, 5 miles from the sea. The population is 70,500.

Q. What are the other large towns?

A. Elvas, Braga, St. Ubes, Evora, and Coimbra; each of which has about 12,000 inhabitants.

Q. What is the state of the Portuguese commerce?

A. It is carried on chiefly with Brazil and England. From the former, are imported gold, silver, pearls, diamonds, precious stones, cottons, indigo, wheat, sugar, and drugs: from the latter, woollens, cottons, linens, hardware, and dried fish. Port wine is annually exported to the amount of 48,000 pipes.

Lisbon wine, to the amount of 10,000 pipes; oil, 1200 pipes; wool, 1,000,000 lbs.; salt, 2,400,000 bushels; and fruits, 95 cargoes.

Q. What is the state of the Portuguese manufactures?

A. The chief articles of manufacture are hats, silks, coarse woollens, cottons, earthen ware, and salt.

Q. What is the government of Portugal?

A. An absolute monarchy. The heir apparent is called the prince of Brazil. The present residence of the government is St. Salvador, in Brazil. It is thought that it will soon return to Lisbon. Portugal is now governed by a viceroy and a regency.

Q. What is the state of the Portuguese finances?

A. The revenue is 16 millions of dollars, and the debt is about 20 millions.

Q. What is the military strength?

A. The army, in 1803, consisted of 52,427 regular troops, and 33,600 militia: in all, 86,027. This is much larger than the ordinary peace establishment. There are no better soldiers in the world than were the Portuguese under *Marshal Beresford.*

Q. What is the naval strength?

A. In 1804, the navy consisted of about 60 vessels of war, manned by 12,000 marines. Of these, 13 were of the line, and 15 were frigates.

OF ITALY.

Q. What is the situation of Italy?

A. It lies on the S. of Europe, between 37° and 46° 35' N.; and between 6° 10' and 18° 35' E. It is 740 miles long, from S. E. to N. W. and in the N. 350 broad. Generally it is narrow.

Q. What is the shape of Italy?

A. It is that of a man's leg and foot.

Q. What are the boundaries?

A. On the N. W. and N. the Alps divide Italy from France, Switzerland and Germany; on the E. is the Adriatic; and on the S. E. and S. W. the Mediterranean.

Q. What is the climate?

A. That of the north is temperate and healthy. In the south the heat is often violent.

Q. What is the soil?

A. It is every where fertile. The north of Italy was long styled the garden of Europe.

Q. What are the rivers?

A. The Po rises in the Western Alps, and runs E. 350.

miles to the Adriatic. The Adige rises in the Eastern Alps, and runs southward 200 miles to the Adriatic ; emptying 12 miles N. of the Po. The Tiber rises in the Appenines, and runs S. W. 180 miles to the Mediterranean. The Arno runs 100 miles in the same direction.

Q. What lakes are there in Italy ?

A. There are three in the N. of some extent : the Maggiore, 27 miles long by 3 ; the Como 32 by 3 ; and the Garda 30 by 8.

Q. What are the mountains of Italy ?

A. The Alps are the northern boundary. Mount Blanc, their loftiest summit, is the highest mountain in Europe.— Mount Vesuvius, a well known volcano in the S. of Italy, is 30 miles in circuit and 3600 feet high. The Appenines run through the middle of Italy, from S. E. to N. W. and in Piedmont join the Maritime Alps.

Q. What are the vegetable productions ?

A. The forest trees on the mountains are the pine, larch, fir, yew, mountain ash, birch, pine, juniper and alder, and lower down the oak, elm, linden, ash, lime and walnut, chesnut, poplar, cork-tree, cypress and ilex. The fruits are apples, pears, plums, cherries, apricots, nectarines, pomegranates, oranges, lemons, figs, dates, palms, pistachios, almonds, olives and grapes ; most of them growing wild in the forests.

Q. What are the animals ?

A. The cattle are large and excellent ; in the N. of a pale rose colour ; in the middle and S. of a light grey.— The horses are indifferent. The buffalo is common. Asses, mules, sheep, goats and hogs abound. Wild boars, wolves and foxes, are found in the mountains.

Q. What is the religion in Italy ?

A. The Roman Catholic is universally the established religion ; and, in many places, to the exclusion of all others.

Q. What is the language ?

A. The Italian, a language derived chiefly from the Latin, is spoken throughout Italy.

Q. What is the population of Italy ?

A. From enumerations made of the different regions at various times within the present century, it was calculated to amount, in 1809, to 16,114,000.

Q. What is the character of the Italians ?

A. They are bigoted Catholics ; and are haughty, irritable, jealous and revengeful.

Q. How is Italy divided ?

F 2

A. By the Act of the Congress of Vienna, Italy is now divided into the following states and territories.

Dominions of Sardinia in the N. W. {	Savoy	296,366
	Piedmont	2,083,099
	Genoa	595,310

Total 2,974,775

Dominions of Austria in the N. E. { Counties of Chiavenna, Bormio and the Valteline, Milan and Mantua, Republic of Venice, including Istria.

Total population, 6,071,927

Duchy of Modena { . Modena, Mirandola, Reggio, Massa and Carrara	470,000
Duchy of Parma—Parma, Placentia and Guastella	300,000
Duchy of Lucca	172,000
Grand Duchy of Tuscany	1,100,000
States of the Church	2,000,000
Kingdom of Naples	4,963,502

Total on the Continent 18,052,204

Sicily to Naples	1,656,000
Sardinia, to the kingdom of Sardinia	520,000
Malta, to Great Britain	89,772
The Seven Islands	187,000

Total in the Islands 2,452,772

Total in Italy 20,484,976

OF THE DOMINIONS OF SARDINIA.

Q. What territories belong to the king of Sardinia ?

A. On the continent, Savoy, Piedmont, including Montserrat and Allesandrine, and Genoa ; and the Island of Sardinia.

Q. What are the situation and extent of the continental possessions of Sardinia ?

A. They lie between 6° and 10° 30' E. long ; and between 43° 40' and 46° 30' N. lat ; and are 200 miles long, and 130 broad ; containing about 15,000 square miles.

Q. How are they bounded ?

A. On the N. by Switzerland ; on the E. by the river Tessino which divides them from the Austrian possessions, and by Parma and Modena ; on the S. by the Gulf of Genoa ; and on the W. by France.

Q. What are the situation and extent of the Island of Sardinia ?

A. It lies between 39° and 51° 15' N. lat. and between 8° 45' and 10° 15' E. long. ; is 160 miles long and 70 broad, containing 7000 square miles. A narrow strait separates it from Corsica.

Q. What is the soil of these territories?

A. Savoy is not fertile, as is true also of the territory of Genoa; but Piedmont and the island of Sardinia abound in corn, wine, oil, silk, maize, rice, hemp, flax and fruits. Sardinia has also immense flocks of sheep and valuable fisheries.

Q. What is the government?

A. An absolute monarchy. Sardinia is governed by a viceroy. The revenue may be estimated at 1,500,000l. sterling. The army, according to the old establishment, will be about 35,000 men.

Q. What is the population?

A. The continental territories contained in 1807, 2,974,775; that of the island was estimated, in 1809, at 520,000 : in all 3,494,775.

Q. What is the capital?

A. Turin, in Piedmont, on the Po, in lat. 45° 8′. It is a strong and beautiful town, and has a population of 73,716.— The houses are of brick and well built.

Q. Describe Genoa?

A. It stands at the head of the Gulf of Genoa, and is a place of great strength. The houses are handsome and lofty, and the harbor is a fine bay, opening to the south. The population 80,156.

Q. What are the other towns?

A. Alexandria on the Tenaro, with 32,225 inhabitants; Asti, a little above, on the same river, with 21,225; Nice, near the mouth of the Var, with 18,473; all in Piedmont; and Chamberg, the capital of Savoy, with 10,800.

Q. What towns are there in the Island of Sardinia?

A. Cagliari, the capital, in the S. has a population of 50,000, a large deep harbor, and an extensive commerce. Sassari, in the N. W. has 30,000 inhabitants. The Sardinians are proud, ignorant and brutish.

OF THE AUSTRIAN DOMINIONS IN ITALY.

Q. What do you say of the Austrian dominions in Italy?

A. They lie in the N. E. part of Italy, N. of the Po and E. of the Tessino, contain about 33,000 square miles, and 6,071,927 inhabitants, and have already been described in the account of Austria.

DUCHY OF MODENA.

Q. What territories belong to the duke of Modena?

A. The duchies of Modena and Minandola, and the territories of Reggio, Massa and Carrara: containing in all about 1800 square miles, and 470,000 inhabitants.

Q. Where are they situated ?

A. Genoa and Parma lie on the W.; Mantua, N.; the States of the Church and Lucca, E.; and the Mediterranean S. The revenue is about 180,000l. sterling. The present sovereign is the archduke Francis D'Este. Modena, the capital, has 26,884 inhabitants.

DUCHY OF PARMA.

Q. What territories belong to the duchy of Parma ?

A. The duchies of Parma, Placentia and Guastella; containing about 1500 square miles, and 300,000 inhabitants.

Q. What is their situation ?

A. Piedmont is W.; Milan, N.; Modena, E.; and Genoa, S. The soil is fertile. Parma, the capital, has 35,000 inhabitants. The revenue is about 200,000l. sterling. _ The present sovereign is the unfortunate Maria Louisa, daughter of the emperor of Austria, and late wife of Napoleon Bonaparte.

DUCHY OF LUCCA.

Q. What is the situation of Lucca ?

A. It lies on the Mediterranean, N. of the Arno, between Tuscany and Modena. It has about 350 square miles and 127,000 inhabitants. Lucca, the capital, has 22,000. The duchess is the Infanta Maria Louisa, with a revenue of about 120,000l. sterling.

GRAND DUCHY OF TUSCANY.

Q. What is the situation of Tuscany ?

A. The Mediterranean and Lucca are S. and W.; and the States of the Church N. and E.; containing about 7000 square miles and 1,100,000 inhabitants. The country is remarkably rich and productive.

Q. What are the towns ?

A. Florence, the capital, on the Arno; has 80,000 inhabitants, and is one of the most beautiful cities in Italy. Leghorn, on the coast, has 58,000, and is the most commercial town. Pisa, N. of Leghorn, has 22,000.

Q. What is the government ?

A. The archduke Ferdinand, brother of the emperor Francis, of Austria, is the present archduke. His revenue exceeds 500,000l. sterling, and he can bring into the field, on an emergency, 30,000 men.

STATES OF THE CHURCH.

Q. Where are the States of the Church situated?

A. In the heart of Italy. The Adriatic is on the N. E.; Naples on the S. E; the Mediterranean on the S.; Tuscany on the W.; and Modena and Mantua, on the N. W.—They contain about 16,000 square miles, and 2,000,000 inhabitants.

Q. What is the soil of this territory?

A. Formerly it was very fertile; but owing to the indolence of the inhabitants, considerable tracts now consist of mere marshes.

Q. What is the government?

A. The Pope is the political as well as spiritual head of these states. In the provinces he governs by legates. The religion is the Catholic. The revenue exceeds 1,000,000 sterling.

Q. What is the capital?

A. Rome, formerly the mistress of the world, is now the chief town of this territory. It lies on both sides of the Tiber, 15 miles from its mouth. It contains 300 churches, 35,900 dwelling houses, and 163,034 inhabitants. St. Peter's church is the noblest specimen of modern architecture.

Q. What are the other towns?

A. Bologna on the Savona, at the foot of the Appenines, with 63,420 inhabitants; and Ferrara, on a branch of the Po, with 24,444.

KINGDOM OF NAPLES; OR, THE TWO SICILIES.

Q. What territories belong to the kingdom of the two Sicilies.

A. Naples and the Island of Sicily.

Q. What are the situation and extent of Naples?

A. It lies between 38° and 42° 50′ N.; and between 13° 15′ and 19° E. It is 320 miles long and 100 broad; containing 25,000 square miles. It is divided into 12 provinces.

Q. How is it bounded?

A. On the N. W. by the States of the Church; on the N. E. by the Adriatic; on the S. E. and S. W. by the Mediterranean.

Q. What is the soil?

A. It is remarkable for its fertility, producing wheat, barley, maize, rice, flax, silk, and every variety of fruits. Iron, woollens, silk and glass are the chief manufactures.

Q. What is the extent of Sicily?

A. It is separated from the foot of Italy by the Straits of Messina; is 170 miles long by 120 in breadth; and contains about 10,880 square miles.

Q. What is the religion?

A. The Catholic. Naples in 1803, had 21 archbishops, 110 bishops, and 72,000 of the inferior clergy. Sicily has 2 archbishops and 7 bishops. The inferior clergy are also numerous.

Q. What is the government?

A. It is nearly despotic.

Q. What is the revenue?

A. In 1808, it amounted to 12,550,000 dollars. Of this sum Naples yields 9,880,000; and Sicily 2,670,000. The national debt of Naples was then 26,000,000.

Q. What is the military strength?

A. 21,000 for Naples and 10,000 for Sicily.

Q. What is the naval strength?

A. One ship of the line, five frigates, and 8 or 10 smaller vessels.

Q. What is the population?

A. That of Naples in 1803, was 4,963,502. Sicily, in 1797, contained 1,655,536 inhabitants, 340 market towns, and 268,000 houses. The united population of the two countries is 6,619,038.

Q. What is the capital?

A. Naples. It is at the head of a large bay, 12 miles in diameter, and 18 miles in circumference. The streets are broad and the houses well paved. The population is 412,-489. It is the fourth city in Europe.

Q. What are the other towns in Naples?

A. Tarranto, with 18,457 inhabitants; Bari, with 18,191, and Reggio with 16,139.

Q. What is the capital of Sicily?

A. Palermo, in the N. with a population of 120,000. It has an extensive commerce.

Q. What are the other towns?

A. Messina, on the straits, with 36,000; Catania, 50 miles S. with 40,000; and Siragoza with 17,044.

Q. What are the principal productions?

A. Silk, wines, salt, corn, fruits, glass and wool.

Q. What islands are off the coast of Naples?

A. In the Adriatic, Tremiti, St. Domino, Capraria, and St. Nicolo; and, on the W. coast, Capri, Ischia, Nicida, Pocida, Ponza, Palmaria and Zanona.

Q. What islands lie off Sicily?

A. The Lipari Isles, with 18,000 inhabitants, 8 in number,

are off the N. coast ; the Egatian Isles, off the W. coast, 3
in number, with a population of 12,000 ; and Pantalaria, half
way between Sicily and Africa, with 3000.

OF MALTA.

Q. Where is the island of Malta?

A. It is 50 miles S. of Sicily, is a solid rock of freestone,
20 miles by 12, and containing 134 square miles. It contains
74,705 inhabitants ; Gozzo in its neighborhood has 12,464 ;
and Comino 603 ; in all 87,772.

Q. To whom does it belong?

A. To Great Britain. It is almost impregnable. Vallette,
the capital, contains 23,680 inhabitants. It bids fair to be
the emporium of the Mediterranean.

OF THE TURKISH EMPIRE.

Q. What territories are under the dominions of the Grand
Seignior ?

A. In Europe, Turkey proper, comprising ancient Greece,
Thrace, Maesia ; and part of Illyricum, Sarmatia and Da-
cia ; and in Asia, Turkey in Asia, including Asia Minor,
Syria, Circassia, Armenia, and Mesopotamia.

OF TURKEY IN EUROPE.

Q. What is the situation of Turkey in Europe?

A. It is the southeastern country of Europe, lying between 36° 30' and 48° 30' north latitude ; and between
16° and 40° east longitude.

Q. What is the extent of Turkey ?

A. Its greatest length from N. to S. is 870 miles, and the
greatest breadth 600. The number of square miles is estimated at 212,410.

Q. What are the boundaries ?

A. On the N. Austria and Russia ; on the E. the Black
Sea, Straits of Constantinople, Sea of Marmora, Dardanelles, and the Archipelago ; on the S. the Archipelago
a d Mediterranean ; and on the W. the Mediterranean,
the Adriatic, Dalmatia and Croatia.

Q. What is the climate ?

A. It is mild, healthy, and serene.

Q. What is the soil ?

A. Few countries are equally fertile. Wheat, barley,
maize, and rice grow in immense quantities even with the
sorry agriculture of the Turks.

Q. What mountains are there in Turkey ?

A. Beyond the Danube, a part of the Carpathian chain

runs about 200 miles on the borders of Moldavia. The long range of Haëmus stretches upwards of 400 miles.

Q. What are the rivers of Turkey?

A. The Dniester, the Danube, the Maritz, and the Vardari.

Q. What is the population of Turkey?

A. About 9,882,000.

Q. What is the capital city of Turkey in Europe?

A. Constantinople.

Q. Give a description of it?

A. It was built by the Roman Emperor Constantine the Great, and stands on the European side of the Bosphorus, on the spot where stood the ancient city Byzantium. It is situated in 41 degrees of north latitude, and 29 degrees of east longitude. It is one of the largest cities in Europe, containing about five hundred thousand inhabitants.—About two thirds of the inhabitants of Constantinople are Greeks and Armenians.

Q. Describe Philippoli?

A. It is a town on the Maritz, lat. 42° 22′ meanly built in a marsh; containing 26,000 houses, and 120,000 inhabitants.

Q Describe Adrianople?

A. It stands on the great bend of the Maritz, in lat. 41° 41′. The houses are chiefly of mud, and the streets narrow and dirty. The population is 100,000.

Q. What are the other towns?

A. Saloniki has 62,000 inhabitants; Bosna Serai 48,000; Sophia 46,000; Bucharest 42,000; and Belgrade 30,000.

Q. What nations people Turkey?

A. The modern Greeks chiefly occupy the province of Albania, comprehending the Morea, Livadia, Thessaly, Macedonia, and Albania proper. They also are almost the only inhabitants of the islands. The Turks are principally embodied in Rumelia. The inhabitants of Bosnia, Servi, Bulgaria, Wollachia, Molda ia and Bessarabia are Sclavonians, descendants of the ancient Slavi.

Q What are the characteristics of the Turks?

A. They are indolent, superstitious, heavy, morose, treacherous, furiously passionate, jealous, unsocial, and unfriendly to all other nations. The Turks are now the only obstacle to the establishment of Christianity in Western Asia; it is believed that the time is at hand, when they will be banished from Europe. The Greeks are enterprising, intelligent, shrewd and industrious.

Q. What are the customs of the Turks?

A. They commonly sit cross-legged in company, and spend much of their time with their women; drink coffee, smoke tobacco, or chew opium. They salute each other by nodding the head and laying the right hand on the breast.— They accustom themselves to frequent bathings and prayers. The lower sort live chiefly on rice; and their meat is always boiled or roasted to rags.

Q. What are their diversions?

A. These are tilting darts, or shooting at the mark, and sometimes hunting; but their common diversion is playing at chess, at which they never bet any money.

Q. What is the Turkish dress?

A. The Turks shave their heads, wear a turban instead of a hat, and a cloak fastened with a sash. Their breeches form but one piece with their stockings. The women dress much like the men, but they wear veils when they go abroad.

Q. What do you say of the Turkish marriages?

A. Their religion allows them only four wives; but as many concubines as they please. The women negociate the match, the men troubling themselves very little about it.

Q. What is the language of Turkey?

A. There are several languages spoken in the country, among which is modern Greek and Arabic.

Q. What is the state of learning?

A. The Turks pay no attention to it, and have no universities. Some of them learn to read the koran, to write a letter and to make verses.

Q. What is the state of the Turkish commerce?

A. Owing to the oppression of the government, the commerce is not flourishing. Their exports are wheat, maize, rice, wool, camel's hair, goat's hair, cotton, hides, leather, silk, flax, coffee, sugar, honey, tobacco, wax, and numerous other articles.

Q. What is the state of the Turkish manufactures?

A. The Turks manufacture carpets of superior beauty, printed muslins, crapes, gauzes, fire-arms, swords and morocco leather.

Q. What is the government of Turkey?

A. An absolute despotism. The despot takes the title of the grand seignior. The succession is limited to the family of the Othmanidae. When the grand seignior dies, the army select the successor out of that family. The prime minister is called the grand vizier. In war he is generalissimo of the armies. The governors of provinces are styled pachas.

Q. What is the revenue of Turkey?

A. The miri or public revenue is estimated at 15 millions of dollars. The hasne, or revenue of the sultan, is said greatly to exceed the other.

G

Q. What is the military strength of Turkey ?

A. In 1804, it included 190,000 infantry and 107,000 cavalry : in all 297,000 men. The horse-guards called spahis, are 20,000 in number ; and the foot-guards called janizaries, are 40.000.

Q. What is the naval strength of Turkey?

A. The Turkish navy, in 1806, comprised 20 ships of the line, 15 frigates, and 32 smaller vessels of war.

Q. How does Turkey lie with respect to the other European countries ?

A. It lies south of Russia, Poland, Prussia and Hungary ; southeast of Norway, Sweden, Denmark, Germany, England, Scotland, Ireland, and France ; and east of Portugal, Spain and Italy.

OF THE TURKISH ISLANDS.

Q. What islands belong to Turkey in Europe?

A. Candia, and those lying in the western half of the Archipelago.

Q. Describe Candia ?

A. Candia, the ancient Crete, lies at the bottom of the Archipelago, in lat. 35° north, and between longitude 23° 30′ and 26° 30′ east. It is 180 miles long, from east to west, and about 40 broad ; containing 4318 square miles, and a population of 280,000. The capital, Candia, is on the northern coast, and has a population of 14,000.

Q. Describe Negropont ?

A. It was anciently a peninsula, called Euboea ; but is now an island, separated from Greece by a long narrow strait, called the Euripus. It is 96 miles long, from northwest to southeast, and from 8 to 16 broad ; and contains 482 square miles, and 40,000 inhabitants. The capital, Negropont, on the Euripus, contains 16,000 inhabitants, and has a good harbour.

Q. What are the other islands ?

A. Lemnos, Andros, Tinos, Thassos, Scyros, Myconi, Naxia, Paros, Antiparos, Nio, Egina, Zea, Thermia, Milo, Santorini, and many of inferior si

OF ASIA.

Q. WHAT is the situation of Asia ?

A. Asia is the northeast division of the eastern continent ; and lies between 2° and 77° north lat. ; and between 26° and 190° east longitude. The most western point of Asia is Cape Baba, in Asia Minor ; the most eastern is East Cape, on the promontory of the Techutski. The most northern limit is Cape Taimura, in the country of the Samoeids, in Siberia; the most southern is the promontory of Malacca, in farther India.

Q. What is the extent of Asia?

A. The greatest length, from E. to W. is about 7500 miles; and the greatest breadth, from N. to S. is 5250. The number of square miles is estimated at 12,000,000. Asia is larger than Africa and Europe united.

Q. How is Asia bounded?

A. On the N. by the Frozen Ocean; on the E. and S. E. by the Pacific Ocean, which divides it from America; on the S. by the Indian Ocean; and on the W. by the Red Sea, Egypt, the Mediterranean, the Archipelago, the Sea of Marmora, Black Sea, Sea of Azoph, and Russia in Europe.

Q. How is Asia divided?

A. The northern part of Asia belongs to Russia, and is called Asiatic Russia or Siberia. Immediately south of this lies Mandsburia, in the east; Mougalia in the middle, and Independent Tartary in the west. The two former constitute Chinese Tartary. Turkey in Asia lies west of Independent Tartary. Arabia, Persia, Hindostan, farther India and China, are in the south of Asia.

Q. What is the population of Asia?

A. If we take Sir George Staunton's account of the population of China at 333,000,000 as accurate, the whole population of Asia will not fall short of 500,000,000.

Q. What are the religions of Asia?

A. About nine tenths of the Asiatics or 450 millions, are heathens. About 47 millions are Mahometans; and about 3 millions are Christians. The Christians are found in Hindostan, Georgia, and Russia in Asia. The Mahometans are found in Turkey, in Asia, Arabia, Persia and Hindostan, and are thinly scattered in farther India, Independent Tartary, and Russia in Asia.

Q. What are the governments of Asia?

A. Asiatic Russia, Turkey in Asia, and a large part of Hindostan belong to Europe. These comprize about half of the continent. The independent governments are all despotic.

Q. What is the nature of the Asiatic commerce?

A. It is almost wholly passive. The ships of Europe and America are their carriers.

Q. How has Asia been distinguished in the history of mankind?

A. It was the scene of all the events recorded in the old testament. Here our first parents were placed by the Creator. Here Noah and his sons planted themselves after the deluge. Here the Assyrian, Babylonian and Persian empires rose and fell. Here all the miracles of the bible were performed. Here our Saviour was born, lived and died, and here the gospel was first published to mankind.

OF TURKEY IN ASIA.

Q. What is the situation of Turkey in Asia?

A. It is the westernmost country of Asia, lying between 26° and 47° east longitude; and between 31° and 45° north latitude. Its highest latitude is the mouth of the Cuban.—Its lowest is the south of Syria.

Q. What is its extent?

A. It is about 1000 miles long, from north to south; and 840 miles broad; comprizing about 470,000 square miles.

Q. How is it bounded?

A. On the N. by the Black Sea and Asiatic Russia; on the E. by Asiatic Russia and Persia, and by the river Tigris; on the S. by Arabia and the Levant; on the W. by the Levant and the Archipelago; and on the N. W. by the Dardanelles, the Sea of Marmora, and the Straits of Constantinople.

Q. How is it divided?

A. Into the following provinces; viz. Anatolia, between the Black Sea and Levant; Scham, or Soria, east of the Levant; Caucasus east of the Black Sea; Armenia south and southeast of Caucasus; Curdistan south of Armenia; Algezira between Curdistan and Syria; and Irak-Arabi south east of Algezira.

Q. To what countries do these divisions correspond?

A. Anatolia is Asia Minor. Soria or Scham is ancient Syria. Caucasus comprizes Dircassa. Algezira and Irak-Arabi are the ancient Mesopotamia.

Q. What is the climate?

A. That of Anatolia is delightful. Some of its western seaports however are unhealthy. In the southern provinces the heats are oppressive.

Q. What is the face of the country?

A. This country is generally mountainous. Particularly is this true of Asia Minor, Armenia and Caucasus. The mountains are intermingled with large and beautiful plains, covered with numerous flocks and herds. Mesopotamia, is generally a plain country.

Q. What is the soil?

A. In the south near Arabia, it is a region of sand. Elsewhere generally the soil is good. The agriculture is deplorably neglected.

Q. What are the mountains of Turkey in Asia?

A. Mount Caucasus, Mount Taurus, Mount Ararat and Mount Libanus.

Q. What are the rivers of Turkey in Asia?

A. The great river of this country, the Euphrates, runs S. E. to the Persian Gulf about 1500 miles.

Q. Describe the river Tigris?

A. It runs S. E. about 1000 miles, and falls into the Euphrates 60 miles above Bassora. The tongue of land between these two rivers is the S. E. limit of Turkey in Asia.

Q. What are the other rivers?

A. The Kizil Irmak, the Sacaria, the Sarabat, the Mender and the Orontes. The river JORDAN issues from Lake Phiala, and soon loses itself in the sand. In 15 miles it reappears and passes through Lake Meron. Again it flows through the Lake of Tiberias and thence runs southward 65 miles and falls into the Dead Sea.

Q. What lakes are there in Turkey in Asia?

A. Lake Van, is 80 miles long and 40 broad. The Dead Sea is 24 miles long and 6 or 7 broad. It occupies the site of ancient Sodom and the cities of the plain. Its waters abound with sulphur and bitumen. No fish can live in them. In the centre of Asia Minor is the Salt Lake, 70 miles long, and 2 or 3 broad.

Q. What are the animals?

A. The lion, the tiger, the leopard, the hyena, the wild boar, the jackal, the ibex, the antelope, the deer and the hare. The cattle of this country are inferior. The mutton is excellent. The best horses are of Arabian descent.

Q. What are the vegetable productions?

A. Among the trees are the weeping willow, the olive, the wild olive, the white mulberry, the storax tree, the pomegranate, almond, peach, cherry, lemon, orange, myrtle, fig, date, the cypress and the cedar. Madder, jalap, castor oil, opium and spikenard are among the vegetable drugs.

Q. What mineral waters are celebrated?

A. Those of the Prusa at the foot of Olympus.

Q. What is the number of inhabitants?

A. It is estimated at about 11 millions. Of these 6 millions are in Anatolia; one and a half millions in Syria; 800,000 in Algezira; 300,000 in Caucasus; one million in Irak-Arabi; half a million in Curdistan; and 900,000 in Armenia.

Q. What is the religion?

A. The Mahometan. In Caucasus is a nation of Christians called Sonnas, about 200,000 in number.

Q. What is the government ?

A. Each province is governed by a pacha. The whole system is a system of oppression and plunder.

Q. What is the capital ?

A. Haleb or Aleppo. It lies in latitude 36° 20' in the north of Syria, about 80 miles eastward from the Mediterranean. It is well built; has an extensive commerce, and large manufactures of silks and cottons ; and contains a population of 250,000.

Q. Describe Damascus ?

A. It lies also in Syria in lat. 33°, and has a population of 180,000. Its manufactures of silks, cottons and soap are extensive.

Q. Describe Smyrna ?

A. Smyrna lies on a gulf of the same name in the Archipelago. Its houses are mud huts, and its streets filthy. Yet it is the chief mart of European commerce in the east; and has 140,000 inhabitants.

Q. What are the other towns ?

A. Angora, Prusa, Tocat, and Bassora.

Q. What celebrated cities were formerly found in this region ?

A. BABYLON, on the Euphrates ; NINEVEH, on the Tigris ; JERUSALEM, in the S. of Syria ; TYRE and SIDON, on the coast of Syria ; PALMYRA, in the desert; and EPHESUS, on the Archipelago. TREBIZOND and SINOPE, were once celebrated ports on the Black Sea.

OF THE ISLANDS BELONGING TO TURKEY IN ASIA.

Q. What islands belong to Turkey in Asia ?

A. Cyprus, Rhodes, Cos, Samos, Chios, Mytilene, and several smaller islands.

Q. Describe Cyprus ?

A. It lies in that part of the Mediterranean called the Levant ; between 32° 20' and 35° E. ; and between 34° 30' and 35° 30' N. It is 160 miles long from E. to W. and 70 broad. The soil is fertile. Silk, cotton, wines, turpentine, timber and fruits are the chief products. The population is 50,000. Nicosia is the capital.

Q. Describe Rhodes ?

A. It lies near the S. W. angle of Asia, a short distance from Cape Cano ; is 36 miles long from N. to S. by 15 ; produces wheat; and has 40,000 inhabitants. Rhodes, the capital is on the north end.

OF RUSSIA IN ASIA.

Q. What is the situation of Russia in Asia?

A. It spreads over the whole northern half of Asia from Europe eastward to the Pacific Ocean. Including the late additions from Persia, it lies between 37° and 77° north latitude, and between 37° and 190° east longitude.

Q. What is its extent?

A. Its length from E. to W. is about 4600 miles; and its breadth 2000.

Q. How is it bounded?

A. On the north by the Northern Ocean; on the east by the same ocean, by Behring's Straits, the Sea of Kamtschatka, and the Sea of Okotsk; on the S. by the Sea of Kamtschatka, the Sea of Okotsk, Chinese Tartary, Independent Tartary, the Caspian Sea, Persia, Turkey in Asia, and the Black Sea; on the W. by the Black Sea, the Sea of Azoph, and Russia in Europe.

Q. How is it divided?

A. Into four governments: Cazan, Astrachan, Tobolsk and Irkutsk. The two latter constitute Siberia.

Q. What is the climate?

A. The governments of Cazan and Astrachan enjoy a mild and temperate climate, as do the new acquisitions from Persia. Those of Tobolsk and Irkutsk lie chiefly between 50° and 77° north latitude, and are therefore rather frigid than temperate.

Q. What is the face of the country?

A. The northern coast presents immense marshy plains covered with almost perpetual snows. Much of the middle and south of Siberia are hilly and mountainous. Here however we find vast plains called steppes, occupying whole provinces.

Q. What are the rivers?

A. The rivers in this country, in their size and length approach those of America. The Unal, the Oby, the Yenisea and the Lena.

Q. What gulfs and seas are there on the coast?

A. On the northern coast, the Sea of Cara, and the Gulf of Oby; on the eastern coast, the Sea of Kamtschatka and the Sea of Okotsk.

Q. What lakes are there in this country?

A. The Caspian Sea, is the largest lake on the globe. It lies between 46° 15′ and 36° 50′ north latitude; and is 650 miles long; and in the north 265, and in the south 235 broad. Its circumference is 2820 miles; and its area is 150,000 square miles.

Q. Describe the Baikal?

A. It is between 51 and 55 north latitude ; is 400 miles long from N. E. to S. W. ; and from 40 to 50 broad.

Q. What are the mountains ?

A. The Altaian Mountains are, after the Andes, the longest chain on the globe. They commence in the country of the Techutski, in the north east of Siberia, and run south west a long distance, till they divide the waters of the Amoor and the Lena. Thence their course is west along the head waters of the Yenisea, the Oby and the Irtish. Their whole length probably exceeds 5000 miles.

Q. Describe the Uralian mountains ?

A. They commence between the Caspian and Lake Aral ; and pursue a northward course of 1800 miles to the sea of Cara, where they terminate in two lofty promontories.

Q. What are the vegetable productions ?

A. The cedar, cypress, savine, red juniper, beech and oak are found on the mountains ; the almond, peach, fig, quince, apricot, pear, vine and olive, are among the fruits.

Q. What are the animal productions ?

A. The rein-deer is common throughout Siberia, and in the south the horse and the ass are found wild. The bison, the wild sheep, the ibex, the stag, the wild boar, the bear, the wolf and the fox are hunted in the mountains.

Q. What are the mineral productions ?

A. The gold mines of Catherinburg on the Uralian mountains, in lat. 57, are of great value. Copper abounds. But the iron mines are of much greater importance. They are very numerous and rich.

Q. What is the population ?

A. The census of 1796, gave a return of 6,893,677, exclusive of savages. Of this number 1,038,359 were in Siberia. To these, by adding the supposed number of savages in each government, and the actual increase ascertained by a register of births and deaths, the population in 1808, is discovered to have been 9,274,000. Of these, 1,510,600 only were in Siberia.

Q. What nations occupy this country ?

A. The Tartars, Monguls, and Mandshuns, are the three great nations of Asiatic Russia, divided each into numerous tribes.

Q. What are the characteristics of these people ?

A. These three principal nations live chiefly in tents, in imaks or clusters of 150 to 300 families. They remove frequently from place to place for pasturage. Their religious books are in the language of Thibet. Each imak has a schoolmaster. They remove from ten to fifteen times a year. Their amusements are races on horseback, archery, wrestling, pantomimes, dances, cards and chess. Their herds consist of horses, camels, oxen, sheep and goats. They live chiefly on their herds and on the animals killed in hunting. All the labour is performed by the women. In the western part of Asiatic Russia, the inhabitants are civilized and stationary resembling their neighbours in Europe.

Q. What is the religion of this country ?

A. In the western cities and towns most of the inhabitants profess the Greek religion. Many of the tribes in the south west are Mahometans. The Mongul tribes worship the Grand Lama. The Mandshuns are Shamanians. Tobolsk is an archbishopric, as are Cazan and Astrachan. There is another see at Irkutsk. At Karass, 530 miles southwest of Astrachan and 260 north of Tifflis, there is an important missionary establishment.

Q. What is the government ?

A. Governors are appointed by the emperor for each of the four governments.

Q. What languages are spoken ?

A. The Sclavonian and the Finnish in the west. The languages of the Mandshuns, the Monguls and the Tartars are each radically different.

Q. What are the large towns ?

A. Astrachan, Azof, Tobolsk, Tefflis, Derbend, Kolyvan and Irkutsk.

Q. Describe Astrachan

A. It is near the mouth of the Wolga, in lat. 46° 40'; is built of wood ; contains 25 Greek churches, beside Armenian, Lutheran and Catholic churches and a Hindoo temple. Its population is 70,000. Its commerce is valuable.

Q. Describe Tobolsk ?

A. It stands at the confluence of the Tobol with the Irtish, and has a population of 15,000 souls. It is the chief town in Siberia, and receives India goods by the Kalmuck and Bucharian merchants.

Q. What are the manufactures ?

A. Leather, salt and nitre are manufactured at Astrachan ; isinglass and kaviar on the Caspian; felts among the Tartars ; and pitch extensively in Siberia.

Q. What is the commerce ?

A. On the Black Sea, furs, kaviar, iron and linen are exported to Turkey, in return for wine, fruits, coffee, silks and rice. An extensive commerce is carried on with the Chinese by land at a town in 106° 32' east and 50° north; called by the Russians Kiachta, and by the Chinese Maimatschin. The yearly amount is two million of roubles.

Q. What is the commerce with Russia Proper ?

A. Siberia annually sends iron, salt, gold, silver, furs, skins, copper, &c. to the value of 12 million of roubles.

Q. What islands belong to Asiatic Russia ?

A. Behrings I. Copper I. and the Kurilian isles.

Q. Describe them ?

A. The two first lie in the Sea of Kamtschatka. The last lie directly south of the peninsula of Kamtschatka, and are about 20 in number. The population of all these islands is estimated at 8000.

OF INDEPENDENT TARTARY.

Q. What is the situation of Independent Tartary ?

A. It is west of the centre of Asia, and is wholly an inland country; lying between 34? and 55° north latitude ; and between 51° and 84° east longitude.

Q. What is its extent ?

A. The length, from the mountains of Guar in the south, to the Russian boundary in the north, is 1500 miles. The breadth from the Caspian to the Chinese boundary, is 900 miles.

Q. How is it bounded ?

A. On the north by the government of Tobolsk in Asiatic Russia ; on the east by Mongolia in Chinese Tartary; on the south by Hindostan and Persia ; and on the west by Persia, the Caspian, and the government of Astrachan. On the Caspian it reaches from the river Tedjen in lat. 39° to the mouth of the Jemba in lat. 46°. The Irtish is the northeast boundary, from its source to the town of Omsk, in lat. 50°.

Q. What are the divisions of Independent Tartary ?

A. In the north, is the immense steppe or desert of Issim, in the southern part of which are the three hordes of Kirguses —the great, in the east ; the middle, and the lesser, on the Caspian. In the S. W. is Karasm, formerly a powerful kingdom. It lies between the Caspian, and the river Gihon on the east. The great horde of Kirguses, reaches S. to the mountains of Argun. All the country south of those mountains is called Great Bucharia. It has the Gihon, on the west ; Persia and Hindostan, on the south ; and the Belur Mountains, dividing it from Chinese Tartary, on the east.

Q. What is the climate ?

A. In general it appears to be excellent. Even in the southern provinces, though in the parallel of Spain, Greece and Turkey, the heat of the summer is mild and temperate.

Q. What is the face of the country ?

A. In the north the steppe of Issim is an immense plain reaching from the northern boundary to below the Lake of Aral. The country between the Lake of Aral and the Caspian is a high level plain. Karazm, on the country south of the Aral, is chiefly a level country. Great Bucharia is a country of mountains, hills and vallies.

Q. What are the rivers of Independent Tartary?

A. The Amu or Gihon runs W. and N. W. to the lake of Aral 900 miles. The Sirr or Sihon, about 550 miles, and falls into the east side of the same lake.

Q. What are the lakes?

A. The lake of Aral lies about 120 miles east of the dead gulf of the Caspian, between 43° and 47° north, and between 58° and 63° east. It is about 250 miles long, and from 70 to 100 broad. Its waters are salt.

Q. What are the mountains?

A. The Belur-Tag, separates Great Bucharia from Chinese Tartary. The Argun Mountains bound Great Bucharia on the north.

Q. What are the cities of Independent Tartary?

A. Bokhara, and Balk, Khiva and Samarcand.

Q. Describe Khiva?

A. Khiva is on a small tributary of the Gihon, about 300 miles east from the Caspian, in lat. 41° 45′; is fortified; and has mud houses with flat roofs.

Q. Describe Samarcand?

A. It is on the south bank of the Sogd, a branch of the Gihon, about 120 miles above Bokhara, in a delightful country. It is the capital of the whole country.

Q. Who are the inhabitants of this region?

A. The Kirguses in the north; the Kievinski Tartars in Karasm; and the Bucharians or Usbeks in Bucharia. There is also a tribe of Turcomans, on the coast of the Caspian.

Q. Describe the Kirguses?

A. From time immemorial, they have been classed in three hordes: the great, the middle, and the lesser. The great horde is considered as the source of the other two. Each horde is governed by its own khan or prince. They live in tents made of felt, and lead a wandering life.

Q. Describe the Turcomans?

A. They spread from the dead gulf along the Caspian, to the bay of Balkan, and occupy the islands in that bay. They are robbers and pirates.

Q. Describe the Kievinski Tartars?

A. They resemble the Kirguses, but surpass them in cunning and treachery. They live in towns and villages. The khan is absolute and resides at Kieva. Much of their country is barren. A small tribe of Usbecks occupy the angle made by the Tedjen and the Caspian.

Q. Who are the Bucharians?

A. In 1494, this country was inhabited by a nation of Monguls. In that year, their sultan Baber was driven with his army from Great Bucharia into Hindostan, where he founded the Mogul empire. The nation which drove him out was a numerous horde of Usbeck Tartars. Many of the Monguls remained in the country. Their descendants and those of the Usbecks now constitute the people of Bucharia.

Q. Describe the Bucharians?

A. Their religion is the Mahometan of the Sunni sect. They are divided into distinct provinces each subject to its own khan. Those of Balk and Samarcand are the most powerful. Each of them is despotic. The whole revenue is estimated at half a million sterling. The country people in summer live in tents but in the winter in villages. They are bold, enterprising and industrious; and often make hostile incursions into Persia. Their language is the Zagathian or Turkish.

Q. What is the population?

A. The middle and lesser hordes of Kirguses are estimated each at 30,000 families or 180,000 individuals. The great horde is about as large as both the others: making a total of 720,000. The population of Karasm has not been estimated. It is not very great. The inhabitants of Great Bucharia are estimated at one million.

Q. What are the manufactures?

A. In Bucharia, silk-paper, silks, soap, calico and fine linen.

Q. What is the commerce?

A. The Kirguses trade with the Russians at Orenberg, on the Ural. The middle horde trade at Omsk. Sheep to the number of 150,000, horses, cattle, lamb-skins, camel's wool and camelets, and Persian and Turcoman slaves are carried to Orenberg. In return they receive cloths and furniture. From Bucharia and Karasm, in return for camels and cattle, they get arms and coats of mail. The Kievinski Tartars carry cattle, furs and hides to Bokhava and Persia. From Bucharia are exported silks, rhubarb, musk, lapis-lazuli, rubies, gold and silver. The Hindoo traders resort chiefly to Balk.

OF THE CHINESE EMPIRE.

Q. What is the situation of the Chinese empire?

A. It occupies the whole of Middle Asia east of Independent Tartary, as well as the southern coast as far west as the Gulf of Tongquin. It reaches from longitude 70° to 144° east; and from latitude 20° 30' to 56° north.

Q. What is its extent ?

A. Its length from east to west is 3600 miles. Its greatest breadth in the east is 2500. Its common breadth is about 1750 miles.

Q. What are the boundaries of the Chinese empire ?

A. On the north, the Altaian mountains divide it from Russia; on the east lie the channel of Tartary, the Sea of Japan, the Straits of Corea, the Yellow Sea, and the Pacific Ocean ; on the south the China Sea, India and Hindostan ; and on the west Independent Tartary. The whole extent of seacoast, from Russia, in the north, to the frontier of Tongquin, is about 4500 miles.

Q. How is this immense region divided ?

A. Into China, Chinese Tartary and the tributary dominions of China.

OF CHINESE TARTARY.

Q. What is the situation of Chinese Tartary ?

A. It lies between 70° and 144° east longitude, and between 35° and 56° north latitude.

Q. What is its extent ?

A. Its length, from east to west is 3600 miles ; its breadth is about 15 degrees of latitude, or 1050 miles.

Q. How is it bounded ?

A. On the north by Asiatic Russia; on the east by the channel of Tartary and the Sea of Japan ; on the south by Corea, the Yellow Sea, China Proper, Thibet and Hindostan ; and on the west by Independent Tartary.

Q. What are the divisions ?

A. The western and largest division of this country is inhabited by Mongul tribes, and the eastern by Mandshurs. Hence the two parts have been called Mongolia and Mandshuria.

Q. What is the climate ?

A. It is much colder here than in the corresponding latitudes of Europe.

Q. What is the face of the country ?

A. The most singular feature is that immense table-land or elevated plain occupying full two thirds of the whole country. This prodigious plain is indeed the country of Mongolia, and lies between 70° and 120° east and 35° and 50° north. Its southern division is the sandy desert of Cobi or Shamo, which is destitute of plants and water, and is safely passed only on camels. Mandshuria is a country of mountains, hills and vallies.

Q. What is the state of agriculture ?

H

A. The southern Mandshurs and the Monguls of little Bucharia pay some attention to agriculture. They cultivate wheat.

Q. What are the vegetable productions?

A. They are little known.

Q. What are the animals?

A. The camel, the ibex or rock-goat, the tiger, the ermine, the wild horse, and the wild ass, are among the animals of this country.

Q. What is the great river of this country?

A. The Amoor, a river which winds in a southeast and north northeast direction, to the channel of Tartary, emptying in latitude 53° after a course of 2000 miles.

Q. What are the other rivers?

A. The Yarkand, and the Ili, the Irtish, the Oby, the Yerisea and the Hoangho, all rise in Chinese Tartary.

Q. What are the lakes?

A. The Balkash, the Zaizan, and the Kokonor.

Q. What are the mountains?

A. The Altaian Range is on the north; and the Belur-Tag on the west. The northern mountains of Thibet, constituting the southern frontiers, are little known. The Bogdo-Alim, or the Almighty Mount, thought to be the highest in Asia, is in lat. 46°.

Q. What are the towns of Mongelia?

A. Cashgar, Yarkand, Turfan and Hami.

Q. Describe them?

A. Cashgar, is on a branch of the Yarkand in little Bucharia, close to the western frontier. It was once a very large town, and still retains considerable commerce. Yarkand is on the river of the same name, and S. S. E. of Cashgar. Kotum and Karia, are S. E. of Yarkand. Turfan is a town of some commerce in longitude 85°. Hami or Chami is a populous place, about half a league in circuit, with two beautiful gates. It is in a large fertile plain forming a kind of island in the desert of Cobi. Naimatchini or Maimatochin is a trading town on the Russian frontier, close to Kiachta.

Q. What are the towns of Mandshuria?

A. Chinyang, in the S. near the Yellow Sea, is the capital of the province of Leaodong. Nincouta, on the Hounha, is a considerable town, and the chief mart of ginseng.

Q. What is the population?

A. It has been estimated at 6,000,000; but this estimate is unquestionably too small. If we estimate the population of Mandshuria at 6,000,000 and that of Mongalia at 3,000,000 it will probably be nearer the truth.

Q. What is the religion?

A. That of the Mandshurs is Shamanism, or a belief in a Supreme Being who governs the world by numerous inferior deities. Many of the Monguls worship the Grand Lama.

Q. What is the government?

A. Mandshuria is divided into three great governments, Chinyang, Kiren-Oula and Tsitican or Daouria. The Monguls are divided into various tribes : the Kalkas in the northeast : the Kokonors in the southeast ; and the Eluts, spread very extensively in the middle and the west.

Q. What is the trade?

A. That of Mandshuria consists in ginseng and pearls.

Q. What large island lies off the coast of Mandshuria?

A. The island of Tchoka or Saghalien.

Q. Describe it?

A. It is between 46° and 54° north ; and is 550 miles long by 80 in breadth. The channel of Tartary, in the narrowest part not more than 20 miles wide, divides it from Mandshuria on the W. ; and the strait of Peyrouse, 20 miles wide, from Jesso on the S. The dress is a loose robe of skins, or quilted nankeen, with a girdle. Their huts are of timber thatched with grass. The people are mild and intelligent. The shores are level ; the centre is well wooded with pine, willow, oak and birch.

OF THE CHINESE TRIBUTARY DOMINIONS.

Q. What are the Chinese tributary dominions?

A. Corea and Tibet.

OF COREA.

Q. What is the situation and extent of Corea ?

A. Corea is a large peninsula on the northeast of China, lying between 34° and 42° north ; and between 125° and 131° east. It is about 620 miles long and 250 broad.

Q. How is it bounded ?

A. On the north by Mandshuria ; on the east by the sea of Japan and the straits of Corea ; on the south by the Pacific ; and on the west by the Yellow Sea.

Q. Describe Corea ?

A. It has its own king, but is tributary to China. It has a population of a million and a half. Kingkitao, the capital, is on a considerable river emptying into the Whanghai or Yellow Sea. The productions are gold, silver, iron, yellow varnish, silk-paper, ginseng, horses, furs and salt.

OF TIBET.

Q. What is the situation and extent of Tibet?

A. Tibet is an inland country of Asia, between 80° and 105° east; and between 27° and 35° north. Its length from east to west is therefore about 1400 miles, and its breadth in the east about 550; but in the west it is narrow.

Q. How is it bounded?

A. On the W. and N. by Mongolia; on the E. by China; and on the S. by Birma, Assam, Bootan and Nepaul.

Q. What is the climate?

A. In the spring the weather is variable, and marked with heat, thunder storms and refreshing showers. From June to September is the rainy season. From October to the beginning of March a clear and uniform sky prevails. During three months of this time the cold is intensely severe.

Q. What is the face of the country?

A. Its strong features are its ranges of mountains and large and numerous rivers. But little of the country is fertile. Most of the vallies are laid under water during winter. Wheat, pease and barley are cultivated.

Q. What are the rivers?

A. The Indus, the Ganges, and the Burrampooter of Hindostan, the Irawaddy, the Thaluan, and the Maykaung or Japanese river of farther India; and the Kian and Hoangho of China, all rise in Thibet. The Indus runs here about 400 miles; the Ganges 800; Burrampooter 1200; the Kian 1200; and the Hoangho 800.

Q. What are the lakes?

A. Lake Terkiri in the north is about 80 miles by 20.—Lake Palte, a little south of Lassa, is a wide trench, about 6 miles broad, every where surrounding an island of about 36 miles diameter.

Q. What are the mountains?

A. The range of Himlab on the south, and the mountains of Kentaisse on the north.

Q. What are the animals?

A. The Tibetians have horses, common cattle, sheep, goats, and a kind of cattle which do not low, but grunt like swine. The musk deer is found in the mountains.

Q. What are the minerals?

A. Gold, lead, cinnabar, rock salt and crude borax.

Q. What is the population?

A. Nothing is known with certainty respecting it.

Q. What is the religion?

A. The Tibetians believe that the Supreme Being is always incarnate. The man with whom they suppose him to be united, they call the Grand Lama, and pay him divine worship. When the body of the Grand Lama is about to die, he selects some other individual, usually an infant, in whom he proposes to dwell. After his death, the new Grand Lama has the power, privileges and worship of the old one. The Tibetians assemble in chapels for divine worship. The inferior priests are called Lamas.

Q. What is the government?

A. The Grand Lama formerly appointed a secular regent, a right which has probably passed to the Emperor of China.

Q. What are the characteristics?

A. A singular kind of polygamy prevails here—a plurality of husbands instead of wives. The inhabitants have made considerable progress in civilization. They reckon by lunar years of 29 days. The dead are usually exposed to beasts and birds of prey.

Q. What is the literature?

A. They have books, chiefly religious, printed with blocks of wood on slips of thin paper. The gylongs or monks educate many of the children.

Q. What are the cities?

A. Lassa, the capital, is near the Burrampooter.

Q. What are the manufactures?

A. Shawls and woollen cloths.

Q. What is the commerce?

A. At Sining, in the west part of the province of Shensee, the Tibetians trade with the Chinese. For tea, they barter gold-dust, diamonds, pearls, lamb skins, musk and woollens. To Nepaul, Tibet sends rock salt, borax, and gold-dust; for rice and cottons. The trade with Bengal is considerable.

OF CHINA.

Q. What is the situation of China?

A. It is the southeast country of Asia, lying between 20° 30' and 41° 30' north; and between 97° and 122° east.

Q. What is its extent?

A. The greatest length from N. to S. is 1400 miles. In the S. the breadth is 1200 miles but in the narrowest part not more than 750. It contains 1,298,000 square miles.

Q. How is it bounded?

A. On the east by the Yellow Sea and the Pacific Ocean; on the south by the China Sea, Tongquin, and Birma in farther India; on the west by Birma, Tibet, and Mongolia; and on the north by the great wall, which divides it from Mongolia and Mandshuria.

Q. What are the divisions?

A. It is divided into seventeen provinces.

Q. What is the climate? H 2

A. In the south, the climate is hot.   That of the north resembles that of New England.

Q. What is the face of the country ?

A. Generally it is level.   Many of the smaller hills have been reduced to plains by the industry of the inhabitants.

Q. What is the soil ?

A. It is naturally fertile, and has been rendered by cultivation much more so.

Q. What is the state of agriculture ?

A. The Chinese agriculture is carried to the highest perfection.   Pulse, grain, yams, sweet potatoes, cabbage, onions, carrots, and turnips, are among the culinary plants. Rice and grain are the most general objects of cultivation.

Q. What are the rivers ?

A. The two great rivers of China are the Hoangho and Kiang.   The Hoangho rises in the mountains north of Tibet, in about lat. 35° long. 94°.   It falls into the Pacific in lat. 33° 30′ after running about 3600 miles.

Q. Describe the Kiang ?

A. Its source is in the same mountains, about 300 miles further west.   It falls into the Pacific in lat. 32° about 100 miles south of the Hoangho.

Q. What are the other rivers ?

A. The Tigris, on which Canton stands, falls into the China Sea.

Q. What are the lakes ?

A. The Tong-tint, south of the river Kiang, is 240 miles in circumference.   The Poyang is about 120.   The Tai-houi is near Kankin.

Q. Are there are any canals in China ?

A. The canals of China are longer and larger than those of any other country.   Some of them exceed 1000 miles in length.

Q. What are the mountains ?

A. Two parallel ranges run eastward from Tibet through the empire.

Q. What are the vegetable productions ?

A. The tea tree is the most interesting.   The camphor tree, tallow tree, banyan, weeping willow, Spanish chesnut, and larch, are among the forest trees.   The fruit trees are the China orange, plantain, tamarind and mulberry.

Q. What are the animals ?

A. The tiger, buffalo, wild boar, bear, rhinoceros, camel, deer and musk deer.

Q. What are the minerals ?

A. Gold, silver, iron, copper, and mercury, lapis-lazuli,

jasper, rock crystal, loadstone, granite, porphyry, marble, and inexhaustible mines of coal.

Q. Describe the great wall of China ?

A. It is among the grandest labours of art, and is conducted over the highest mountains, the deepest vallies and the largest rivers. At the distance of almost every hundred yards is a tower 48 feet high, and 50 square. The wall is generally 25 feet high and 15 wide at the top. It separates China from Mandshuria and Mongolia, and is about 1500 miles in length. It is believed to have been built about the year 1160.

Q. What are the other antiquities and curiosities of China ?

A. Numerous ancient coins, artificial mountains, remarkable bridges, triumphal arches, splendid sepulchral monuments, and upwards of eleven hundred towers scattered over the empire.

Q. What is the religion of the Chinese ?

A. Shamanism was anciently the religion of the empire. The Supreme Deity was called Chang-Ti. About A. D. 65, the worship of the idol Fo was introduced and became general. Numberless subordinate idols are admitted. The Chinese believe in the transmigration of souls. A colony of Jews settled in China about 200 years before Christ. A few of them still remain at Caifong in Honan, on the Hoangho.

Q. What is the government ?

A. It is patriarchal. The emperor is absolute but rarely tyrannical. Public officers are called mandarins. Each province is under a governor who has absolute power. Rebellions against the governors are not unfrequent. Bribery is universal.

Q. What are the laws ?

A. They are exceedingly numerous and minute. The revenue laws resemble those of Europe. The interest of money is 36 per cent.

Q. What is the population ?

A. Sir George Staunton, from the information of a mandarin of high rank, ascertained the number of inhabitants to be 333 millions. This is almost half the human race.

Q. What is the revenue ?

A. It is estimated by Sir George Staunton, at 66,000,000 pounds sterling.

Q. What are the manners and customs ?

A. The Chinese are mild and tranquil. The upper classes are indolent, and the lower filthy. The merchants are fraudulent and dishonest. The complexion in the north is fair ; in the south swarthy. They are of small stature,

with broad faces, small black eyes, and short flat noses.
The chief amusements are dramatic exhibitions, fire works,
and slight-of-hand tricks. Parents are allowed to cast their
female children into the rivers.

Q. What is their dress?

A. In the winter furs are generally worn; in the summer, cottons and silks. The dress is long with large sleeves,
and a flowing girdle of silk. The houses are chiefly of
wood or brick, some are of clay, and usually of a single
story. Tea is drank at every meal, usually cold.

Q. What are their marriages?

A. The parents make the match before the parties have ever
seen each other. Polygamy is allowed, but it is not common.

Q. What is the manner of their funerals?

A. People commonly have their coffins made in their life
time, and all persons are buried without the wall of the city.
There is a peculiar custom prevailing among them; every man keeps a table on which are written the names of
his father, grandfather, and great grandfather; and when
the father of the family dies, the great grandfather's name
is erased, and his own inserted by his children.

Q. What is the Chinese language?

A. The alphabet contains 214 letters. Each letter has a
distinct meaning by itself. When two letters are joined, the
meaning of the compound partakes of the meaning of the
two letters.

Q. What are the great cities in China?

A. Pekin, Nankin and Canton.

Q. Describe Pekin?

A. It is in latitude 40° N.; longitude 116° 30' E. about 30
miles south of the great wall on the Pay-ho. It covers a
very large space of ground. The streets are wide. The houses rarely exceed one story. The number of inhabitants is
about 3,000,000. Pekin is the residence of the court.

Q. Describe Nankin?

A. It is on the Kiang, about 150 miles from the ocean,
and was formerly the capital. The walls are 17 miles in
circumference. It is the largest city of the empire. The
population is computed at 4,000,000. The porcelain tower
of Nankin is celebrated for its beauty and splendor.

Q. Describe Canton?

A. It is at the mouth of the Tigris on Canton bay, in the
south of China, is surrounded by walls, has 1,500,000 inhabitants, and is the most commercial city in the empire. It
is the emporium of the European trade.

Q. What is the number of walled cities?

A. It is said to exceed four thousand four hundred. Some
of them exceed Canton in population, and Singan is esteemed equal to Pekin.

Q. What are the manufactures?

A. Porcelain or China ware, nankeens, silks, cottons, paper, ink, blocks of wood for printing types, and gunpowder.
The Chinese invented printing and gunpowder before they
were known in Europe.

Q. What is the commerce?

A. The internal trade is immense. An overland trade
with Russia is carried on at Maimatochin. The Japanese
have a scanty trade with the eastern coast. Europeans
trade only with Canton. About 20 millions of pounds of tea
are annually exported, as are porcelain and nankeens extensively.

Q. What islands belong to China?

A. Hainan, Taiwan or Formosa, and the Leeo-Keeo isles.

Q. Describe Hainan?

A. It lies between 18° and 20° north, forming the eastern
side of the Gulf of Tongquin. It is 150 miles long from
southeast to northwest, and 80 broad. The southern part is
mountainous. The northern is more level, and produces
rice. Kiongtcheou in the north is the capital.

Q. Describe Formosa?

A. It is attached to the province of Foochien on the southeast coast, and stretches from north to south between 22°
and 26° north. Its length is 250, and its breadth 60 miles.
A chain of mountains runs from north to south.

Q. Describe the Leeo-Keeo isles?

A. They lie in the Pacific between 24° and 28° north;
500 miles east of China; and are about 36 in number. The
largest Kientsbing, is about 125 miles by 30. The people
are mild, affable, gay and temperate. Sulphur, copper, tin,
and mother of pearl, are the productions.

OF THE EMPIRE OF JAPAN.

Q. What is the situation of the empire of Japan?

A. This empire is composed of numerous large and
small islands in the Pacific Ocean, lying eastward of Mandshuria, and forming the eastern boundary of the sea of Japan. It lies between 30° and 46° north; and between 131°
and 150° east.

Q. What islands compose this empire?

A. The island of Niphon, larger than all the rest, is 750
miles long from south to northeast; by an average breadth
of 80. Kiusiu, south of Niphon, is 140 by 90. Sikoke

northeast of Kiusiu, is 100 by 60. Jesso, north of Niphon, is 350 miles long, and its greatest breadth not far from 200. There are numerous smaller islands around all of these.

Q. What is the climate ?

A. Both the heat of summer and the cold of winter are extreme. The weather is variable, and rain falls abundantly. Thunder, tempest, hurricanes and earthquakes are common.

Q. What is the face of the country ?

A. Generally these islands are a succession of mountains, hills and vallies.

Q. What is the agriculture ?

A. Except the most barren mountains, the earth is universally cultivated. The soil has been rendered rich. Rice is the chief grain. The sweet potatoe abounds, as do beans, pease, turnips and cabbage. The ginger, black pepper, sugar, cotton and indigo, are most abundant.

Q. What are the trees ?

A. The varnish and camphor trees, the cedar, the tea tree, the vine, and the bamboo reed, are abundant. The sweet and the China orange, the mulberry, the plantain, and cocoa-nut tree, are among the fruit trees.

Q. What are the animals ?

A. The Japanese have a few horses, and still fewer cattle and swine, but no sheep or goats. Hens and common ducks abound. The wolf and the fox are among the wild animals.

Q. What are the minerals ?

A. Gold, silver, copper, brimstone and pit-coal.

Q. What is the government ?

A. Before 1595, the daira, or supreme pontiff, was also the emperor. He was chosen by the high ecclesiastical court. Since that time the kubo has had the whole secular power. His power is absolute and his office hereditary.— His court is at Jeddo. The daira still holds an ecclesiastical court at Miaco, which is chiefly occupied with literary pursuits. The government is feudal in its character.— Most crimes are punished with death, but the privy council at Jeddo must sign the sentence.

Q. What is the religion ?

A. There are two sects, that of Sinto and that of Budsho, each believing in Polytheism. Formerly some of the inhabitants embraced Christianity ; but in 1638, all the Christians were massacred.

Q. What is the population ?

A. It has been estimated, with much probability, as not less than 30 millions. Every part of Japan is crowded with inhabitants.

Q. What is the military strength ?

A. Varenius states it 468,000 infantry and 58,000 cavalry. A considerable part of this force is maintained by the princes and governors.

Q What is the revenue ?

A. According to Varenius, it is about 28,340,000*l.* sterling.

Q. What is the character of the Japanese ?

A, They are industrious, active, free and easy in their motions. Their complexion is yellowish. Their eyes are black but oblong, small, flat, and sunk deep in the head.— Their noses are thick and short. Tea is universally used. Sacki or a beer made of rice is the common drink.

Q. What are their houses ?

A. They are of wood, painted white and covered with tiles or clay. Each house constitutes a single room divided into apartments by moveable partitions. They sit on mats.

Q. What is their dress ?

A. Trowsers, and open gowns of silk or cotton. Their shoes are of rice straw.

Q. What is the state of learning ?

A. In the sciences and literature the Japanese yield to few of the Asiatics. Most of the children are taught to read and write.

Q. What are the chief towns ?

A. Jeddo, Miaco and Nagasaki.

Q. Describe Jeddo ?

A. It is at the head of the Gulf of Jeddo, on the southeast side of Niphon. The houses are of two stories. Its extent and population are very great.

Q. Describe Miaco ?

A. Miaco, the spiritual capital, is 160 miles southwest of Jeddo, and about 30 from the Gulf of Osaca. It is the first commercial city of the empire, and is celebrated for its manufactures. In 1674, it contained 405,642 inhabitants.

Q. Describe Nagasaki ?

A. It is on the island of Kiusiu on the S. side, and is the only harbor in which foreign ships may anchor. It is a town of great size. Osaca and Sakai are also imperial cities.

Q. What are the manufactures ?

A. Japanned ware, silks, cottons, glass, porcelain and swords.

Q. What is the state of the commerce ?

A. The internal commerce is very important. The harbors are crowded with large and small vessels. Bar copper and lacquered ware are sent to China, for silks, sugar, turpenine and drugs. The Dutch trade with the Japanese was formerly valuable.

OF FARTHER INDIA; OR, INDIA BEYOND THE GANGES.

Q. What is the situation of farther India?

A. It is a large peninsula in the south of Asia, lying between 2° and 27° north, and between 92° and 109° east.

Q. What is its extent?

A. The greatest length is 1750 miles from south to north, and in latitude 22°: the breadth is about 1000. Below latitude 10° it is every where narrow.

Q. How is it bounded?

A. On the north by Tibet; on the east by China, the Gulf of Tongquin, and the China Sea; on the south by the Indian Ocean; and on the west by the Bay of Bengal, the province of Bengal and Assam.

Q. Into what territories is this region divided?

A. Tongquin, Cochin-China, and Ciampa on the eastern coast; Cambodia, Siam and Malaya on the southern; Laos in the interior west of Tongquin; and the Birman empire in the west, and of more consequence than all the others.

Q. What are the great rivers of farther India?

A. The Irawaddy, the Thaluan, the Meinam or Maygue, and the Maykaung or Japanese river.

OF TONGQUIN.

Q. Describe the situation and boundaries of Tongquin?

A. It has China N.; the Gulf of Tongquin E.; Cochin China S.; and Loas W. It is between 17° and 23° N.; and is 420 miles long, and 350 broad. In the south it is narrow.

Q. Describe the inhabitants?

A. They resemble the Chinese, but are less civilized. The products resemble those of China. Kesho, the capital, is on the Holi-Kian, a river from China. It has a considerable population.

OF COCHIN CHINA.

Q. Describe the situation and boundaries of Cochin China?

A. It reaches from 12° to 17° north, and is about 60 miles wide. The China Sea is east; Ciampa south, Cambodia west, and Tongquin north; from which the river Sungen separates it. It is divided into 12 provinces, all maritime.

Q. What is the climate?

A. The rainy season is the winter months. March, April and May, form a delightful spring.

Q. What are the vegetable productions?

A. Yams, sweet potatoes, greens, pumpkins, melons, the

sugar cane, the mulberry, ebony, and the colamboe wood; also the fruits of Hindostan and China.

Q. What are the animals?

A. Horses, asses, mules, and goats, tigers, elephants, and monkies.

Q. What is the government?

A. An absolute monarchy. Caun-Shung, the king, in 1800, was a man of great talents and wisdom.

Q. What is the military strength?

A. In 1800, it amounted to 113,000 men.

Q. What is the naval strength?

A. The monarch in 1800, had a fleet of 1200 war-boats, manned by 26,800 mariners. Three of the vessels were built on the European plan.

Q. What is the language?

A. It is that of China. As written it is pure; but the pronunciation is incorrect.

Q. What is the religion?

A. It is like that of the Hindoos.

Q. What is the population?

A. The country is populous. The number of inhabitants has been estimated at 13,000,000.

Q. What are the manners of the people?

A. The people go bare legged and bare footed. Their houses are four mud walls thatch'd. Polygamy is common, and gross licentiousness prevails. They have dark complexions, red lips, and black teeth.

Q. What towns are there?

A. Turon is the principal seaport. It has an excellent harbour. Silks, sugar, ebony, colamboe wood, edible bird's-nests, gold dust, metallic gold, copper, and porcelain, are exported. The imports are saltpetre, sulphur, lead, fine cloths and chintzes.

OF CIAMPA.

Q. Describe Ciampa?

A. It has Cambodia west; Cochin China north: and the China Sea east and south. The coast is sandy and rocky. Feneri is the capital. The inhabitants are large, muscular and well made, have reddish complexions, flat noses, and black hair. The country produces cotton, indigo, and silk.

OF CAMBODIA.

Q. What is the situation and extent of Cambodia?

A. It has Laos north; Cochin China and Ciampa east;

I

the China Sea south ; and the Gulf of Siam and Siam west. It is about 560 miles long, and where widest 350 broad ; and is between 9° and 17° north latitude. High mountains limit it on the east and west.

Q. Describe the country ?

A. The coast is low, and the climate very hot. The soil is fertile, yielding corn, rice, legumes, sugar, indigo, opium, camphor, and various drugs, and among others the gum camboge. The Maykaung runs through the territory.

Q. Describe the inhabitants ?

A. They are well made, of a dark yellow hue, with long black hair. Their dress is a long loose robe. Their religion is idolatry. They manufacture fine cloth. Their numbers are not great. The government is an absolute monarchy.

Q. What are the commerce and productions ?

A. Gold, ivory, and precious stones, are among the exports. Elephants, lions, and tigers, are among the animals.

OF LAOS.

Q. What are the situation and extent of Laos ?

A. It has China north; Tongquin east; Cambodia south ; and Seim and Birmah west. It is about 500 miles long from southeast to northwest ; and about 150 wide. It has a chain of mountains as its eastern and western limits. The Maykaung runs through its whole length.

Q. What are the climate and soil ?

A. The climate is temperate and healthy. The soil is fertile, yielding rice in abundance. Musk, benzoin and lacca, are among the drugs. Iron, lead, tin, gold, silver, rubies, and pearls, are among the minerals.

Q. Describe the inhabitants ?

A. They are well shaped, robust, and of an olive complexion ; upright, faithful, affable, and good natured. They are long-lived, and in number about three millions. They live by agriculture and fishing, but are not very industrious. They believe in witchcraft and magic.

Q. What are their customs ?

A. Their food is rice, fish, legumes, and buffalo flesh.— They wear gowns close to their bodies. Polygamy is not lawful ; Though lewdness is general. Funerals are celebrated with great magnificence. Their language is the Siamese.

Q. What is the government ?

A. The king is an absolute independent prince. The property in lands is wholly in him. The capital is Leng or Laung, on the Maykaung.

OF SIAM.

Q. What are the situation and extent of Siam ?

A. Siam has Birmah north ; Laos and Cambodia east ; the Gulf of Siam south ; and Birmah west. On each side of the Gulf it is supposed to reach down as far as latitude 12°. Its northern limit is believed to be in latitude 18° A chain of mountains, on the east, separates it from Laos and Cambodia ; and another on the west from Birmah. Its length is about 420 miles and its breadth 200. It is an extensive valley through the middle of which runs the Meinam.

Q. What is the climate.

A. Winter lasts through December and January, and is mild and dry. February, March and April, is spring, and the rest of the year is summer.

Q. What is the face of the country ?

A. It is a valley, gradually swelling into hills and mountains on each side, near the frontiers.

Q. What is the soil ?

A. On and near the river it is a very rich and pure mold, and is in a high state of cultivation. Near the mountains it is less fertile, and is chiefly covered with forests.— Rice, maize and pease, are cultivated.

Q. What are the animals ?

A. Elephants, wild boars, tigers, buffaloes, deer and monkeys. The horses are few and indifferent. Poisonous serpents infest the rivers, and fire-flies illumine the meadows.

Q. What are the minerals ?

A. Gold, copper, tin and lead ; the loadstone, agates, and sapphires.

Q. What is the religion ?

A. Like that of the Hindoos.

Q. What is the government ?

A. It is despotic. The throne is hereditary in the male line. The laws are very severe and sanguinary.

Q. What is the population ?

A. It has been vaguely estimated at eight millions.

Q. What is the military strength ?

A. Heretofore it has been 60,000 men, and from three to 4000 elephants. The king of Siam has also a number of small vessels of war. His power and his territories have been much curtailed by the king of Birmah.

Q. What is the character of the Siamese ?

A. The men are generally indolent ; labour being chiefly performed by the women. Their complexion is of a reddish brown. They are small, but well made. They are fond of theatrical amusements, also of races of oxen and of boats, combats of elephants, cock-fighting, rope-dancing, and fire-works.

Q. What are their marriages and funerals ?

A. They marry early. Polygamy is allowed. They burn the bodies of the dead on funeral piles.

Q. What are their food and dress ?

A. They live on rice and fish. Their dress is very slight, the heat rendering clothes almost unnecessary.

Q. What is the language ?

A. The alphabet has 37 letters. The words are chiefly of one syllable. The verbs and nouns have no inflections.

Q. What is their literature ?

A. Children are extensively taught to read and write.— The Siamese have books of history, and a published code of laws ; also poetry, tales and mythologic fables.

Q. What is the capital ?

A. Yuthia, about 80 miles up the Meinam. It is a town of some extent. Bankok, is a town at the mouth of the Meinam. Ogmo, is on the east side of the gulf.

Q. What is the trade ?

A. The Siamese trade chiefly with the Hindoos, Chinese, Japanese and Dutch. The exports are grain in prodigious quantities, cotton and benzoin ; sandal, aguallo and sapan woods ; antimony, tin, lead, iron, load-stone, gold and silver ; sapphires, emeralds, agates, crystal, marble and tembac.

OF MALAYA.

Q. What are the situation and extent of Malaya ?

A. It is a long narrow peninsula, the most southern country of Asia, reaching from 2° to 12° north ; and is about 700 miles long, by 150 of medial breadth. It has Birma north ; the Gulf of Siam and the China Sea east ; and the Bay of Bengal west. Its northern limit is not accurately defined. It is said to be divided into two kingdoms : Patani in the north ; and Yohof in the south.

Q. Describe the country ?

A. The centre of the peninsula is said to be mountainous. The tiger, elephant and civet-cat, are among the animals. Pepper and other spices, gums and woods, are among the productions.

Q. Describe the inhabitants ?

A. They are small, have tawny complexions, and flatten their noses. They are fond of war and plunder ; and are universally ferocious and treacherous. Many of them are pirates. Their language is melodious, and is spoken every where in these seas.

Q. What are the towns ?

A. Malacca, in the south, is the largest. In the last century it was thought to contain 12,000 inhabitants. Patani is a town on the eastern coast.

Q. What islands are on the western coast ?

A. The Andaman Isles and the Nicobans.

Q. Describe the Andaman Isles ?

A. They are the Great and Little Andaman, and a number of islets, about 350 miles west of Malaya. Great Andaman is 140 miles long by 20, has excellent harbours and extensive forests. The inhabitants are negroes and cannibals, and in number about 2000. A British settlement is formed on the larger isle.

Q. Describe the Nicobans ?

A. They are S. S. E. of the Andamans, about 300 miles from the coast, and are three in number : the largest being five leagues in circumference. They produce cocoa and areca trees, yams and sweet potatoes. The people are of a copper colour. Swine and dogs are the only quadrupeds.

OF THE BIRMAN EMPIRE.

Q. What is the situation of the Birman empire ?

A. It is on the western part of farther India, lying between 92° and 101° east longitude, and between 12° and 27° north latitude.

Q. What countries does it comprehend ?

A. Cassay in the north ; Arrakan in the west; Ava in the middle, and Pegu in the south ; together with a considerable part of the territory formerly subject to Siam. The whole is now called Birmah.

Q. What is the extent of Birmah ?

A. It is 1050 miles long from N. to S. and 450 broad.

Q. What are the boundaries ?

A. Tibet is on the north ; China, Laos and Siam east ; Malaya and the Gulf of Rangoun south ; the same Gulf, the Bay of Bengal, Hindostan and Assam west.

Q. What is the climate ?

A. It is healthy ; the seasons are regular ; and the extremes of heat and cold are unknown.

Q. What is the face of the country ?

A. In the north and east it is irregular and mountainous. The valley of the Irawaddy is remarkably fertile, as is much of the upper country. The sugar-cane, tobacco, indigo, cotton, and the tropical fruits, are all indigenous.— Wheat and rice, are grown with much success.

I 2

Q. What are the vegetable productions ?

A. The teak tree, the most valuable of all timber, the sandal wood, the ebony, the sycamore fig, the Indian fig, the banyan, the vine, the orange, the lemon, the lime, the mango,
the pine-apple, ginger, candamon, turmeric, pepper, the sugar-cane, the bamboo and spikenard.

Q. What are the animals ?

A. Elephants abound. The horses are inferior.

Q. What are the minerals ?

A. Gold, silver, tin, iron, lead, antimony, arsenic, amber,
rubies, sapphires and sulphur.

Q. What is the religion of the Birmans ?

A. With the Hindoos they worship Boodha as the Supreme
God. They believe in the transmigration of souls.

Q. What is the government ;

A. An hereditary despotism. The king however consults
a council of nobles.

Q. What is the population ?

A. Symes states it at 17,000,000 ; of whom 14,000,000 are
in Ava and Pegu, and 3,000,000 in Arracan. The number of
cities, towns and villages, he states to be 8,000.

Q. What is the military force ?

A. The regular army is small. Every man is liable to be
called into the service. The royal magazines contain about
20,000 indifferent fire-locks.

Q. What is the naval strength ?

A. The king has about 500 war canoes.

Q. What is the revenue ?

A. It is very great, but not certainly known as to its
amount. The monarch possesses immense treasures.

Q. What is the language ?

A. The Birman alphabet has 33 letters, written from left
to right.

Q. What is the state of literature ?

A. The Birmans have many books. Every kioul or mo-
nastery has a library. The royal library has 100 large chests
of books.

Q. What are the character of the Birmans ?

A. They are a lively inquisitive race ; active, irascible and
impatient. They are fond of poetry and music. The women
are generally occupied in the labours of the loom.

Q. What is the capital ?

A. Ummerapoora. It is a city of modern date, on a tributary of the Irawaddy. The city is of considerable extent, and
is ornamented with spires, turrets and obelisks. The other
towns are Ava, Pegu, Rangoun, Martaban and Aracan.

Rangoun, near the mouth of the Irawaddy, has a population of 30,000.

Q. What are the manufactures?

A. The natives excel in gilding. Their temples and barges are constructed with singular elegance. They manufacture marble divinities.

Q. What is the state of commerce?

A. An overland trade is carried on with the province of Yunnan in China. Cotton, amber, ivory, precious stones, and the betel-nut, are sent thither.

OF HINDOSTAN.

Q. What is the situation of Hindostan?

A. It is on the southern coast of Asia, about midway from west to east; lying between 8° and 36° north, and between 66° and 93° east.

Q. What is its extent?

A. Its length from north to south is 2000 miles. Its breadth in lat. 25° is 1700. Generally it is much less.

Q. How is it bounded?

A. On the northwest by Independent Tartary; on the northeast by Mongolia, Sirinagur, Kemaoon, Nepaul, Bootam, and Assam; on the east by Birmah; on the southeast by the Bay of Bengal; on the southwest by the Arabian Sea; and on the west by Persia.

Q. What are the divisions of Hindostan?

A. Rennel, the geographer of Hindostan, has divided it into four parts: Sindetic Hindostan, or that portion watered by the river Sinde or Indus, in the northwest; Gangetic, or that watered by the Ganges, in the N. E.; Central Hindostan, on the country S. of the two first and N. of the river Kistna; and the Deccan, or the country S. of the Kistna.

Q. What are the provinces in Sindetic Hindostan?

A. Sindy, on the coast; the large province of Moultan, stretching from Persia across to Mongolia; Candahar also in the west; Cabul bounding on Independent Tartary; Cuttore, Cashmere and Lahore, bounding on Mongolia.

Q. What are the provinces in Gangetic Hindostan?

A. Bengal, Bahar, Allahabad, Oude, Agra, Delhi, Agimeve and part of Malwa.

Q. What are the provinces of Central Hindostan?

A. Guzzerat, on the west part of Malwa, Candeish, Dowlatabad, part of Golconda, Berar, Orissa and the Circars.

Q. What are the provinces of the Deccan?

A. Visiapour, part of Golconda, the Carnatic, Mysore, and several smaller districts.

Q. What are the rivers of Hindostan ?

A. Those that empty into the Bay of Bengal, are the Burrampooter, the Ganges, the Godavery, the Kistna and the Cavery. Those that empty into the Arabian Sea, are the Nerbudda, the Caggar and the Indus.

Q. Describe the Burrampooter ?

A. It rises in the northwest part of Tibet in Mount Kentaisse, winds southeast through Tibet about 1200 miles, and then through Assam 400; and S. through Bengal 400.

Q. Describe the Ganges ?

A. It issues from the opposite side of Mount Kentaisse, runs in Tibet and Mongolia about 800 miles, and southeast through Hindostan about 1200.

Q. Describe the Indus ?

A. It rises in Mongolia, and runs south southwest to the Arabian Sea about 1300 miles.

Q. What are the mountains ?

A. The Western Gauts run from Cape Comorin to Surat, from 40 to 70 miles from the coast. The Eastern Gauts are parallel with the eastern coast. The sandy desert east of the Indus, is about 450 miles long and from 60 to 150 broad.

Q. What are the vegetable productions ?

A. The teak tree, the ebony, and the ironwood, are among its choicest timber trees.

Q. What are the animals ?

A. Horses, asses, mules, large cattle, sheep, antelopes, apes, monkeys, dogs of various species, the elephant, camel, wild boar, bear, wolf, fox, jackal, hyena, leopard, panther, lynx, and musk-weasel.

Q. What are the minerals ?

A. Diamonds, sapphires, rubies, gold and iron.

Q. What is the population ?

A. It is believed to amount to 60 millions.

Q. What is the religion ?

A. It is a species of Polytheism. Boodha is the Supreme God. Brahma is the immediate agent of creation. This religion divides the Hindoos into four casts : Brahmans or priests; Chehterees or warriors; Brices or writers; and Sooders or slaves. The Baptist missionaries in Bengal have had encouraging success. The bible is now published or publishing, in all the languages of Hindostan. The Danish mission in the south, at Travancore, has been established more than a century, and has been the means of converting hundreds of thousands to Christianity.

Q. Are there any native Jews in Hindostan ?

A. At Cochin, in Travancore, on the S. W. coast, in lat. 10° there is a nation of white Jews, and another of black Jews. The latter came here long before the Christian era.

Q. Are there any native Christians?

A. There is a numerous body of Syrian Christians also at Cochin. The colony was led hither by St. Thomas.

Q. What are the languages?

A. The Sanscrit is the learned language of Hindostan. The Bengalee is spoken in Bengal and along the Ganges. The Hindostanee or Devangaric, is spoken at Benares, and extensively over the north of Hindostan. The Nepalic or language of the Nepauls is much like it. The Guzaratic, spoken in the west, from Surat to Persia. The Talenga, spoken on the eastern coast, from Bengal to the Kistna. The Marahda, spoken throughout the Mahratta country. The Tamulian, used in the Deccan east of the Western Gauts. The Malabar and Canara on the Malabar coast. The latter south of Cochin.

Q. What is the state of literature in Hindostan?

A. The Brahmans have many curious books but of little value.

Q. What are the universities?

A. At Benares, on the Ganges, is the most ancient and celebrated university of Hindostan.

Q. What are the manufactures?

A. Muslins, calicoes and silks. The shawls of Cashmere are of remarkable beauty.

Q. What are the exports?

A. Muslins, calicoes, silks, spices, drugs, rice and sugar.

Q. By whom is Hindostan chiefly possessed?

A. By the British and their allies; the Mahrattas; the Soubah of the Deccan; the Seiks; and the king of Candahar.

Q. What provinces belong to the king of Candahar?

A. Cashmere, Cuttore, Cabul, Candahar, Moultan, west of the Indus and Sindeh; as well as about half of Persia. These provinces border on Mongolia, Independent Tartary and the whole Persian frontier.

Q. What are the towns in his territories?

A. Cabul, the capital, is on the river Kameh, a branch of the Indus not far from Tartary. Cashmere, in the vale of Cashmere, is on the Jalum, a branch of the same river and close to Mongolia. It extends three miles on either bank. The houses are two and three stories high. The Valley of Cashmere is the paradise of the Hindoos. Tatta, the capital of Sindeh, is on the Indus, and has been celebrated for its manufactures and commerce.

Q. What provinces belong to the Seiks?

A. Moultan, east of the Indus, Lahore, and the western part of Delhi, Agimeve and Guzerat. These provinces lie immediately east of the king of Candahar's dominions.

Q. What are the towns?

A. Lahore, on the Rauves, is their capital. Moultan is on the Chunab. Sirhind is on the Caggar. We know not whether Delhi, late the capital of the Great Mogul, now belongs to the Seiks, or not.

Q. Where is the territory belonging to the Mahrattas?

A. The Mahrátta country is bounded by the territory of the Seiks on the N. W.; the government of Bengal on the N. E.; the Bay of Bengal on the east; the dominions of the Soubah of the Deccan on the S. E.; those of the rajah of Mysore on the S.; and the Gauts on the W.

Q. How are the Mahrattas divided?

A. Into the Poona-Mahrattas on the west, and the Berar-Mahrattas on the east. The Poonas occupy the largest extent of country, and are most numerous.

Q. Which are the Mahratta provinces?

A. The Poonas possess the eastern parts of Agimeve and Guzerat; the western half of Agra and Allahabad; Malwa; Candeish; the western parts of Dowlatabad, Visiapour and the Dooab. The Berars possess the extensive provinces of Berar and Orissa.

Q. What are the Mahratta cities?

A. Poona, on the river Beemah in Dowlatabad, is the capital of the western Mahrattas; as Nagpour, on the Bain-Gonga, the central city of Hindostan, is of the eastern. Amedabad in Guzerat, is a large well-fortified town. Cambay is its port. Agra on the Jumna has lost much of its importance.

Q. What is the government of the Mahrattas?

A. They are divided into two states or empires, each having its paishwa or sovereign. The paishwa of the western Mahrattas resides at Poona; that of the eastern at Nagpour.

Q. What is the religion of the Mahrattas?

A. They are the worst of idolaters. The infamous temple of Juggernaut is in Orissa on the coast.

Q. What territories belong to the Soubah of the Deccan?

A. The eastern parts of Dowlatabad; Visiapour, and the Dooab; also Golconda; and several towns in the eastern part of Mysore.

Q. What are the principal cities?

A. Aurungabad, on a branch of the Godaveny; Hydrabad, on an arm of the Kistna close to Golconda, and the present capital of the Soubah.

Q. What are the British possessions ?

A. 1. The government of Bengal including the provinces of Bengal, Bahár, and the eastern half of Allahabad, now called Benares. 2. The Circars a long narrow tract on the eastern coast. 3. The Jaghire of Madras a smaller tract in the Carnatic farther south, on the same coast. 4. The southern half of Mysore. 5. A long narrow tract on the coast of Malabar reaching from Chilwa to Carwan about 350 miles, and eastward to the Gauts, about 60 miles. 6. The island of Bombay and a considerable district in the neighborhood. 7. It is believed that Surat is now a British factory.

Q. What is the extent of these territories ?

A. The government of Bengal is about 550 miles from east to west, and 300 broad ; and contains about 11 millions of native subjects. The Circars, from Gamjam to Mootapilly, are about 400 miles in length along the coast, and from 25 to 75 broad. The Jaghire of Madrass is 108 miles long, and 50 broad. The tract on the Malabar coast reaches from Chilwa to Carwar about 350 miles, and eastward about 60 to the Gauts. All the territories subject to Britain are computed to contain 212,000 square miles, and 14,000,000 inhabitants.

Q. What is the revenue of the British provinces.

A. That of the government of Bengal is 4,310,000l. sterling. That of the others is not known.

Q. What is the government ?

A. That of Bengal is supreme, and is in the hands of a governor general and four councillors. Those of the other provinces are subordinate to Bengal.

Q. Is there any college in Bengal ?

A. That of Fort William, in Calcutta, is a very promising institution.

Q. What is the army ?

A. In time of peace about 25,000 men.

Q. What are the cities belonging to the British ?

A. Calcutta in Bengal is the largest city of Hindostan.— It stands in 22° 38' N. ; and in 88° 28' E. The houses are built some of brick, others of mud ; and many more of bamboos and mats. The houses inhabited by Europeans, are all of brick. It is on the Hoogley, the western arm of the Ganges, 100 miles from the sea, and contains about one million of inhabitants. Its commerce is immense. Dacca and Hoogley are other towns in Bengal.

Q. Where is Patna ?

A. About 400 miles northwest of Calcutta on the Ganges.

It is the chief town of Bahar, and celebrated for its very extensive manufactures of saltpetre.

Q. Where is Benares ?

A. About 100 miles west of Patna on the Ganges. It is a rich, compact and populous city.

Q. What town is there in the Circans ?

A. Masulipatam is a town of some note.

Q. Where is Madras ?

A. It is in the Jaghire, has an extensive trade, and a population of 100,000.

Q. Describe Seringapatam ?

A. It is in the south of Mysore, on a small island in the river Caveri, and is a large and populous town ; lately it was the capital of the dominions of Tippoo Saib. Calicut is a town of some note on the Malabar coast.

Q. Describe Bombay ?

A. It is a large city on the island of Bombay in lat. 19°; and has a capacious fortress, a dock-yard, and marine arsenal. It is the seat of the government of Bombay.

Q. Describe Surat ?

A. It is a large town in the estuary of the Taptea near the west coast, 180 miles north of Bombay, and contains 500,000 inhabitants, who are chiefly Arabs, Persians, Moguls and Turks. The commerce is considerable.

Q. What are the British allies ?

A. The nabob of Oude, the rajah of Mysore, the nabob of Arcot, and the rajah of Travancore and Cochin.

Q. What territory belongs to the nabob of Oude ?

A. The province of Oude and the district of Rohilla, both north of the Ganges, and near Nepaul. Lucknow is the capital. Fyzabad and Allahabad are towns of some note.

Q. What are the dominions of the rajah of Mysore ?

A. They are the northern and larger half of the province of Mysore.

Q. What is the territory of the nabob of Arcot ?

A. The Carnatic, a narrow province on the east coast, reaching from the Cicars south, to Travencore about 500 miles, by a breadth of from 70 to 100. In this district, however, the Jaghire of Madras belongs to the British ; and Tanjore, farther S. to Denmark. Arcot is the nabob's capital.

Q. Where is Travencore ?

A. It reaches from Cape Comorin to Tanjore on the east coast about 250 miles, and on the west coast about 300, to the British Malabar possessions. Cochin, the well known residence of the Jews and Syrian Christians, is in latitude 10° on the western coast.

Q. Have the Portuguese any possessions in Hindostan?

A. They own the small government of Goa, on the western coast. Goa, the capital, is a large town on an island in a noble bay. Its harbour is one of the first in India.

Q. Have the Danes any possessions in India?

A. They possess the town of Serampore in Bengal, near Calcutta, where is the chief establishment of the Baptist Missionaries; also the district of Tangore in the south.

OF THE ISLAND OF CEYLON.

Q. What are the situation and extent of Ceylon?

A. It lies off the S. E. coast of Hindostan, 50 miles from Cape Calymere; between 6° and 10° N. and between 79° 40' and 82° E.; is 280 miles long, and 150 broad. A ridge of rocks, called Adam's Bridge, in lat. 9° connects it with the main.

Q. What are the climate and soil?

A. The climate is cool and healthy. The country is a high table land in the centre, surrounded with low shores about 6 or 8 leagues in breadth. The soil of the vallies is a rich fat loom, fertile in rice and other vegetables. The most important productions are the spices.

Q. What is the chief river?

A. The Mowil-Ganga, which runs north, and empties on the east side at Trincomali.

Q. Are there any mountains?

A. A chain of mountains runs from N. to S. The highest summit is Adam's Peak in the middle of the island.

Q. What are the animals?

A. The elephant, buffalo, wild boar, tiger, bear, jackal, and many tribes of deer and monkeys. The Ceylon alligator reaches the length of 18 feet. The peacock is in the forests.

Q. What the are minerals?

A. The ruby, sapphire, topaz, crystal, amethyst, emerald, cat's eye, iron, and gold. The pearl fishery on the N. W. shore is of great value.

Q. What is the government?

A. The centre of the island was till within a few months under the dominion of a native king, whose capital was Candy, on the Ganga, and who was called the king of Candy. His authority was absolute. He and his golden throne are now in England. The coast of the whole island for an indefinite extent inward belongs to the British. They have a governor-general at Colombo on the W. coast, who is not dependent on the government of Bengal. Since the capture of Candy, the whole island is a colony of the British.

Q. What is the religion?

K

A. That of the natives is the worship of Boodh, whose images are found every where. Many of them have however been converted to Christianity.

Q. What is the population ?

A. That under the British government is 500,000. That of the king of Candy's late dominions is unknown.

Q. Describe the natives ?

A. They are called Cingalese, and are less black than the inhabitants of Malabar. Polygamy both of men and women is common. The morals of the people are exceedingly loose.

Q. What are the towns ?

A. Candy is a small town of no consequence except as having till lately been the royal residence—Colombo on the W. coast is a handsome well-fortified town in lat. 7°. Jaffnapatam, Trincomali, and Bataccla, are seaports.

Q. What are the exports ?

A. Cinnamon, pepper, and other spices, pearls, and precious stones.

Q. What other isles are near the coast of Hindostan ?

A. The Laccadives and Maldives.

Q. Describe the Laccadives ?

A. They are 30 in number, of a small size, and form an extended groupe between 10° and 12° N. ; to the W. of Calicut. The inhabitants trade in cocoa-nuts and fish.

Q. Describe the Maldives ?

A. Their number is said to be 1300. They form an oblong inclosure of small low regular isles around a clear space of sea with very shallow water between each. They are governed by a chief called Atole. The trade is in cowrie shells, with cocoa-nuts and fish. The language is Cingalese.

OF THE DISTRICTS BETWEEN HINDOSTAN AND THE HIMLAH MOUNTAINS.

Q. What territories lie between Hindostan on the south, the Himlah mountains on the north ?

A. Assam, Boutan, Nepaul, Kemaoon and Sirinagur.

OF ASSAM.

Q. How is it situated ?

A. Tibet is on the N. ; Birma on the E. and S. E. ; Bengal on the S. and S. W. ; and Boutan on the W. It is 300 miles long from E. to W. and 200 broad. It is between 25 and 28 N. lat. The Burrampooter, running nearly from E. to W. through the whole district, divides it in into two provinces, Uttercul on the N. and Dachincul on the south.

Q. Describe the country?

A. It is fertile and well cultivated. Among the products are valuable fruits, pepper, cocoa-nuts, sugar, and ginger. The silk equals that of China. The musk deer is found in the forests. Gold and silver are found in the sand of the rivers.

Q. Describe the inhabitants?

A. The Assamese are a stout brave race, and have resolutely maintained their independence. Their dialect resembles the Bengalee. Their king has his residence at Ghargon on the Burrampooter. That part of the Himlah range which lies N. of Assam is called the Duleh mountains.

OF BOOTAN.

Q. What is the situation of Bootan?

A. Tibet is on the N.; Assam, E.; Bengal, S.; and Nepaul, W. It reaches from 26° to 28° N. lat. The Himlah mountains are the northern boundary.

Q. Describe the country?

A. It is mountainous, but covered with constant verdure. Tassaseudon is the capital. The sides of the mountains are covered with orchards, fields and villages. The climate is mild. The government is vested in a prince called Daeb.

OF NEPAUL.

Q. What are the situation and extent of Nepaul?

A. It is between 27° and 29° N.; has Bahan and Oude in Hindostan S.; Kemaoon, W.; Tibet, N.; and Bootan, E. It is a valley of several hundred miles in circuit.

Q. What are the productions?

A. The productions are the fruits and vegetables of Europe, such as the peach, pine-apple, raspberry, mulberry, orange and walnut; turnips, pease, cabbages and rice.

Q. Describe the people?

A. The religion is like that of Bengal. The government is vested in a rajah and numerous petty chieftains. The population is estimated at a million. They are divided into three casts, Brahmans, Cshatrigas, and Newans, or commonalty. Their food is exclusively rice, milk, honey, and fruits: Animal food is prohibited.

Q. What are the cities?

A. Lelit-Pattan, Catmandu, and Bhatgung. The population of the first is stated by Kirkpatrick at 240,000; of the second at 180,000; and of the third at 120,000. If this be correct, the population of the country must exceed one million. Catmandu, the royal residence, in on a branch of th Ganges. Nepaul has lately been subdued by the British arms

OF KEMAOON.

Q. What is the situation of Kemaoon?

A. It lies between Nepaul on the E. and Sirinagur on the W. Its capital is Balsora, on the Gogra, the great northern arm of the Ganges. The Gogra runs S. E. through the whole territory.

OF SIRINAGUR.

Q. What is the situation of Sirinagur?

A. It has Mongolia on the N. W. and W.; Tibet on the E.; Kemaoon on the S. E.; and Moultan, in Hindostan, on the S. W. The Ganges passes through it in a S. E. direction. The Himlah mountains are the N. and N. E. frontier. In the N. W. in lat. 33, the Ganges passes through a celebrated cavern in Mount Himlah, called the Gangoutna or Cow's mouth. Sirinagur, the capital, is on the Aluknumdra, a tributary of the Ganges.

OF PERSIA.

Q. What is the situation of Persia?

A. It lies on the southern coast of Asia, W. of the middle longitude, between 25° and 41° N.; and between 45° and 68° E.

Q. What is the extent of Persia?

A. The length from S. E. to N. W. is about 1300 miles; and the greatest breadth is about 1100. In the year 1814, Persia ceded the whole country W. of the Caspian to Russia; so that the Kizil Ozan, emptying at the S. W. angle of the Caspian, is now a frontier river on the side of Russia.

Q. What are the boundaries?

A. On the N. Asiatic Russia, the Caspian, and Independent Tartary; on the E. Independent Tartary and Hindostan; on the S. the Arabian Sea, and Persian Gulf; and on the W. Arabia and Turkey in Asia.

Q. What are the provinces?

A. Khosistan, Fars, Laristan, Kerman, Maknan, Irak-Ajemi, Segistan, Khorasan, Cohestan, and Mazendran. The provinces ceded to Russia were Ghilan, Aderbijian, Erivan, and Georgia or Gurgistan.

Q. What is the climate?

A. In the north and middle, the winters are severe. In the south, the heat is temperate.

Q. What is the face of the country?

A. Generally it is mountainous. All the extensive plains are deserts. Perhaps no country has fewer rivers.

Q. What is the soil?

A. Generally unfertile. The most common grain is wheat. Rice, barley and millet are also sown.

Q. What are the rivers?

A. The Euphrates and the Tigris, are frontiers 100 miles each. The Ahwaz, the Rud, the Makshid, the Araba and the Himmend. The Tedjen and the Gihon in the northeast.

Q. What are the lakes?

A. The lakes of Durrah and Baktegan.

Q. What are the mountains?

A. The range of Caucasus, the mountains of Elevend, and the Gaur mountains.

Q. What are the deserts?

A. The Great Saline desert reaches from Kom E. to the lake of Durrah, about 400 miles by a breadth of 250. The desert of Kirman, of Khosistan and Mekran.

Q. What are the vegetable productions?

A. The cypress, cedar, pine, lime, oak, acacia, chesnut, sumach and manna-ash grow in vast abundance. The fig, pomegranate, mulberry, almond, peach, apricot, orange and citron, are among the fruits. The vine, liquorice, sugar-cane and cotton tree are generally cultivated. The jasmine, anemone, tulip and ranunculus are among the wild flowers.

Q. What are the animals?

A. The Persian horse is remarkably beautiful. The ass and mule are common. The cattle are like the European. Swine are scarce. The large tailed sheep abound; camels, deer, antelopes, wild goats, wild asses, hyenas and jackals, hares, bears, boars, lions, leopards, and tigers are in the forests. Seals are caught in the Caspian.

Q. What are the minerals?

A. Silver, lead, iron, copper, the turquoise stone, pearls, sulphur, nitre and naphtha.

Q. What is the population of Persia?

A. It has been estimated at 22 millions.

Q. What are the two great divisions of Persia?

A. West Persia, and East Persia or Candahar.

Q. What are the dominions of the king of Candahar.

A. The Hindoo provinces of his kingdom have been already mentioned. According to Rennel the meridian of 57 on a line passing due N. from Cape Task through Tershiz and Meshid is the western boundary. Mekran, and part of Kerman on the coast, Segistan, and the greater part of Cohestan and Corasan are his Persian provinces. To these should be added the province of Gaur, a large territory in the S. W. of Great Bucharia.

Q. What is the extent of the whole dominions of the shah of Candahar?

A. They lie chiefly between 57° and 70° E.; although Cashmere and Sindy in Hindostan transcend the latter limit. The length from N. to S. is about 1100 miles, and the breadth

900. The Bucharians, Seiks, and Mahrattas border on the E.

Q. What provinces belong to Western Persia?

A. Cossistan, Fars, Laristan, Irak-Ajemi, Mazendran, and the western parts of Mikran, Cohestan, and Corasan.

Q. What is the extent of the dominions of the shah of Persia?

A. His dominions are all in Persia, and are about 1000 miles in length by 700. Both of the shahs are absolute monarchs. The administration of the eastern government is represented as uniformly mild.

Q. What is the religion of Persia?

A. The Persians are Mahometans of the sect of Ali. The Afghans are the ruling nation in East Persia or Candahar. They are now ascertained to be the descendants of the Ten Tribes of Israel who revolted from Rehoboam.

Q. What is the military strength?

A. The shah of Ispahan is said to be able to raise an army of 100,000 men, and the shah of Candahar of 300,000. The dominions of the latter, owing to the numerous wars in West Persia, are far the most populous.

Q. What are the revenues?

A. That of Candahar is estimated at 3 millions sterling and that of Persia at 2 millions.

Q. What is the language of Persia?

A. The Parsi or proper Persian is of the same origin with the Gothic or German. The Pehlavi or ancient Persian is Assyrian or Chaldaic. The modern Persian excels all the languages of the east in strength, beauty and melody. It is very extensively spoken, being understood from Calcutta to Damascus.

Q. What is the state of Persian literature?

A. The literature of Persia approaches that of Europe in solid good sense, and clearness of thought and expression.

Q. What is the education of the Persians?

A. It is chiefly military.

Q. What are the cities of Western Persia?

A. Ispahan, Shiraz, Kom, Gombroon and Busheer.

Q. Describe Ispahan?

A. In the time of Chardin, it was 24 miles in circuit and had a population of 600,000. It is on the river Zenderud.

Q. Describe Shiraz?

A. It is in a fertile valley of 26 miles in length by 12 in breadth, and bounded on all sides by lofty mountains. The city is 4 miles in circuit, surrounded by a wall of 25 feet high and 10 thick.

Q. Describe the other towns?

A. Kom is a large city, half way from Ispahan to the Caspian, containing 15,000 houses. The manufactures are porcelain, soap and sword blades. Gombroon and Busheer are towns on the coast.

Q. What are the cities in East Persia ?

A. Cabul, the royal residence, is in Hindostan. Candahar is on the frontiers of the two countries within the limits of Persia, and is a large and commercial town. Herat, near the source of the Tedjen, is considerable for its trade and size. Meshid, a larger town, is the capital of Corasan.

Q. What are the manufactures of Persia ?

A. Embroidery in cloth, silk and leather, porcelain, shagreen leather, braziery, bows, sabres, razors, cottons, wooliens, goat's and camel's hair shawls, silks, brocades, velvets, and carpets.

Q. What is the commerce ?

A. Tobacco, preserves, horses, porcelain and leather, are sent to Hindostan ; tobacco and kitchen utensils to Turkey ; and silks to Russia by the Caspian and Wolga.

Q. What islands belong to Persia ?

A. Ormuz, Kishma, and Karek in the Persian Gulf.

OF ARABIA.

Q. What is the situation of Arabia ?

A. It is the southwest country of Asia ; lying between 12° 30' and 34° 30' N. lat. and between 32° 30' and 59° 14' E. longitude.

Q. What is the extent ?

A. The length is 1600 miles, and the medial breadth 800 ; making 1,280,000 square miles. The breadth from Suez to the Euphrates, is 550 miles, and on the southern coast it exceeds 1100.

Q. How is Arabia bounded ?

A. On the N. W. by the Mediterranean for about 100 miles, and by Syria ; on the E. by the Euphrates, which divides it principally from Turkey in Asia, and about 100 miles below the Tigris from Persia by the Persian Gulf, and by the Bay of Ormus ; on the S. E. by the Arabian Sea ; and on the W. by the Red Sea and Egypt.

Q. What are the divisions ?

A. Arabia is divided by the inhabitants themselves into eight districts, viz. Yemen in the S. W. ; Hadramaut, Oman, Lahsa ; the country of the Bedouins ; Hajar in the northwest ; Hedjas along the Red Sea ; and Nedsied, central between Hedjas and Lahsa.

Q. What is the climate ?

A. There is a regular rainy season on the coast, but prevailing at different periods. The samiel, or hot wind of the desert, prevails in the north. The sky is usually clear.

Q. What is the face of the country?

A. The northern and central parts of Arabia are chiefly a desert, with a few fertile isles or oases. The mountains are usually destitute of trees. No country is more badly watered.

Q. What is the soil?

A. The soil, where capable of cultivation, is rarely fertile. Wheat, barley and durrah are the grains cultivated.

Q. What are the rivers?

A. The Euphrates is the northeast frontier for an extent of 600 miles. The Sana is a river of about 300 miles in length in the south, emptying at Macula into the Bay of Hadramaut. The Aftan, a longer stream, empties at Lahsa into the Persian Gulf.

Q. What are the mountains?

A. Mount Sinai is in the north, between the two arms of the Red Sea. Mount Horeb is in full view from it. The chain of Mount Arsa runs nearly parallel with the west coast from Medira to Yemen. The southern coast is chiefly mountainous.

Q. What are the vegetable productions?

A. The cotton-tree, pomegranate, banyan, coffee-tree, opobalsamum or balm of Mecca, date, cocoa-nut, great fanpalm, sycamore-fig, plantain, almond, apricot, tamarind, peach, pear, filbert, bread-tree and orange. The smaller plants are the sugar-cane, frankincense, spikenard, cinnamon, cassia, cardamum, pepper, myrrh and aloes.

Q. What are the animals?

A. The Arabian horses surpass all others. The ass, camel, rock-goat, jackal, hyena, jerboa, antelope, wild ox, wolf, fox, wild boar and panther.

Q. What is the religion of the Arabians?

A. The Mahometan. Mahomet was born at Mecca in the year 569. The religion which he introduced spread extensively about the time of his flight to Medina, or A. D. 622. This year, which the Arabians call the *Hegira*, or *The Flight*, is the Mahometan Æra. Before the time of Mahomet, the religion of the Arabians was the Sabian.

Q. What is the government?

A. Arabia is governed by numerous independent shekhs, who have no common head. Within a few years the Wahabees, a powerful tribe, under a prince of superior talents, have possessed themselves of Medina and all the north of Arabia. They are said not to be Mahometans. Among the Bedouins, the government is strictly patriarchal.

Q. What is the population ?

A. Arabia is thinly peopled, but no tolerable estimate can be made of the number of the inhabitants. Prodigious numbers of the Bedouins, or wandering Arabs, roam over the deserts of Africa.

Q. What is their character ?

A. The Arabians as a nation are distinguished for their intelligence and quickness of apprehension. They are polished in their manners and hospitable ; but at the same time faithless and revengeful.

Q. What are their houses ?

A. In the towns they are of stone, but meanly constructed ; the apartments of the men being in front, those of the women behind. The Bedouins live in tents.

Q. What is the language ?

A. The Arabic, or ancient language of Arabia, has long been a dead language. The modern language, or Arabesque, is spoken very extensively over the south of Asia and the north of Africa.

Q. What are the large towns of Arabia ?

A. Mocha, and Suez, in the W.; Medina, Jedda, Mecca, Sana, Rostak, Maskat and Lahsa.

Q. Describe the towns in the west.

A. Suez, is at the head of the Red Sea, and is a place of some commerce. Medina is a small town 40 miles from the Red Sea, and contains the tomb of Mahomet. Jedda the port of Mecca is the most commercial place on the Red Sea, and has a fine harbour. Mecca, 200 miles S. of Medina, is 40 miles from the coast. The houses are mud or stone, in a plain 2 miles long and one broad. Sana, at the foot of Mount Nikkum, about 4 miles in circuit, has considerable commerce, and is called the chief city of Arabia. Mocha, a little N. of the Straits, is well built, and has a valuable commerce.

Q. Describe the other towns ?

A. Rostak, is the residence of the iman of Oman and is near the coast. Maskat on the coast is a large town, and has an extensive trade with Arabia, Persia, and Hindostan. Lahsa is built near the mouth of the Aftan, on the gulf, an impetuous torrent falling into the bay of Lahsa. In this bay is a valuable pearl-fishery.

Q. What are the manufactures ?

A. They are of no consequence.

Q. What is the state of the Arabian commerce ?

A. From Yemen are exported coffee, aloes, myrrh, olibanum, senna, ivory, and gold.

Q. What islands belong to Arabia ?

A. The largest is Socotra, 240 miles from the Arabian coast, and 120 from Cape Guardefoi. It is about 100 miles by 30, and is celebrated for the production of aloes. The inhabitants are Arabs. Bahrin is an isle in the bay of Lahsa, in the Persian Gulf, remarkable for its pearl-fishery.

OF THE ASIATIC ISLANDS.

Q. What are the Asiatic Islands ?

A. The Isles of Sunda, Borneo, the Manillas, the Celebes, and the Spice Islands.

OF THE SUNDA ISLES.

Q. What is the situation of the Sunda Isles ?

A. They are in the Indian Ocean S. of Malaya, Borneo, and the Celebes, and N. W. of New-Holland ; between 6° N. and 10° S. ; and between 95° and 129° east longitude.

Q. What islands compose this chain ?

A. Sumatra, Java, Bally, Lombok, Sumbawa, Floris, Timor, Madura, Banka, and many smaller Isles.

OF SUMATRA.

Q. What is the situation of Sumatra ?

A. It forms the N. W. part of the Sunda Chain, lies between 6° N. and 6° S. and is 1000 miles long and 200 broad. The straits of Malacca separate it from Malaya.

Q. Describe the country ?

A. A chain of mountains runs through the island about 20 miles from the W. coast. Mount Ophir, under the equator, is 13,842 feet high. The rainy monsoon lasts from May to September ; the dry, from November to March. Most of the island is forested. There are many mines of gold, iron and tin.

Q. Describe the inhabitants ?

A. They are estimated to amount to 2,250,000. The coast is occupied by Malays. The interior by numerous tribes of natives who are pagans. Menang-Cabou, on the Straits of Malacca is the chief native sovereignty. The complexion of the natives is yellow. Acheen is a considerable kingdom at the north end.

Q. What are the products ?

A. Pepper, camphor, cassia, rattans, silk and cotton.

Q. What settlement have the British in Sumatra ?

A. Bencoolen in the southwest. It is important as the emporium of the Sumatran commerce.

Q. What isles are contiguous to the coast ?

A. Banka in the S. E. celebrated for its inexhaustible mines of tin ; Billeton, E. of Banka ; the Pitti Isles in the Straits of

Malacca; and the Poggy Isles, 20 leagues off, on the west coast.

OF JAVA.

Q. What is the situation of Java ?

A. It is S. E. of Sumatra, and S. S. W. of Borneo ; between 105° and 115° E. and in 8° S. It is 650 miles long and 100 broad. It abounds with forests, and presents an enchanting verdure.

Q. What is the chief town ?

A. Batavia, on the middle of the N. coast. It is large and populous ; but very unhealthy. Its commerce is highly important.

Q. To whom does Java belong ?

A. The British took Batavia in 1811. It is now to be restored to the Dutch. There are three or four petty native sovereigns.

Q. What are the products ?

A. The same as those of Sumatra. The Buhon-Upas, or poisonous tree of Java, has been often described.

OF THE SMALLER ISLES.

Q. Describe the smaller isles ?

A. Madura, N. E. of Java, has an independent prince. Bally, E. of Java, furnishes slaves, cotton yarn and pickled pork. The inhabitants are black and pagans and are very numerous. Lombok is E. of Bally ; Sumbawa, of Lombok ; and Florez, a larger island, of Sumbawa. Of these little is known. Timor, S. E. of Florez, is 200 miles by 60. It bears the white sandal wood. Numerous little isles lie N. E. and N. W. of Timor.

OF BORNEO.

Q. What is the situation and extent of Borneo ?

A. It is at the bottom of the China Sea, E. of Malaya and Sumatra, and N. E. of Java ; is 900 miles long by 600 in its greatest breadth.

Q. Describe the country ?

A. Most of the coast consists of swamps covered with forests, and numerous rivers. Lofty mountains rise in the interior.

Q. What are the products ?

A. Gold, diamonds, pepper, dragon's blood, camphor, sandal wood and edible bird's nests.

Q. Describe the inhabitants ?

A. The natives called Biajos are black, with long hair, and occupy the interior. The coasts are held by Malays, Macassars and Japanese. The whole population is estimated at five millions.

Q. What are the towns ?

A. Borneo on the northwest has 3000 houses, built on posts fixed in rafts. Bender-Massin in the south is at the mouth of a considerable river.

Q. What are the Bornean Islands ?

A. N. E. of Borneo are the Sooloos, rich in pearls, the largest of which is 30 miles by 12. Tawee lies between.—— Balambancan is near the north extremity. The groupes of Anamba and Natura are on the west.

OF THE MANILLLAS OR PHILLIPPINE ISLANDS.

Q. Where are the Manillas ?

A. They are N. E. of Borneo and S. E. of Canton, between 5° and 19° N. latitude. Luzon the largest, in the N. is 450 miles long and 100 broad. Mindanao in the S. is the second in size. The other chief islands are Mindore, Pani, Buglas, Zebu, Leyte, and Samar, between the two larger and Palawa in the W. nearer Borneo. These islands belong to Spain.

Q. Describe the country ?

A. The soil is fruitful. Sugar, cocoa-nuts, rice, cotton, and the bread-fruit ; gold, copper, iron, and sulphur ; the wild-boar and the deer, horses and buffaloes, are among the productions. Several volcanoes are found.

Q. Describe the inhabitants ?

A. They are called Tagals, are of a mild character, and a tawny complexion, tall, well made, and live on rice and salted fish. Their dress is a shirt and loose drawers. A commerce, still valuable, is carried on between Manilla and Acapulco in Mexico. Manilla the capital in Luzon, contains 12,000 Christian inhabitants.

OF CELEBES.

Q. What is the situation of Celebes ?

A. The Straits of Macassar on the W. separate it from Borneo, and the Manillas are directly N. It is between 1° 30' N. and 5° 30' south. Is 500 miles long, but divided into four peninsulas by great bays, so that it is every where narrow.

Q. Describe the country ?

A. It is lofty and mountainous and contains several volcanoes. The soil is fertile. Rice grows most abundantly.—— Many poisonous trees are found in the forests, and among others the Buhon-Upas.

Q. Describe the people ?

A. They are called Macassars ; are bold and ferocious, and

in great numbers freebooters and tyrants. Their houses are raised on pillars. The population is great. Maccassar the chief port is in the southwest. Here the Dutch have a trading establishment.

Q. What are the Celebezian Isles?

A. Sanguy in the north; the Shullus and Peling in the east; and Boutan and Sala in the south:

OF THE MOLUCCAS; OR, SPICE ISLANDS.

Q. Where are the Moluccas?

A. They are between 5° S. and 3° N. lying E. of Celebes and W. of New-Guinea. They are Gilolo, Ceram, Bouro, Mortay, Oubi, Mysol, Bouro, Amboyna, the Banda Isles, and five islands west of Gilolo, viz. Ternat, Tidore, Motin, Makian, and Bakian.

Q. Describe Gilolo?

A. Like Celebes it is divided into four peninsulas by bays, and is 230 miles long and 40 broad. Ceram is 190 by 40; and Bouro is 90 by 50. Amboyna is 60 by 40.

Q. What is the chief produce of these islands?

A. Cloves and nutmegs, indigo, sugar and coffee.

Q. To whom do these islands belong?

A. The king of Ternat possesses Maklan, Motin, Bouro, and the N. of Gilolo. The king of Tidore holds the S. of Gilolo. The king of Bakian has Ceram and Oubi. Amboyna and the Bandas, a numerous groupe of islets in the S. E. belong to the British. They are populous. Amboyna, in 1796, had 45,252 inhabitants, of whom 17,813 were protestants and the rest Mahometans.

OF AUSTRAL-ASIA.

Q. What territories have geographers included under the name of Austral-Asia?

A. Various large islands and their dependencies lying S. of the equator and S. E. of the Asiatic Isles; viz. New-Holland; Van Diemen's Land; New-Guinea; New-Britain; New-Ireland, with the Solomon Isles; New-Caledonia with the New-Hebrides; and New-Zealand.

OF NEW-HOLLAND.

Q. What is the situation and extent of New-Holland?

A. It is between 110° and 153° E.; and between 11° and

L

39° south; it is 2730 miles long from E. to W. and 1960 broad.

Q. What part of New-Holland has been explored?

A. A considerable tract of country in the S. E. round Port Jackson?

Q. What are the rivers, lakes and mountains?

A. Hitherto they have not been explored. There is a very large bay in the N. called the Gulf of Carpentaria.

Q. What are the vegetable productions?

A. The botany of no country in the world is more rich and varied than that of New-Holland.

Q. What are the animals?

A. The opossum, kargoroo, jackal, weazel, and ant-anter; the brown eagle, falcon, parrot, and cassowary.

Q. What are the minerals?

A. Coal and rock-salt.

Q. Describe the inhabitants?

A. Those near Port Jackson are of a low stature, ill-made, nearly black, with flat noses, wide nostrils, and thick lips.— They are remarkably ignorant and live by hunting and fishing.

Q. What is the language?

A. That of the different tribes is said to be radically different.

Q. Describe Port Jackson?

A. It is on the S. E. coast, in lat. 84°, has one of the noblest harbours in the world extending about 14 miles, and is regularly laid out and flourishing. It is the place of transportation for British convicts.

OF VAN DIEMEN'S LAND.

Q. What is the situation and extent of Van Diemen's Land?

A. It is an island on the S. E. of New-Holland and separated from it by Bass' Straits, which are about 90 miles wide.— It is 160 miles long by 80. The land is fertile and verdant, and well wooded. The inhabitants are black, slender, and woolly-headed.

OF PAPUA; OR, NEW-GUINEA.

Q. What is the situation and extent of New-Guinea?

A. It is in the same meridian with the eastern half of New-Holland and the Japan Isles; and is 1200 miles long from N. W. to S. E. and 300 broad.

Q. Describe the country?

A. The coasts are lofty and the interior mountainous.—

The whole country is verdant and beautiful, and clothed with woods. Cocoa-trees abound on the coast. This island is the chosen resort of the Bird of Paradise.

Q. Describe the inhabitants?

A. They have stout bodies, flat noses, thick lips, woolly hair, and skins of a shining black. They live on fish and sago. The Chinese bring instruments and utensils, and carry away ambergris, tortoise-shell, pearls, and birds of paradise.

Q. What are the Papuan Isles?

A. At the N. W. end of Papua are Waijoo and Salwatti. The former has 100,000 inhabitants. Mysori and Jobi are on the N.; and Timorlaut is on the S. W.

OF NEW-BRITAIN AND NEW-IRELAND.

Q. What is the situation of these islands?

A. Dampier's Straits separate New-Britain, from Papua on the S. W. New-Ireland is N. E. of New-Britain, and is separated by a narrower strait. They are mountainous, woody and fertile, and produce cocoa-nuts, ginger, pepper, nutmegs and yams.

Q. Describe the people?

A. They are black and woolly headed, but have not the negro features. They are very hostile, and have lances headed with flint. The Solomon Isles lie far off in the S. E.

OF NEW-CALEDONIA.

Q. What is the situation and extent of New-Caledonia?

A. New-Caledonia lies E. of New-Holland, about 800 miles off, and half way between New-Britain in the N. W. and New-Zealand in the S. E. The country is barren and rocky. The people are of a brown complexion and muscular. They live on roots and fish. Their houses are wigwams. The New-Hebrides is a cluster of isles N. of New-Caledonia.

OF NEW-ZEALAND.

Q. What are the situation and extent of New-Zealand?

A. New-Zealand consists of two large islands, separated, by a very narrow strait called Cook's Strait; each about 600 miles long and 150 broad.

Q. Describe the country?

A. These islands are fertile and enjoy a temperate climate, Storms are frequent and violent. The soil is yellow marl. The country is covered with verdure. The flax has a beautiful silky appearance. Mount Edgecumbe is a lofty mountain in Cook's Strait.

Q. Describe the natives?

A. They are tall, well made, of a dark brown colour and regular features. They bury their dead. Suicide is common. Their years are lunar. Their large canoes will carry 30 men. Their weapons are spears, javelins and battle-axes. They are cannibals.

OF POLYNESIA.

Q. What territories are included in that part of the world which geographers have called Polynesia ?

A. Numerous clusters of islands in the Pacific Ocean, lying E. N. E. and N. of Austral-Asia, between 50° S. and 35° N. ; and between 170° E. and 130° W.

Q. What are the names of these clusters ?

A. On the N. of the equator are the Ladrones, the Pelew Islands, the Carolines, and the Sandwich Isles ; and on the S. the Friendly Isles, Navigator's Isles, Society Isles and Marquesas.

OF THE LADRONES.

Q. What is the situation of the Ladrones ?

A. They are in 15° N. and 127° E. lying N. of Papua, and S. S. E. of Japan.

Q. Describe them ?

A. They are about 12 or 14 in number. Only 4 are inhabited. Guam the largest is 120 miles in circuit and has 30,000 inhabitants. They resemble those of the Manillas.—Here are oranges, lemons, cocoa-nuts and the bread-fruit. Between these islands and Japan are numerous little islets.

OF THE PELEW ISLANDS.

Q. What is the situation of the Pelew Islands ?

A. They are between 5° and 9° N. and between 130° and 136° E. ; and lie N. of the W. end of Papua. They are small, of a moderate height, and well covered with wood. The cocoa-nut and sugar-cane are indigenous.

Q. Describe the people ?

A. They are nearly black, have long flowing hair, are mild, affable and industrious; tatoo their bodies, and dye their teeth black. The men go naked. The women wear two little aprons. Polygamy is allowed. They bury their dead. The king of Ooolong, the largest isle, is monarch of the whole groupe. Their chief nourishment is fish.

OF THE CAROLINES.

Q. What is the situation of the Carolines ?

A. They are a long, extensive range, about 30 in number;

S. E. of the Ladrones, in the same longitude with Kamtschat ka and about 10 degrees N. of the equator. Hogoley, the largest, is 90 miles long by 40.

Q. Describe the people?

A. They are of a deep tawny, live on fish and cocoa-nuts, allow polygamy, have negro slaves, and are armed with lances. Each island has its monarch.

OF THE SANDWICH ISLES.

Q. What is the situation of the Sandwich Isles?

A. They are in the Pacific Ocean, in the latitude of 20 north, about as far again from China as from the American coast. Owyhee the largest is 280 miles in circuit. Here Capt. Cook was killed.

Q. Describe them?

A. The climate is temperate. Hogs, dogs and rats are the only quadrupeds. They produce the bread fruit, sugar-cane and yams.

Q. What is the government?

A. These islands are subject to a powerful monarch called Tamahama. He has numerous war-boats, some of a large size and armed with cannon and muskets. The inferior chiefs are styled Eroes.

Q. Describe the inhabitants?

A. The natives are of a dark complexion, of pleasing features, and of a mild character. They wear their beards and tatoo their bodies. They offer human sacrifices.

OF THE MARQUESAS.

Q. What is the situation of the Marquesas?

A. They are just south of the equator, about 2500 miles southwest from California, and 2000 S. S. E. from the Sandwich Isles. Noabeva the largest is about 60 miles in circuit.

Q. Describe the natives?

A. They are tawny, well-made, and have handsome features. They believe in numerous deities, and bury their dead. Their canoes are made of wood and bark and are 29 feet in length. They tatoo their bodies.

OF THE FRIENDLY ISLES.

Q. What is the situation of the Friendly Isles?

A. They are S. of the Marquesas, are between 12° and 30° S. and 110° and 160° west, and are about 70 in number. Otaheite the largest is only 120 miles in circuit, and consists of two peninsulas joined by a neck of land three miles across,

All the habitations on these islands are on the coast. The interior of each is forested.

Q. Describe the people?

A. They are of a dark olive complexion, have fine black eyes, white teeth, and are tall and well shaped. Their voice and speech are soft and harmonious. Their houses are about 18 feet long.

Q. What is their religion?

A. They believe in a superior deity, and numberless subordinate ones; and admit a future state of rewards and punishments. They are ferocious and treacherous in their dispositions and licentious in their manners. Missionaries have met with no success.

Q. What are the productions?

A. The bread-fruit, cocoa-trees and plantains. Hogs, dogs and poultry are the chief animals. The sea swarms with fish. The soil is remarkably fertile, and the climate delightful.

OF THE FRIENDLY ISLES.

Q. What is the situation of the Friendly Isles?

A. They are a numerous groupe, including both the Feejee Isles and the Navigator's Isles, and lying between the Society Isles and New-Guinea.

Q. Describe them?

A. They are fertile and well cultivated; yielding flax, the bread fruit, cocoa-nuts, the banana, guava, and orange. Hogs, dogs, fowls and pigeons abound.

Q. Describe the people?

A. They are industrious, expert in sailing their canoes, of remarkable stature, strength and ferocity, and at the same time licentious. They live in villages.

OF AFRICA.

Q. What is the situation of Africa?

A. Africa lies south of Europe, southwest of Asia, and east of S. America. Cape Serra, its northern limit, is in 37° 18′ north; and Cape L'Anguillas, its southern, is in 34° 50′ south. Cape Verd, its western, is in 17° 33′ west; and Cape Guardafui, its eastern, is in 51° east.

Q. What is its extent?

A. It is 5000 miles long from north to south, and in its greatest breadth, 4,600 broad. Its extent is estimated at 6,500,000 square miles.

Q. What are the boundaries?

A. On the N. the Mediterranean; on the E. Arabia, the

Red Sea, and the Indian Ocean ; and on the W. the Atlantic.

Q. What are the great natural features of Africa ?

A. Sahara, or the Great Desert ; Jibbel-Kumra, or the Mountains of the Moon ; the Chain of Mount Atlas ; and the rivers Niger and Nile.

Q. Describe Sahara or the Great Desert?

A. It lies south of the Barbary states, and north of the country of Soudam ; and reaches from the Atlantic on the west to the borders of the Nile. Near the eastern extremity it pushes northward, between Egypt and Tripoli, to the Mediterranean. Its length from east to west is about 3400 miles, and its breadth from 800 to 900. It is interspersed with numerous oases or islands of verdure, which serve as resting places to the caravans.

Q. Describe the Jibbel-Kumra or Mountains of the Moon ?

A. They commence in the west of Africa, separating Soudan on the north, from Guinea on the south; and passing eastward through many unknown regions, appear again in Abyssinia, at the sources of the Nile in lat. 7°. Their whole length exceeds 2700 miles.

Q. Describe the chain of Mount Atlas?

A. It begins in the S. W. part of Morocco, runs N. E. to lat. 33?, and then E. on the southern frontier of Algiers and Tunis, to the Mediterranean.

Q. Describe the river Niger ?

A. It rises in the W. of Africa, from a spur of the Jibbel-Kumra, and pursues an easterly course through the country of Soudan. No European traveller has traced its whole progress. The Arabs assert, that it is the great western branch of the Nile. Either this is true, or it is lost in the sands; or it bends southward, breaks through the Jibbel-Kumra, and falls into the Gulf of Guinea. If it is true, the length of the whole river is about 4800 miles : the longest though not the largest river on the globe.

Q. Describe the Nile ?

A. Its eastern branch rises in Abyssinia, in 11° N. and 36° 55' E. In Sennaar, in lat. 15° 45', it receives the western and far the largest branch, supposed to be the Niger. Hence, its course is northward to the Mediterranean. Its whole length, from the source of the eastern branch, is about 2500 miles.

Q. What are the divisions of Africa?

A. Most of the interior is unknown. In the N. are Egypt and the Barbary states, including Morocco, Algiers, Tunis, and Tripoli. South of the Barbary states is the Saharia ;

south of that, Soudan; and south of that, Guinea. Sennaar lies S. of Egypt, and Abyssinia S. of Sennaar. The eastern coast S. of Abyssinia; and the western S. of Guinea, are divided into petty states, having no common name. On the S. coast, is the colony of the Cape of Good Hope.

OF MAROCCO.

Q. What is the situation of Marocco?
A. It is the N. W. country of Africa, having the Atlantic W.; the Mediterranean N.; Algiers and Biledulgerid E.; and Sahara S. It is 630 miles long from S. W. to N. E.— Its breadth in the middle and south is 350, on the N. coast 240. That extensive tract lying S. of Algiers and E. of the S. part of Marocco called Biledulgerid is said to be tributary to Marocco. It is extensively a desert and but little known.

Q. What are the divisions?
A. Fas in the N.; Marocco in the middle; Terodant in the S.; and Tafilet in the E.

Q. What is the climate?
A. The dry season is from March to September, and is exceedingly hot. The Shume or poisonous wind of the desert is frequent in the S. The country is unhealthy. The leprosy is very common.

Q. What is the face of the country?
A. Fas and Marocco are pleasant champaign countries, covered with vegetation. Terodant and Tafilet approximate too nigh to the level of the desert.

Q. What are the rivers of Marocco?
A. The Fillelly E. of the Atlas is the largest. It is lost in the sands. The Mulwia is a frontier on the side of Algiers. The Tensift runs near Marocco, and the Seboo near Fas.

Q. What are the animals?
A. Horses, mules, asses, camels, and cattle abound. The lion, hyena, leopard, rhinoceros, wild-cat, antelope, fox, camel of the desert, and horse of the desert. Noxious insects and poisonous reptiles are common.

Q. What are the minerals?
A. Gold, silver, iron, copper, lead, antimony and mineral salt.

Q. What is the population?
A. Jackson, a late traveller, states it at 14,886,600.

Q. How is the population divided?
A. Jackson divides it into Moors, Arabs, Berebbers and Shullahs. The Moors are the descendants of those who were driven out of Spain. The Arabs are emigrants from the

Bedouins of the desert. The Berebbers inhabit Mount Atlas N. of the city of Marocco, and are descended from the ancient Mauretani. They are very imperfectly subdued. The Shullahs occupy the south part of Atlas and the territory of Terodant. Negroes are also numerous.

Q. What is the religion ?

A. The Mahometan. Great numbers of Jews are found here.

Q. What is the government ?

A. It is despotic. The laws are very severe.

Q. What is the military strength ?

A. The army amounts to 36,000 men.

Q. What is the naval strength ?

A. There are 10 frigates, and 14 galliots, manned by 6000 mariners.

Q. What is the revenue ?

A. Upwards of a million of dollars ; and the expenses about 300,000.

Q. What are the languages ?

A. That of the Moors is Arabic intermixed with Spanish. That of the Arabs is a corrupt Arabusque or modern Arabic. That of the Berebbers is probably derived from the language of the ancient Mauretani. That of the Shullahs is a peculiar dialect from the others.

Q. What are the dress and dwellings ?

A. That of the Moors is a shirt and drawers, a close coat and shawl, a red cap and turban. The Arabs omit the shawl and coat. The Moors and Shullahs live in houses with flat roofs ; the Arabs and Berebbers in tents.

Q. What are the manners of the people ?

A. All complexions are found here. They are short but well-made. The beauty of the women decays early. It is lawful for each man to have four wives. The situation of the women is deplorable. Both sexes are cleanly. In their houses they sit cross-legged, and eat with their fingers.

Q. What are the large towns ?

A. Marocco, Fas, Mequinas, Terodant, and Rabat.

Q. Describe Marocco ?

A. It is about 120 miles from the sea, not far from a spur of Mount Atlas, and is surrounded by a thick strong wall. It has numerous mosques and contains 270,000 inhabitants. The palace is of hewn stone. The streets are filthy.

Q. Describe Fas ?

A. Fas is in the north, contains numerous splendid mosques, about 200 caravanseras, and 380,000 inhabitants. It is generally well built.

Q. Describe Mequinas?

A. It is near the Seboo, and not far from Fas, in the midst of a beautiful valley, ornamented by groves. The population is 110,000.

Q. What are the manufactures?

A. Shawls and sashes of silk and gold; shawls of cotton, of silk, and of woollen; Marocco leather; gun-powder; and carpets.

Q. What is the state of commerce?

A. Marocco has a passive commerce by sea, and an over-land commerce with Soudan by caravans.

Q. What are the exports?

A. To Europe, fruits, gums, bees-wax, leather, oil, wool, ostrich feathers, ivory, and tallow; and to Timbuctoo in Sou-dan, linens, cottons, muslins, silks, coffee, tea, sugar, spices, ornaments, and salt.

Q. What are the imports?

A. From Europe, woollens, linens, silks, nankins, cottons, gin, sugar, tea, cloves, potatoes, tin, iron, steel, mirrors, hard-ware, and china-ware: from Timbuctoo gold dust, gold bars, ivory, gums, grains of Sahara and slaves.

OF ALGIERS.

Q. What is the situation of Algiers?

A. It has Marocco W.; the Mediterranean N.; Tunis E.; and Mount Atlas S. It lies between 1° 30' W. and 9° 16' E.; is 610 miles long from E. to W. and 100 broad.

Q. What are the divisions?

A. Constantia in the E.; Tlemsen in the W.; and Titeri in the S. W.

Q. What is the climate?

A. Generally hot. The Shume (or wind of the desert) is not common, but is very oppressive.

Q. What is the soil?

A. Generally fertile. Wheat, beans, barley, rice, millet, and maize are cultivated. Figs and dates grow in the S.

Q. What are the rivers?

A. The Haregal, the Mina, and the Gemar.

Q. What are the mountains?

A. Mount Atlas in the S. Jurjura a spur from the main range, and the highest mountain in Barbary, is 60 miles S. of Algiers.

Q. What is the population?

A. It is estimated at 1,500,000.

Q. What is the military strength?

A. In peace 6500 ; in war 25,000.

Q. What is the navy ?

A. It consists of 8 frigates, 12 sloops of war and 30 gunboats.

Q. What is the revenue ?

A. About 670,000 dollars.

Q. What is the government ?

A. A military despotism. The chief magistrate is the dey, who is chosen by the soldiers. His divan is composed of the mufti and cadi, and about 30 bashaws or officers of the army.

Q. What is the religion ?

A. The Algerines are bigotted Mahometans.

Q. Into how many classes are the inhabitants divided?

A. Turks born in Turkey about 10,000, and their descendants called Coloris ; Moors descended from those who were driven out of Spain ; Cabyles or Berebbers in Mount Atlas ; Arabs and Jews.

Q. What is the character of the inhabitants ?

A. The Turks are proud, indolent, voluptuous, jealous, and revengeful. The Coloris are generally like them but less indolent. The Moors are industrious. Those in the cities are merchants. The Cabyles live in tents, chiefly in the mountains, and are slightly dependent on the dey. The Arabs live in tents. The Jews are much oppressed.

Q. What are the large towns ?

A. Algiers, Tremesen, Oran, and Bleeda.

Q. Describe Algiers ?

A. Algiers is on a good and well-fortified harbour of the Mediterranean, and is surrounded by walls 12 feet thick. The houses are of brick or stone. The population is 80,000. Lat. 36° 50′, long. 2° 13′.

Q. What are the manufactures ?

A. Silks, cottons, woollens, leather, and carpets.

Q. What is the commerce ?

A. The exports are ostrich feathers, wax, leather, wool, copper, silk sashes, dates and slaves.

OF TUNIS.

Q. What is the situation of Tunis ?

A. Tunis has Algiers on the W. ; the Mediterranean on the N. ; the same sea and Tripoli on the E. ; and the chain of Mount Atlas S. It is 300 miles from N. to S. and 170 broad.

Q. What is the climate ?

A. It is healthy and pleasant. From October to April is the rainy season.

Q. What is the soil ?

A. Fertile and productive, and yields wheat, barley, maize and olives ?

Q. What are the animals ?

A. Horses, mules, asses, cattle, goats, sheep and the wild animals of Marocco.

Q. What is the principal river ?

A. The Mejerda.

Q. What is the population ?

A. It is estimated at 1,000,000.

Q. What is the religion ?

A. The Mahometan. There are about 200,000 Jews in this country.

Q. What is the government ?

A. An hereditary despotism. The Bey nominates his successor.

Q. What is the military strength ?

A. The bey has a body guard of 6000 Turks, and can muster a force of 50,000 militia, three-fourths cavalry.

Q. What is the revenue ?

A. It is considerable, but the amount is not known ?

Q. What is the capital ?

A. Tunis. It stands on a rising ground on the W. bank of a lake 6 miles from the bay of Tunis, and communicating with it by a narrow outlet. The population is about 150,000. Jerba is an inland town.

Q. What are the manufactures?

A. Scull caps, woollens, and morocco leather.

Q. What is the commerce ?

A. The exports are oil, wool, hides, wax, soap, dates, senna, madder, coral, oil of roses, and ostrich feathers. A valuable overland commerce is carried on with Timbuctoo by caravans.

OF TRIPOLI INCLUDING BARCA.

Q. What are the situation and extent of Tripoli ?

A. The length of the coast, from the Gulf of Cabes in the W. to the tower of the Arabs in the E. is 1100 miles. The breadth is about 200. Tunis is W. ; Sahara S. ; Egypt E. ; and the Mediterranean N. Tripoli Proper is the western and much the smaller part. Barca is chiefly a desert.

Q. What is the soil?

A. Chiefly barren. The civilized inhabitants live in towns along the coast.

Q. What is the religion ?

A. Mahometan.

Q. What is the government ?

A. A despotism. The sovereign is styled the bashaw of

Tripoli. He has 6000 troops ; one 50 gun ship and 6 galliots ; and a revenue of 150,000 dollars.

Q. What is the population ?

A. About one million. The great body of them are the Bedouin Arabs, and live in tents in the desert.

Q. What is the capital ?

A. Tripoli. It is on a good harbour, 270 miles from Tunis and 570 from Algiers. The houses are low and mean, and the streets narrow and dirty. Derne is the chief town of Barca 500 miles east of Tripoli.

OF EGYPT,

Q. What is the situation of Egypt ?

A. It is the N. E. country of Africa, lying between 23° 30' and 31 3' N.; and between 29° 48' and 32° 30' east.

Q. What is the extent ?

A. The length from N. to S. is 560 miles. The breadth on the Mediterranean is 280. S. of the Delta Egypt is a narrow strip along the Nile.

Q. What are the boundaries ?

A. On the N. the Mediterranean ; on the E. Arabia and the Red Sea ; on the S. Nubia ; and on the W. the desert.

Q. What are the divisions ?

A. Egypt is divided into Lower and Upper Egypt. Lower Egypt is the country N. of Cairo ; and Upper Egypt the country to the S. The tract between Cairo and Assiut or Siut is called Vostant. The rest o' Upper Egypt is called Said.

Q. What is the climate ?

A. Very hot and unhealthy. Winds of a northerly direction are most common. There are no rains except in winter and then they are uncommon.

Q. What is the face of the country ?

A. The habitable part of Egypt is a narrow valley through which runs the Nile. Two chains of mountains bound it on the E. and W. the whole distance. It is from 12 to 30 miles wide. North of Cairo it becomes of much greater width. W. of the western range is the Sahara ; and E. of the eastern, a desert that reaches to the Red Sea.

Q. What is the soil ?

A. The soil of the valley of the Nile is remarkably rich and fertile. The river annually overflows and leaves a sediment richer than the richest manure.

Q. What is the agriculture ?

A. Rice, wheat and barley grow in vast abundance. Maize, flax, hemp, tree-sugar, lentils, onions, leeks, the vine, privet, and various medicinal plants, are extensively cultivated.

M

Q. What are the lakes ?

A. Menzala, E. of the Nile, is 60 miles long and 12 broad. Lake Berelos, in the Delta and near the coast, is 32 miles by ten.

Q. What are the trees of Egypt ?

A. The fig, date, orange, lemon, olive, pomegranate, banana, apricot, peach, almond, and pistachio-nut. The cotton tree and sugar-cane ought also to be mentioned.

Q. What are the animals ?

A. The horse, ass, mule, fawn coloured cattle, buffalo, dogs, cats, sheep and goats, the tyger, jackal, antelope, deer, fox, and hare ; the crocodile and the ichneumon ; cameleons, scorpions, and insects without number.

Q. What are the minerals ?

A. Marble, phorphyry, granite, and the Egyptian pebble.

Q. What is the population ?

A. It is estimated at 3,500,000.

Q. How is the population distributed ?

A. Into the Copts chiefly in the Said ; the Arabs ; the Turks ; the Mamelukes ; the Jews ; and the Berebbers in the upper part of the Said and in Nubia.

Q. What is the religion ?

A. Most of the inhabitants are Mahometans. The Copts are Monophysite Christians, and have a patriarch at Cairo. It is doubted whether all the Berebbers of Africa both of Egypt and Barbary are not Pagans.

Q. What is the government ?

A. It is in the hands of the Mamelukes, who are natives of Georgia and Circassia, and sold as slaves in Egypt. The Bedouin Arabs are divided into tribes, each having its own shekh.

Q. What is the military force ?

A. It should be about 20,000 infantry, and 12,000 cavalry.

Q. What is the revenue ?

A. About 2,000,000*l.* sterling.

Q. What is the appearance of the natives ?

A. The Turks and Moors are swarthy. The Mamelukes incline to yellow and have flaxen hair. The Copts are of a dusky brown. The Arabs are of a very deep tawny. The Berebbers are of a shining jet black, with sharp noses, deep sparkling eyes, small lips and remarkably spare persons.

Q. What are the languages ?

A. The modern Arabic is spoken by the Arabs, Copts, Jews, Turks, and Mamelukes. The Berebbers have a peculiar language. The Copts use the ancient Coptic in their religious services. The Turks also speak Turkish.

Q. What are the manners and customs ?

A. The Copts of the Said are husbandmen. Those of Cairo and the cities are writers. The Turks are artisans, priests, and military officers ; are not numerous ; and have no influence. The Saracenic Arabs are husbandmen and artists. The Mograbian Arabs are in the Said, and are artisans, and husbandmen. The Bedouins live in tents, and are mere marauders. The Mamelukes are soldiers. The Jews are merchants and manufacturers.

Q. What are the cities ?

A. Cairo, Alexandria, Damietta, and Rosetta.

Q. Describe Cairo ?

A. It is on the east side of the Nile, a mile from its bank, and 10 from the Delta, and is 9 in circumference. The streets are crooked and narrow, and the houses of earth and brick. The population is 300,000. The body of the people are Saracenic Arabs. About 12,000 are Mamelukes. The commerce is very extensive. Boulac, a large suburb of Cairo, is on the river's bank.

Q. Describe Alexandria ?

A. It is 12 miles W. of the W. branch of the Nile, is on the shore, and is 6 miles in circuit.

Q. Describe Damietta ?

A. It is on the E. bank of the E. branch of the Nile, 2 miles from its mouth ; is healthy and well built ; and has 80,000 inhabitants.

Q. Describe Rosetta ?

A. It is on the W. bank of the W. branch of the Nile, 6 miles from its mouth ; and is 3 miles long and 1 wide. It is well built, and has an extensive trade.

Q. What are the other towns ?

A. Cosseir on the Red Sea, Siut, Girgeh, and Syene.

Q. What is the commerce ?

A. From the cities on the Mediterranean, are exported drugs, linseed, linens, flax, sugar, grain, fruits, coffee, spices, hides, and precious stones. The imports are cloths, hardware, gun-powder, arms, wines, silks, paper, money, mirrors, and china-ware. Caravans go from Cairo to Marocco, to Mecca, to Damascus, to Sennaar, to Abyssinia and to Fezzan.

OF NUBIA.

Q. What is the situation of Nubia?

A. Nubia is a country of indefinite extent, lying S. of Egypt and N. of Abyssinia. The Red Sea, is its eastern boundary and the desert its western.

Q. What are the divisions

A. From the tropic in 23° 30' as far S. as Goos, in lat. 18° the Nile flows through a mere desert. This desert westward is a part of the Saharra; eastward, it reaches to the Red Sea. From Goos, southward as far as Abyssinia, is the country of Sennaar.

Q. What is the climate?

A. It is neither pleasant nor healthy. The thermometer often rises to 120.

Q. What is the soil?

A. The country in Sennaar appears in the dry season a barren waste. In August and September it is every where verdant. Millet, wheat and rice are cultivated.

Q. What are the rivers?

A. The two great branches of the Nile, the Asrek or White river from the east, and the Abiad or Black river from the W. unite in 15° 45' N. lat. The latter is supposed to be the Niger. It is much the largest branch. The Atbara is a large tributary from Abyssinia.

Q. What is the population?

A. The number of inhabitants is unknown. They are of three classes: the Berebbers, the Arabs, and the Shillooks. The Berebbers are the aborigines, and live in villages along the banks of the Nile. The Arabs live chiefly in tents; some of them also in towns, as at Gerri and Herbagi. The Shillooks are the ruling nation, and came in 1504 from the banks of the Abiad or Black river, and subdued the country.

Q. What is the religion?

A. All the inhabitants are Mahometans.

Q. What is the government?

A. The king of Sennaar is monarch of the whole country, and has absolute power. The kingly office is hereditary. The Arabs are divided into 10 tribes, all subject to a prince called the Welled Ageeb, who is a descendant of Mahomet. He is tributary to the king of Sennaar.

Q. What is the military strength?

A. The king of Sennaar has 14,000 infantry, armed with javelins and shields; and 1800 cavalry.

Q. What is the revenue?

A. It is paid in gold, and probably exceeds L.2,500,000 sterling. That of the Welled Ageeb is also very considerable.

Q. Describe the inhabitants?

A. The Arabs are of a light copper complexion. The Berebbers and Shillooks are black.

Q. What are the towns?

A. Sennaar is on the W. bank of the Nile, in lat. 13° 35', and covers considerable ground. El-Aice on the Abiad is the capital of the Shillook country in lat. 13° 30'. Herbagi, on the W. bank of the Nile in lat. 14° 39' is the residence of the Welled Ageeb. Suakem is a port on the Red Sea.

Q. Is there any commerce ?

A. A small caravan goes yearly from Goos to Suakem, and the Arabs carry ivory to Abyssinia.

OF ABYSSINIA.

Q. What is the situation and extent of Abyssinia ?

A. The S. W. limit is in lat. 7° N. ; the N. E. on the Red Sea in lat. 16° N. It is between 35° and 44° E. Its length from E. to W. is 560 miles ; and its breadth from N. to S. 420.

Q. What are the boundaries ?

A. Nubia is on the N.; the Red Sea E. ; Adel, on the S. E.; and the Nile W.

Q. What are the divisions ?

A. The country is divided into 12 provinces.

Q. What is the climate ?

A. There are two rainy seasons. The hill country is generally healthy.

Q. What is the face of the country ?

A. The middle and south is rugged and mountainous. The north is chiefly a flat country.

Q. What is the soil ?

A. It is thin, but rendered very productive by the rains.— Barley, fitches and wheat are cultivated.

Q. What are the rivers ?

A. The Asrek or E. branch of the Nile rises in lat. 11.— The Atbava, a tributary of the Nile, runs about 800 miles.

Q. What lakes are there in Abyssinia ?

A. Lake Dembea, S. W. of Gondar, is 50 miles long and 35 broad. The Asrek or Nile passes through it.

Q. What are the mountains ?

A. A chain of mountains runs along the coast of the Red Sea the whole distance from Suez to Babelmandel. In lat. 13° a spur pushes westward and crosses the Nile at its cataracts in 11° 35'. The mountains in the S. are part of the Jibbel Kumra, or mountains of the moon.

Q. What is the population ?

A. It is estimated at 3,000,000.

Q. What is the religion ?

A. Professedly Christian. The patriarch is styled the Abuna, and always comes from Egypt. It is a very corrupt branch of the Greek church. The clergy are numerous and

M 2

very licentious. Few countries have as many churches.

Q. What is the government ?

A. An absolute hereditary monarchy. The Abyssinians believe their reigning family to be descended from Solomon by the queen of Sheba. Formerly all the blood royal except the reigning monarch were imprisoned in the high mountain of Geshen in Amhara.

Q. What is the military strength ?

A. In peace 20,000 ; and in war 40,000. The country is almost always distracted by civil wars.

Q. What is the revenue ?

A. It is paid partly in gold and partly in produce.

Q. What is the dress ?

A. A pair of breeches, a long wrapper of cotton cloth round the body, and a girdle.

Q. What are their marriages ?

A. The husband receives a dowry with the wife, and is obliged to give security to refund the goods if they separate. Marriage is dissolved by the dissent of either party. Nothing like personal purity is known.

Q. What is the manner of living ?

A. The houses are of clay with thatched conical roofs.— Cakes of unleavened bread and raw flesh are the chief articles of food. Their feasts always terminate in riot and debauchery.

Q. What is the capital ?

A. Gondar. It is in lat. 12° 34' and long. 37° 33! on a hill of considerable height. It contains 10,000 houses and 50,000 inhabitants.

Q. What are the other towns ?

A. Axum the ancient capital, 140 miles N. E. from Gondar and 120 from the coast, has 600 houses. Masuah and Arkeeko are seaports.

Q. What is the commerce ?

A. Gold, ivory, slaves, elephants and buffaloes' hides are exported. The imports from Arabia are blue cottons, Surat cloths, beads, cotton, mirrors, glass and antimony. A caravan goes yearly to Cairo.

OF THE EASTERN COAST OF AFRICA.

Q. What country lies S. E. of Africa ?

A. Adel. It reaches from the Straits of Babelmandel E. and S. to Magadexo in about 5° N. The country is populous and productive. The people are of a deep tawny. Adel the capital is in lat. 8° 5' and long. 44° 20' on the Hawash, a large river emptying a little E. of the Straits.

Q. Describe Magadoxo?

A. It extends from Adel to the mouth of the Jubboo under the equator. The people are black and are Mahometans. Magadoxo is 2° 30' N. and is a large commercial town. The country is not very fertile. Melinda bounds it on the S.

Q. Describe Melinda?

A. Melinda or Zanguebar reaches south to the Portuguese territory of Mambaza. The people are chiefly Mahometans, and are black. The king is absolute. Melinda the capital is a well built commercial town. Many Arabs and Portuguese reside here. It is thought to have been the Tarsish of Solomon.

Q. Describe Mombaza?

A. Mombaza and Juiloa are two Portuguese towns on the coast, and each constituting a government. The country between Melinda and Mozambique belongs to them. These towns are well built, healthy and commercial, and the territory is fertile. Millet, rice and fruits are the products.

Q. Describe Mozambique?

A. It extends from lat. 10° to 18° along the coast, and is fertile. Mozambique the capital is on a small island, is well built and fortified. The people are black. The king is dependent on the Portuguese. Monomotapa, Safala, Sabia and Inhanbane lie S. of Mozambique. S. of these the coast of Natal reaches to the colony of the Cape of Good Hope.

OF THE COLONY OF THE CAPE OF GOOD HOPE.

Q. What is the situation of this colony?

A. It lies on the S. coast of Africa, between 29° 55' and 34° 50' S.; and between 17° 30' and 28° 20' E.

Q. What is the extent?

A. On the W. coast it reaches 315 miles to the river Koussie in lat. 30. Great Fish river is the boundary on the S. coast in long. 28° 20'. The length from west to east is 580 miles, the mean breadth 223; and the number of square miles 128,150.

Q. How is it divided?

A. Into 4 districts: Cape District in the S. W.; Stellenbosh in the W.; Zwellendam in the S.; and Graaf-Reynet in the E.

Q. What is the climate?

A. The climate is healthy and pleasant. Violent storms are not uncommon.

Q. What is the face of the country?

A. The country is chiefly made up of chains of mountains running from E. to W. and broad vallies between them.

Q. What is the soil?

A. About half of the land in the colony is an unprofitable waste consisting of arid plains or mountains.

Q. What are the productions?

A. Wine, barley, flax, cotton, coffee, sugar, hemp and indigo, and immense numbers of cattle.

Q. What are the rivers?

A. Great Fish river in the E. Sunday river, Great river, Lion's river, and the Gauritz, all on the S. coast; and elephants' river on the W. coast.

Q. What are the mountains?

A. Table mountain reaches from the Cape of Good Hope N. to Cape Town 30 miles. The South mountains are a low range 60 miles from the south coast, and parallel with it.— The Zmartberg is a parallel range about 60 miles north, and parallel. The Nieuwveld is the northern boundary running generally from east to west, and is 10,000 feet high.

Q. What is the population?

A. In 1797, it was 60,000; of whom 22,000 were whites, and the rest slaves and Hottentots. Now it is far greater.

Q. What are the classes of people?

A. Those of European extract are chiefly Dutch, by whom the colony was planted. The wine growers are of French descent.

Q. What is the government?

A. This is a British colony, and is entrusted to a governor and lieutenant-governor.

Q. What is the religion?

A. The Hottentots were originally Pagans. Many of them have been converted to Christianity through the benevolent labours of Moravian and English missionaries. The established religion of the colony is Calvinism.

Q. What is the revenue?

A. In 1801, it amounted to 90,142*l*. 13*s*. 4*d*. sterling.

Q. What is the capital?

A. Cape Town on Table Bay, about 30 miles N. of the Cape. The harbour is bad. Here are four churches and a government house. In 1797 it had 1145 houses, 5,500 whites, and 12,000 blacks: in all 17,000.

Q. What is the trade?

A. The exports are wines and brandy, aloes, skins, dried fruits, ivory, and ostrich feathers.

OF THE WESTERN COAST AND INTERIOR OF AFRICA.

Q. What is the country N. of the Cape Colony on the western coast?

A. From the frontier river Koussie in lat. 29° 55' S. to the River St. Francisco in 13° S. or about 1100 miles, the coast is chiefly a desert. The most distinguishing feature of this tract is the Great Orange River, which rises in the N. E. angle of the Cape Colony, and runs westward to the Atlantic about 1000 miles. The first country N. of this desert is Benguella.

Q. Describe Benguella?

A. The Coanza in 9° 54' south divides it from Angola, leaving a coast of 250 miles. St. Philip is a Portuguese town on a large bay. Benguella is a town on a high mountain north of the other. Provisions and ivory are exported.

Q. Describe Angola?

A. The river Dando on the north separates it from Congo. Its seacoast reaches only 120 miles. The Portuguese have forts on the coast.

Q. Describe Congo?

A. It extends to the river Zair which divides it from Loango. The king is by profession a Catholic, as are many of the inhabitants; though the majority are heathens. St. Salvador the capital 40 miles up the Zair has 40,000 inhabitants.

Q. Describe Loango?

A. It probably reaches north to the southern limit of Biafra. The king is powerful. Polygamy is common. Loango the capital is a large and populous town, two leagues from the sea on a large river. Slaves and copper are exported.

Q. Describe Biafra?

A. The Del Rey or King's river separates it from Guinea on the northwest. Its capital, Biafra, is on a bay called the Bite of Biafra.

Q. What is the extent of Guinea?

A. The whole coast from the Del Rey to the Mesurada, about 500 leagues, is called the coast of Guinea. The land of Guinea reaches north to the Jibbel Kumra, which separates it from Soudan.

Q. Into what territories is it divided?

A. Benin on the east; Guinea Proper in the centre; and Malaqueta in the west.

Q. Describe Benin?

A. It reaches westward to the river Volta, about 220 leagues. Benin, the capital, is on the river Benin.—The king is a powerful monarch and can bring 100,000 men into the field. Polygamy is common. The inhabitants are heathens. Whidah and Ardra, two districts in the west of Benin, are said to be governed by their own monarchs.

Q Describe Guinea Proper?

A. It reaches west to Cape Palmas 180 leagues. The eastern half is called the Gold Coast, and the western the Ivory Coast. The natives are of a jet black. The country is divided into petty principalities. Slaves, ivory and gold are exported. The Guinea slaves are called Koromantyns in the West Indies, and are distinguished for superior firmness, activity and intelligence.

Q. Describe Malaqueta?

A. It is 100 leagues in extent from Cape Palmas to the Mesurada. It produces Guinea pepper or the grains of Paradise, and hence is often called the Grain coast. The people are heathens. The English engross the whole commerce.

Q. What is the country north and northwest of Guinea?

A. Soudan. On the coast it extends from the Mesurada, to beyond the Senegal; and eastward to an indefinite extent along the Niger. It is the tract lying between Saharra north, and the range of Jibbel Kumra or mountains of the moon S.

Q. What part of Soudan has been explored?

A. The western part as far east as Tombuctoo.

Q. Who inhabit Soudan?

A. Negroes and Moors. In the west and south all the districts as far as they have been explored are inhabited by negroes. In the east the Moors and negroes are intermixed.

Q. What are the Moors?

A. About the year 650 the Saracens or Arabs conquered the Barbary states, the inhabitants of which were then called Mouri or Moors. To avoid the fury of the Arabs many of them retired across the desert into Soudan. Their descendants are the present Moors.

Q. Into what tribes are the negroes divided?

A. The Foulahs, Feloops, Mandingoes, Jaloffs, and Serawoolies.

Q. Describe the Southern Foulahs?

A. They occupy the coast from the Mesurada to the river Grande 500 miles, and the interior to the mountains of the moon. Teembo is their capital. They can raise 16,000 cavalry, and are chiefly Mahometans. The English colony of Sierra Leone is on their coast, in lat. 8° N.

Q. Where are the Northern Foulahs?

A. Between the river Senegal and the desert and on both banks of that river as far up as Kassom. They are also extensively dispersed among the Moors. They are Mahometans and read the Koran. Many of them are robbers.

Q. Where are the Feloops?

A. On the coast. They reach from the river Grande northward nearly to the Gambia. They are wild, unsocial, fierce, and unrelenting, and occupy themselves in collecting honey in the woods.

Q. Where are the Mandingoes?

A. They occupy both banks of the Gambia from its mouth to its source, and eastward to the Niger, together with Kaarta and Kasson on the Senegal, and the western half of Bambarra on the Niger.

Q. Describe the Mandingoes?

A. They are strong, well-shaped, dress in cotton of their own manufacture, live in mud huts with conical roofs, practise polygamy, are occupied in agriculture and pasturage, are gentle, cheerful and hospitable, and practise circumcision.

Q. Where are the Jaloffs?

A. On the coast, between the Mandingoes and Northern Foulahs. They are active, powerful and warlike; and of a jet black. They manufacture fine cotton cloths.

Q. Where are the Serawoolies?

A. They are embodied on the Senegal in Kajaaga, which is W. of Mandingo and S. of Kaarta, but are dispersed extensively over the rest of Soudan, as merchants, brokers and slave-drivers.

Q. What districts are possessed by the Moors?

A. Trasant, H-braken, and Jaffro, all on the confines of the desert; Ludamar N. of Kaarta; Beeroo of Bambarra: and Tombuctoo farther E. on both sides of the Niger.

Q. Describe Bambarra?

A. It is an extensive and powerful kingdom on both sides of the Niger from Mandingo and Kaarta in the W. to Tombuctoo E. The Negroes are dominant, but the Moors are very numerous. Sego the capital on the Niger, in lat. 14° 15' N. contains 50,000 inhabitants.

Q. Describe Tombuctoo?

A. It reaches eastward to Houssa, and is a large and powerful kingdom. Tombuctoo the capital is in a large plain, 12 miles N. of the Niger, in 1° 30' E. long. and 90 miles S. of the desert. Its commerce is very extensive. Caravans go from it to Morocco, Algiers, Fezzan and Cairo. The soil is fertile. Rice, millet, maize, coffee and indigo are the products.

Q. Describe Houssa?

A. It reaches from Tombuctoo eastward to a great distance. The Niger flows through the middle from W. to E. Houssa, a large and commercial city, is 60 miles N. of the Niger. The city of Kashna said to be the largest in the interior of Africa, is on the Niger. The Houssians are chiefly negroes. Bournou bounds Houssa on the E.

Q. Describe Bournou?

A. It is a very extensive country E. of Houssa. Beyond it are Dar-Baghorme and Dar-Fur, which are the western bounds of Abyssinia.

Q. Who are the inhabitants of the Sahara?

A. The Tuaricks and Tibboos, both roving nations; and the inhabitants of the Oases or fertile islands.

Q. Describe the Tuaricks?

A. They are a numerous people divided into various tribes, and occupying the desert N. of Houssa and Tombuctoo, and probably westward to the coast. They are tall, firm, honest, intelligent, and warlike; are chiefly Mahometans, and carry on commerce with Soudan, Fezzan, and Gadamis.

Q. Describe the Tibboos?

A. They are E. of the Tuaricks and N. of Bournou, and are wanderers in the desert.

OF THE OASES OF THE GREAT DESERT.

Q. What are the principal oases or fertile districts in the desert?

A. Fezzan, Gadamis, Augila and Siwah.

Q. Where is Fezzan?

A. Between long. 14° and 17° E. and about 150 miles S. of the Mediterranean. It is of an oval shape, 300 miles long from N. to S. and 200 broad. The Tuaricks are S. and S. W.; the Tibboos E. and S. E. It contains 100 towns and villages.

Q. What are the climate and soil?

A. The weather in summer is intensely hot and unhealthy, in winter damp and chilling. Dates are the staple produce; vegetables, wheat, barley and senna are cultivated.

Q. Describe the people of Fezzan?

A. They are about 75,000, and are Mahometans; are of a deep tawny complexion, and are engaged in agriculture and commerce. Their morals are loose.

Q. What is the government of Fezzan?

A. The sultan is of the family of the Sherreefs, and is absolute. The crown is hereditary. The revenue is small. The sultan pays a yearly tribute of 4000 dollars to the bashaw of Tripoli.

Q. What are the towns of Fezzan?

A. Mourshuk, in 27° 23' N. and 15° 40' E. 500 miles S. E. of Tripoli is the capital, and the emporium of the caravans. Zeula is 70 miles E. of Mouzuk.

Q. What is the commerce of Fezzan?

A. Caravans come hither from Cairo, Benghazi, Tripoli, Gadamis and Soudan.

Q. Where is Gadamis?

A. It is an oasis near the southwest corner of Tripoli, in lat. 31° 30' N. ; long. 11° E. It is said to contain 92 villages. Little is known respecting it.

Q. Where is Augila ?

A. In east longitude 23°, 160 miles from the coast, and in 29° 30' north latitude, and 450 miles E. N. E. of Mourzuk. It is governed by a viceroy from Tripoli. The country is flat, well watered, and fertile.

Q. What are the towns ?

A. Augila, Mojabra, and Meledilla. Augila is a mile in circumference, and is badly built. The common language is the Tuarick ; but Arabesque is spoken.

Q. Where is the Siwah ?

A. It is an oasis 50 miles in circumference, 210 miles E. of Augila, 260 W. S. W. of Cairo, and 150 from the Mediterranean. The hills of Mogurnah reach from Siwah eastward 200 miles. The road to Cairo lies at their foot. The soil is a sandy loam, yielding corn, oil, vegetables and dates.

Q. Describe the people ?

A. They are all Mahomedans, and speak the Tuarick language. They wear a shirt, breeches, cloak and cap. They are great thieves. The government is in the hands of 32 shekhs.

Q. Describe the capital ?

A. Siwah the capital is in the centre of the oasis, and is built upon a round mass of rock shaped like a bee-hive. The caravan from Siwah to Cairo follows the hills of Mogurnah, and in Egypt crosses the Natron Valley.

OF THE ISLAND OF MADAGASCAR.

Q. What is the situation and extent of the island of Madagascar ?

A. It is off the E. coast of Africa, and separated from it by the channel of Mozambique, 90 leagues across. It is between 11° 20' and 25° 40' S. lat.; and between 41° 14' and 48° 14' E. long. It is 980 miles long, and has a medial breadth of 250 miles, containing about 250,000 square miles.

Q. How is Madagascar divided ?

A. Into 28 provinces.

Q. What is the climate ?

A. It is healthy, the heat being tempered by the sea-breezes.

Q. What is the face of the country ?

A. It is extensively hilly and mountainous, has numerous rivers, and is well forested and fertile. It produces pepper, cotton, rice, barley, beans and pease. The banana, the citron, and the orange flourish. Oxen, sheep and goats abound.

Q. What is the population ?

A. It is stated by Rochon, at four millions. They have all one language. Many of them also speak Arabesque. They are generally of an olive colour, in the north approaching to black.

Q. What is the religion ?

A. They are heathens but not idolaters. They call their supreme being Zanhare, and sacrifice sheep and oxen. They believe the soul immortal.

Q. What is their mode of life ?

A. They live in towns and villages. Their houses are of wood covered with straw and leaves. They have manufactures of iron and steel, and weave fine linens. They have books in their own language and in the Arabic.

Q. What is their character ?

A. They are hospitable, friendly, intelligent, honorable and grateful. The French have heretofore stolen them for slaves and carried them to Bourbon and Mauritius.

OF THE SMALLER AFRICAN ISLANDS.

Q. Where is Socotra ?

A. In the Indian Ocean, east of Cape Gardefui, and has already been described.

Q. Where are the Comoro Isles ?

A. They are four small isles west of the north Cape of Madagascar, between 11° and 13° south latitude. They are inhabited by Arabs and natives, and are verdant and fertile. The East India ships touch here for refreshment.

Q. Where are Monfia, Zanzibar and Pemba ?

A. They are little isles close to the coast of Zanguebar.

Q. Where is Mauritius or the Isle of France ?

A. It is 400 miles east of Madagascar, in latitude 20° south, longitude 57° east ; and is 150 miles in circuit. It has a healthy climate ; an indifferent soil, yielding indigo ; a town called Port Louis ; 8000 white inhabitants, and 12,000 blacks. It belongs to the English.

Q. Where is Bourbon ?

A. It is W. S. W. of Mauritius and 370 miles E. of Madagascar ; is 60 miles long and 40 broad ; and contains 60,000 blacks and 5000 whites. St. Dennis is the chief port.

Q. Where is the Isle of Desolation ?

A. It is S. E. of the Cape of Good Hope, and S. W. of New-Holland, in lat. 48°.

Q. Where are Prince Edward's and Desert Islands ?

A. Between Desolation and the Cape of Good Hope.

Q. Where are Gough's Island, Diego, Tristran de Cunha, and Saxemberg ?

A. W. of the Cape of Good Hope and nearly its latitude.

Q. Where is St. Helena ?

A. In lat. 15° 55' south and 5° 59' W ; about 1200 miles from the coast of Africa. The land is so elevated as to be visible 20 leagues off at sea. It is 20 miles in circuit, has 2000 inhabitants, and is fertile and productive, but much infested with rats. It was formerly the stopping place for the India ships, and belongs to the English. It is now the prison of Napoleon Buonaparte.

Q. Where is Ascension ?

A. N. W. of St. Helena, in 7° 56' S. It is 10 miles long, and is barren and desolate.

Q. Where is St. Matthew ?

A. In 1° 45' south and northeast of Ascension.

Q. Where are Annabon, St. Thomas, Prince's Island, and Fernando Po ?

A. In the Gulf of Guinea.

Q. Where are the Bissages ?

A. In 11° N. ; near the mouth of Rio Grande.

Q. Where is Bissao ?

A. Just N. of Rio Grande, in 11° 30' N. It is 80 miles in circuit and belongs to the Portuguese.

Q. Where is Goree ?

A. Close to the coast S. of Cape Verd, and belongs to the English.

Q. Where are the Cape Verd Isles ?

A. About 130 leagues W. of Cape Verd, a promontory on the W. coast of Africa, in lat. 14° 45' ; lon. 17° 35'. They contain about 100,000 inhabitants, a mixed race of Portuguese and natives. There are 5 of considerable size. Leather and salt are the principal riches.

Q. Where are the Canary Isles ?

A. They are 13 in number, off Cape Nun, in Marocco, between 27 and 30° N. and 13 and 17° 30' W. Six are small and uninhabited. The other seven are Lancerotta, Forteventura, Canary, Teneriffe, Gomera, Ferro, and Palma.

Q. Describe Teneriffe ?

A. It is central ; having the three first named on the east, and the three last on the W. ; is 70 miles by 22 ; and has a capital called Santa Cruz. Its soil is exceedingly productive. About 40,000 pipes of wine are made here annually. The Peake of Teneriffe is a well known land-mark in these seas. The population it 100,000.

Q. Describe Canary?

A. Is is 70 miles W. of Teneriffe, and 100 in circuit. Palma its capital on the S. W. has 12,000 inhabitants, and the island 40,000.

Q. What is the population of all the Canaries?

A. It is 195,500. The natives are almost extinct. The inhabitants are Spaniards, and the islands belong to Spain. The religion is the Catholic. The government is entrusted to a governor and royal audience.

Q. What is the produce?

A. Wine, sugar, cotton, wheat, barley and rice. The exports, in 1788, amounted to 88,255l. sterling, and the imports to 71,856l.

Q. Where is the Isle of Madeira?

A. It is a triangle of 150 miles in circuit, in lat. 32° 30' N. and lon. 17° W. The population is 70,000, chiefly Portuguese. Funchal the capital has 15,000 inhabitants. The exports are 20,000 pipes of Madeira annually, sweet-meats and fruits. It belongs to Portugal.

Q. Where is Porto Santo?

A. It is N. E. of Madeira, about 50 miles, and belongs also to Portugal.

OF AMERICA.

Q. WHAT is the situation of the continent of America?

A. It reaches from Cape Isidro, the southern extremity of the continent, in lat. 54° S. to about 80 degrees of north latitude. If Greenland be a part of the continent, its eastern limit is 4° W. ; if not, its eastern limit is Cape St. Roque, on the coast of Brazil, in 34° 30' W. Its western limit is Cape Prince of Wales, or Behring's Straits, in 168° W.

Q. What is the extent?

A. Its length from N. to S. is 9400 miles. Its greatest breadth, from Labrador to the Pacific, is about 4600 ; and its least, across the Isthmus of Darien, in only 34. Exclusive of its islands it contains about 14,000,000 square miles.

Q. How is it divided?

A. Into North and South America.

Q. How is it bounded?

A. On the N. by the Northern Ocean ; on the E. by the Atlantic ; on the S. by the Straits of Magellan ; and on the W. by the Pacific. In the N. W. Behring's Straits, 48 miles across, separate Cape Prince of Wales from East Cape in Asia. N. of those Straits the Frozen Ocean is the western boundary.

Q. What large bays and gulfs are on the coast?

A. In the Atlantic, Baffin's bay, W. of Greenland; Hudson's bay, W. of Labrador; the gulf of St. Lawrence, W. of Newfoundland; the gulf of Mexico, opening between Florida and Yucatan in Mexico; and the Caribbean sea, inclosed by the West India Islands: and in the Pacific, the gulf of California, in Mexico: and the sea of Kamschatka, N. of the promontory of Alaska.

Q. What range of mountains traverses the American continent?

A. The Andes commence at Cape Isidro in lat. 54° S. and run N. to the Isthmus of Darien, about 4600 miles. Here they take the name of the Cordillera of Mexico and pursue a N. W. course, and nearly parallel with the western coast, to lat. 40° N.; where they begin to be called the Rocky Mountains, and whence they run N. N. W. to the Frozen Ocean. No river divides them throughout their whole length, which is about 12,000 miles.

OF NORTH AMERICA.

Q. What is the situation of North America?

A. It lies between 8 and 80° of N. latitude; and if Greenland do not belong to it, between 55 and 168° W. longitude. Its length, from N. to S. is 5200 miles: and its greatest breadth is 4600. It contains about 7,500,000 square miles.

Q. What are the boundaries?

A. On the N. the Frozen Ocean; on the E. the Atlantic; on the S. the gulf of Mexico, and South America; and, on the W. the Pacific, Behring's Straits, and the Frozen Ocean.

Q. How is it divided?

A. Into Russian America, in the N. W.; Danish America in the N. E.; the British possessions; the United States; and the Spanish possessions.

OF RUSSIAN AMERICA.

Q. What part of America is claimed by Russia?

A. The N. W. coast, from Portlock Harbor in lat. 58° to Cape Prince of Wales in Behring's Straits; together with several islands on that coast.

Q. What are the Islands?

A. The Aleutian or Fox Islands, stretching W. from the promontory of Alaska; and Kodiak, 150 miles long and 70 broad, together with some small islets S. of that promontory.

Q. What is the population of these islands?

A. That of the Aleutian Isles is 2500; and that of Kodiak 5000.

N 2

Q. What do you say of the natives on the coast?

A. They are very numerous. In 1784 about 50,000 were tributaries to Russia.

Q. What settlements have the Russians in these seas?

A. The principal settlement is on the E. side of Kodiak.— There is one on Unalashka, one of the Aleutian Isles, one at Portlock harbor, and several others on the coast.

OF DANISH AMERICA; OR, GREENLAND.

Q. What country does Denmark possess in N. America?

A. Greenland. In the south it is separated from the continent by Baffin's Bay; and it is not known whether it is a peninsula or island.

Q. What is the situation and extent of Greenland?

A. Its southern point, Cape Farewell, is in 59° 38! N.; and it reaches farther N. than lat. 80°. The west coast is in 55° W; and the E. coast in 4° W. If an island, it is the largest in the world except New Holland; being certainly upwards of 1500 miles from N. to S. and about 1200 in breadth.

Q. What is the climate?

A. The E. coast, inhabited in the 10th century by Norwegian colonies, has for centuries been rendered inaccessible by mountains of ice. On the W. coast, between 64 and 68° N. the weather is comfortable from May to September.

Q. What is the face of the country?

A. Generally mountainous. A range of lofty mountains runs N. and S. through the country. They are always covered with ice and snow. The two divisions, lying E. and W. of this range, are called East and West Greenland.

Q. What are the productions?

A. The hardier vegetables, a few oaks, juniper, and a few other shrubs. The animals are the rein deer, foxes, hares, dogs, and white bears.

Q. What is the population?

A. Nothing is now known of the E. coast. Those of European descent on the W. coast are about 10,000, and are Lutherans; and the natives, about 20,000 in number, are partly heathens and partly Moravian converts. They are the same race, and speak the same language with the Esquimaux of Labrador, are short and brawny, have flat noses, thick lips, and a tawny complexion.

Q. What is the chief settlement?

A. Good Hope on Baffin's Bay, in lat. 64°.

OF THE BRITISH POSSESSIONS.

Q. What territories in N. America belong to Great Britain?

A. New-Britain, Lower Canada, Upper Canada, Nova-Scotia, New-Brunswick, and the Islands of New-Foundland, Cape Breton and St. John's.

Q. What is the situation of the British possessions?

A. They lie N. of the United States. The most southern limit, Cape Au-Plait, in Lake-Erie, is in lat. 41° 40'; and the eastern limit of Labrador is in lon. 54° W. They extend N. and W. indefinitely.

Q. What is the population?

A. That of all these territories is about 620,000.

Q. What is the government?

A. The governor-general of all British America resides at Quebec, and is also governor of Lower-Canada; which, as a government, includes New-Britain and New-Foundland. Upper Canada is a distinct province. Nova-Scotia, Cape Breton and St. John's compose one government. New-Brunswick is a separate government.

OF NEW-BRITAIN.

Q. What is the situation of New-Britain?

A. It lies N. of Upper and Lower Canada, and has the Atlantic and Baffin's Bay on the east. It includes Labrador on the peninsula E. of Hudson's Bay; and New-South and New North Wales, or the country S. W. and W. of that Bay.

Q. What is the face of the country?

A. The country W. and S. W. of Hudson's Bay is chiefly a flat country. Labrador is generally rocky or mountainous.

Q. What are the rivers?

A. Churchill river runs E. N. E. to the W. side of Hudson's Bay, about 750 miles, emptying at Fort Churchill. Nelson's river rises in the Rocky Mountains, and runs N. E. through Lake Winnipec to Hudson's Bay, after a course of 1200 miles. Severn, Albany and Moose rivers fall into the same bay.

Q. What are the lakes?

A. Lake Winnipec, 280 miles long and 100 broad; and Lake of the Hills, 180 long but narrow, are claimed as belonging to New-Britain. Slave lake, 1000 miles in circumference, in 60° N. and 115° W. is beyond its pretended limits.

Q. What is the population?

A. The whole country is thinly peopled. Small detachments of troops are found at forts Churchill, York, Severn, Albany, and Moose, on Hudson's Bay. The rest are natives. Those of Labrador are called Esquimaux, are short and tawny like the Laplanders.

Q. What is the religion ?

A. The Moravians have missions in Labrador. Numbers of the Esquimaux here have embraced Christianity.

OF LOWER CANADA.

Q. What is the situation and extent of Lower Canada ?

A. It is between 45° and 52° N. and between 61 and 71 W.; and is 800 miles long from E. to W. and 450 broad.

Q. What are the boundaries ?

A. New-Britain is on the N. ; the Gulf of St.Lawrence E. ; New-Brunswick, New-Hampshire, Vermont, and New-York S. ; and Upper Canada S. W. and W.

Q. What are the divisions ?

A. This province is divided into 21 counties.

Q. What is the climate ?

A. The winters are severely cold. The spring is short, and vegetation is surprisingly rapid.

Q. What is the face of the country ?

A. It is hilly and frequently mountainous. Most of it is still forested.

Q. What is the soil ?

A. Very fertile. Wheat, barley, rye, tobacco, and vegetables are raised. The meadows yield excellent grass.

Q. What are the rivers ?

A. The St. Lawrence and Utawas run a considerable distance here. The Sorel is the outlet of Lake Champlain.

Q. What are the mountains of Canada ?

A. A chain of mountains runs parallel with the St. Lawrence.

Q. What are the productions ?

A. The vegetable and animal productions of Lower Canada are like those of the New-England states. Few minerals are found.

Q. What is the population ?

A. About 300,000. The greatest part are descendants of the original French colonists. French is universally spoken.

Q. What is the religion ?

A. About nine tenths are Roman Catholics. The rest are chiefly Episcopalians.

Q. What is the government ?

A. The government of this colony is vested in a governor-general appointed by the crown ; a council of 15 members appointed by the king for life ; and a house of assembly of 50 members chosen yearly by the people.

Q. Are there any colleges ?

A. There is one at Quebec and one at Montreal, both Catholic.

Q. What is the capital?

A. Quebec is the capital of this province and of all British America. It is on the N. bank of the St. Lawrence, 320 miles from the sea, and contains about 18,000 inhabitants.

Q. Describe Montreal?

A. It is on the east end of a large island in the St. Lawrence, 200 miles below Lake Ontario, and 180 above Quebec. It contains about 18,000 inhabitants, and has a very extensive commerce. It grows faster than Quebec.

Q. What are the manufactures?

A. Ship building, biscuits, potash, maple sugar and course linens and woollens.

Q. What is the commerce?

A. In 1810 the exports exceeded a million sterling. The fur trade is an object of immense importance.

OF UPPER CANADA.

Q. What are the situation and extent of Upper Canada?

A. It lies S. W. and W. of Lower Canada, being separated by the Utawas; has the St. Lawrence, Lakes Ontario, Erie, Huron, and Superior S.; and reaches W. to Lake Winnipec and Red River. New-Britain is on the N. It is about 1000 miles long from E. to W. and 250 or 300 broad.

Q. What are the divisions?

A. It is divided into 19 counties, and again into townships, like the New-England states.

Q. What is the climate?

A. Much milder than that of Lower Canada.

Q. What is the face of the country?

A. It is generally level. The soil is good. Wheat, maize, flax, grass, hops, plums, mulberries, blackberries, raspberries, grapes, apples, peaches, cherries and currants, are the productions.

Q. What are the rivers?

A. The St. Lawrence is the southern boundary. The Utawas is the north-eastern. It runs 600 miles E. S. E. and falls into the St. Lawrence opposite Montreal Island.

Q. What are the lakes?

A. The northern half of Lakes Ontario, Erie, Huron, Superior, Rainy Lake, and Lake of the Woods, belong to Upper Canada; as does a part of Lake Winnipec in the west.

Q. Where is the bay of Quinti.

A. On the north shore of Lake Ontario, and is made a peninsula which puts out eastward 50 miles.

Q. What is the population?

A. About 120,000. They are chiefly emigrants from New-England and New-Jersey.

Q. What is the religion?

A. The inhabitants are chiefly Methodists.

Q. What is the government?

A. It is vested in a governor appointed by the crown; a legislative council of 7 members appointed by the crown for life; and a house of assembly of 16, chosen by the people. The people pay no taxes but town and county taxes.

Q. What are the towns?

A. York, the seat of government, is on the N. W. shore of Lake Ontario. Kingston is at the mouth of the same lake.

OF NEW-BRUNSWICK.

Q. What is the situation of New-Brunswick?

A. It has Maine on the W.; Lower Canada N.; the Gulf of St. Lawrence E.; and Nova-Scotia, the Bay of Fundy and the Atlantic S.

Q. What are the rivers?

A. St. John's rises in Maine, and runs S. E. 350 miles to the Bay of Fundy. The St. Croix divides it from Maine.

Q. What is the population?

A. It is thought to exceed 60,000

Q. What are the towns?

A. St. John's, on the mouth of the St. John's, has about 1000 inhabitants. Fredericktown, the seat of government, is 80 miles up that river.

OF NOVA-SCOTIA.

Q. What are the situation and extent of Nova-Scotia.

A. It is between 43° 30' and 48° N. and between 58° 50' and 67° W.; is 307 miles long from east to west, 154 broad; and has 14,000 square miles.

Q. What are the boundaries?

A. On the N. and N. W. are the Bay of Fundy, New-Brunswick and the Gulf of St. Lawrence; and on the east, south and west the Atlantic Ocean.

Q. What are the divisions?

A. It is divided into 8 counties and 37 townships.

Q. What is the climate.

A. The winters are mild and healthy; the spring usually rainy; the summer warm; and the two first months of autumn mild and pleasant.

Q. What is the face of the country ?

A. Eastward of Halifax it is hilly and rocky ; westward it is fertile and agreeably diversified. The soil here is productive.

Q. What large bay is on the coast?

A. The Bay of Fundy, 150 miles long, and from 36 to 100 wide. Verte Bay on the opposite side of the isthmus. The width of the isthmus is 18 miles.

Q. What is the population ?

A. About 100,000 ; almost all of English descent.

Q. What is the religion ?

A. The Episcopalians are most numerous.

Q. What is the government ?

A. It is vested in a governor appointed by the crown ; a council, and an assembly of 59 members.

Q. Is there any college ?

A. One is established at Windsor, and is flourishing.

Q. What is the capital ?

A. Halifax, on the S. E. coast, in lat. 44, 40, has a noble harbor, is regularly built, has a valuable commerce, 1000 houses and 8000 inhabitants. Picton and Liverpool are flourishing towns.

Q. What is the trade of Nova-Scotia ?

A. The exports are timber, fish and lumber. Those from Halifax amounted in 1810 to 600,000l. sterling ; and the imports into the whole province to 1,200,000l.

OF NEWFOUNDLAND.

Q. What is the situation of the island of Newfoundland ?

A. It is the N. E. boundary of the Gulf of St. Lawrence.

Q. What is the extent ?

A. It is 381 miles long and from 40 to 287 broad.

Q. What is the climate ?

A. The winters are severe. Fogs are customary on the coast. The soil of the coast is barren.

Q. Describe the banks of Newfoundland ?

A. The great bank, 60 miles from the S. E. shore, is 300 miles long and 75 wide. Eastward of this is green bank, 240 miles long and 120 broad. These are the two largest.

Q. Give an account of the fisheries ?

A. They employ 3000 sail of small craft and 100,000 hands ; and yield about 450,000 quintals of dried fish, and 3000 tons of oil.

Q. What is the population ?

A. About 30,000, and about 1000 Indians.

Q. What are the towns ?

A. Placentia, in the southeast, has a fine harbor, and a population of 3000 inhabitants. St. John's, not far off, is about as large.

OF CAPE BRETON.

Q. What is the situation of the island of Cape Breton ?

A. It is the S. E. boundary of the Gulf of St. Lawrence, and separated from Nova-Scotia by the Gut of Canso. It is 109 miles long and 84 broad.

Q. Describe the country ?

A. The shores are bold and have good harbours. Much of the land is arable. Here are valuable coal mines.

Q. What is the population ?

A. About 3000. It is governed by a governor and council appointed by the king. The chief towns are Sidney and Arichat.

OF ST. JOHN'S.

Q. What is the situation of the Island of St. John's ?

A. It is at the bottom of the Gulf of St. Lawrence, and is 103 miles long and 35 broad. The soil is rich. Charlestown is the capital. The whole population is 5000. It is under the government of Nova Scotia.

Q. What other isles are in the Gulf of St. Lawrence ?

A. Anticosti, in the river's mouth, is 120 by 30. The Magdalen Isles, and Isle Percee.

OF THE UNITED STATES.

Q. What territories belong to the United States ?

A. The United States Proper, or the territory relinquished by Great Britain at the close of our revolutionary war; and the country of Louisiana.

Q. What are the boundaries of these territories ?

A. On the N. undefined tracts, and the British possessions ; on the E. New-Brunswick and the Atlantic ; on the S. Florida, and the Gulf of Mexico ; on the S. W. Mexico ; on the W. the limits are not settled. The government of the United States claim that the Pacific Ocean is the western boundary.

Q. What is the extent of these territories ?

A. If the Pacific be taken as the western boundary, the length across the continent from E. to W. exceeds 2500 miles, while the breadth from N. to S. is 1350. The square miles comprised in these limits probably exceed 3,000,000.

A. What is the situation of the United States Proper ?

A. They are on the eastern coast of America between, 31°

and 49° 37' N. lat. and between 67° and 95° 6' W. longitude.

Q. What is their extent ?

A. The length from N. to S. is 1350 miles ; their breadth in the N. is 1300, and on the S. line 620. They contain one million square miles.

Q. What are the boundaries ?

A. On the E. New-Brunswick, and the Atlantic ; on the S. Florida ; on the W. the Missisippi, which divides it from Louisiania ; and on the N. the Lake of the Woods, Rainy Lake, Lakes Superior, Huron, Erie, and Ontario, the River St. Lawrence and Lower Canada.

Q. How are the United States divided ?

A. Into the following states and territories, viz.

Maine	Pennsylvania	Kentucky
New-Hampshire	Ohio	North-Carolina
Massachusetts	Michigan Territory	Tennessee
Vermont	Illinois Territory	South-Carolina
Rhode-Island	Indiana Territory	Georgia
Connecticut	Delaware	Mississippi Terr.
New-York	Maryland	Louisiana (State)
New-Jersey	Virginia	Missouri Terr.

The two last include the whole country of Louisiana.

Q. You have mentioned the lakes in the north ; describe the Lake of the Woods.

A. It is in the N. W. corner of the United States, 75 miles in diameter, and flows into Lake Winnipec.

Q. Describe Rainy Lake ?

A. It is E. of the Lake of the Woods, flows into it, and is 45 miles in diameter.

Q. Describe Lake Superior ?

A. It is the largest body of fresh water on the globe, is 400 miles long, and 1600 in circumference, and flows through St. Mary's river 70 miles into Lake Huron.

Q. Describe Lake Michigan ?

A. It is S. of Superior, and W. of Huron, 300 miles long, 950 in circumference, and empties through the Straits of Michilimackinac into Lake Huron.

Q. Describe Lake Huron ?

A. It is 250 miles long from N. to S. 1000 in circumference, and flows S. through St. Clair river 40 miles, into Lake St. Clair ; a small lake 30 miles in diameter, which empties through Detroit river, 28 miles long, into Lake Erie.

Q. Describe Lake Erie ?

A. It is 210 miles long from E. to W. 710 in circuit, and flows N. through Niagara river 30 miles to Lake Ontario.

Q. Describe Lake Ontario ?

A. It 160 miles long from S. E. to N. W. and 450 in circumference, and flows through the river St. Lawrence a N. E. course of 690 miles to the sea.

Q. What are the great rivers of the United States ?

A. The St. Lawrence, the Missisippi, the Missouri, and the Ohio.

Q. Describe the St. Lawrence ?

A. Its remotest source is the river St. Louis, a tributary of Lake Superior. It runs through the lakes just mentioned and their outlets, and empties into the Gulf of St. Lawrence : exceeding 2000 miles in length.

Q. Describe the Missisippi ?

A. It rises in lat. 47° 38' N. and long. 95° 6' W. and runs S. about 3050 miles into the Gulf of Mexico.

Q. Describe the Missouri ?

A. It rises in the Rocky Mountains, about 50 . lat. runs S. E. 3106 miles, and falls into the Missisippi. It is much larger than the Missisippi. From its source to the gulf of Mexico is 4500 miles, surpassing the length of any river on the globe, unless the Nile and Niger are the same river.

Q. Describe the Ohio ?

A. It rises in Pennsylvania, and runs W. S. W. 1433 miles to the Missisippi ; emptying 193 miles below the Missouri.

Q. What are the mountains ?

A. The Allegany mountains run parallel with, and about 250 miles from the coast in the middle and southern states.

Q. What are the bays ?

A. Chesapeake bay, 200 miles long ; Delaware bay, 65 miles long ; and Massachusetts bay, 60 miles long.

Q. What are the sounds ?

A. Long-Island sound 140 miles long ; Pamlico sound ; and Albemarle sound.

Q. What is the population ?

A. In 1790 the United States contained 3,929,328 inhabitants ; in 1800, 5,305,666 ; and in 1810, 7,239,903 ; of whom 1,377,810 were blacks. To these ought to be added about 60,000 Indians. In 1815 the population is probably about 8,540,000.

Q. What is the form of government ?

A. The United States consist of 18 sovereign independent states, united in one Federal Republic. The supreme power is vested in a president and congress. The president is chosen for 4 years, senators for 6, and representatives for 2.

Q. What is the religion of the people ?

A. All religions are tolerated. Congregationalists and

Presbyterians are the most numerous sect ; then Baptists, Methodists, and Episcopalians.

Q. What is the military strength ?

A. In time of peace about 10,000 regular troops. The militia of the United States amounted in 1813, to 600,538 infantry : 28,219 cavalry : and 11,815 artillery ; aggregate including officers, 719,449.

Q. What is the naval strength ?

A. The navy of the United States consists of 3 ships of the line ; 12 frigates ; 8 brigs and 40 smaller vessels : in all 63.

Q. What is the revenue ?

A. In ordinary years it may be estimated at 14 millions of dollars.

Q. What is the national debt.

A. Before the war, it was $50,897,617.06. Now it is not fully ascertained, but there is reason to believe it is not less than 150 millions of dollars.

Q. What is the annual amount of American manufactures ?

A. By the returns in 1810, it appeared to exceed 150 millions of dollars. Since that time it has greatly increased.—— The great articles are cottons, woollens, leather, ships, linens, iron, spirituous liquors, hats and candles.

Q. What is the state of American commerce ?

A. The exports in 1810, amounted to $66,757,970.

Q. What is the number of tons of shipping ?

A. In 1810 it was 1,350,281 tons.

OF THE DISTRICT OF MAINE.

Q. What are the situation and extent of the District of Maine ?

A. It is 240 miles long, and 200 broad. It is between 43° and 48° 12' north latitude, and between 64° 54' and 70° 40' west longitude ; and contains 40,000 square miles.

Q. How is it bounded ?

A. By Lower Canada, from which the highlands separate it on the N. ; by New-Brunswick, E. ; by the Atlantic, S. ; and by New-Hampshire, W.

Q. How many counties are there ?

A. In the District of Maine there are 8 counties, viz: York, Lincoln, Cumberland, Hancock, Washington, Kennebeck, Oxford and Somerset.

Q. What are the rivers of this province ?

A. St. Croix, Penobscot, Kennebeck and Saco rivers are all large, and furnish fine inlets into the country.

Q. What are the principal bays in the province ?

A. The largest are Passamaquoddy, Penobscot, Broadbay, Sagadahok, Casco and Well's bay.

Q. What capes are there in this province?

A. Cape Pemaquid, Cape Elizabeth, Cape Small Point, Cape Neddick, and Cape Porpoise.

Q. What mountains are there in this province?

A. Mount Agamenticus, in the town of York, is a landmark for seamen.

Q. What is the capital town of the province?

A. Portland. It is a neat growing town, and has some commerce. In 1810 it contained 7169 inhabitants. There are also the towns of York, Bath and Wiscasset.

Q. What is the climate of this province?

A. It is temperate in summer, and cold in winter. It is however healthy, though subject to fogs from the sea.

Q. What is the face of the country?

A. It has in it many swamps and rising grounds, and a number of pine plains.

Q. What is the state of the soil?

A. The seacoast is rocky; the interior parts are fertile in many kinds of vegetable productions, such as grass, Indian corn, rye, oats, barley, pease and fine potatoes. A great part of it is covered with large and useful timber of various kinds.

Q. What is the state of trade and manufactures?

A. Their trade consists principally in lumber, of which large quantities are annually exported to various parts of the United States, and to foreign countries. The principal manufactures are ship building and lime burning.

Q. Are there any minerals in this province?

A. Iron, copperas and sulphur are found in some parts of it.

Q. What are the animal productions of this province?

A. Deer, moose, otters, beavers, sables, squirrels, rabbits, bears, wolves, catamounts and hedge hogs. There are partridges, wild geese, and ducks, with most other kinds of water fowls, in great plenty.

Q. What number of inhabitants are there in the province?

A. In 1790 there were 96,540. In 1800 there were 151,719. In 1810 it had 228,705.

Q. What is their character?

A. Though many of them are well educated, yet the want of schools is more evident here than in any other part of New-England. They are hardy, industrious and humane. Their religion is the same with that of New-England in general.

OF NEW-HAMPSHIRE.

Q. What are the situation and extent of New-Hampshire?

A. It is situated between 42° 41' and 45° 11' north latitude, and between 70° 40' and 72° 20' west longitude. It is 168 miles long, and from 90 to 19 broad.

Q. How is New-Hampshire bounded ?

A. On the north by Lower Canada ; east by Maine and the Atlantic ; south by Massachusetts ; west by Connecticut river, which separates it from Vermont. It has 18 miles of seacoast.

Q. Into how many counties is New-Hampshire divided ?

A. Into 6 : Rockingham, Strafford, Hillsborough, Cheshire Grafton and Coos.

Q. What are the shire towns ?

A. Portsmouth and Exeter in Rockingham ; Dover and Durham in Strafford ; Amherst in Hillsborough ; Keene and Charlestown in Cheshire ; Haverhill and Plymouth in Grafton ; Lancaster in Coos.

Q. What is the seaport town in New-Hampshire ?

A. Portsmouth, which stands on the southwest side of the Piscataqua river, containing in 1810, 6933 inhabitants. There are 4 churches. It is two miles from the sea.

Q. What other towns of consequence are there in New-Hampshire ?

A. Exeter, Dover and Concord.

Q. What rivers are there in New-Hampshire ?

A. The Piscataqua and the Merrimack.

Q. Are there any lakes in New-Hampshire ?

A. In the northeast corner of the state is Umbagog ; in the interior is Winipiseogee, which is 24 miles long, and from 3 to 12 broad.

Q. What mountains are there in New-Hampshire ?

A. The White hills, so called from the snow and ice which cover them almost all the year. They stand about seventy miles from the shore, and are about eleven thousand feet above the level of the sea. They are without exception, the highest mountains in the union. In the county of Cheshire is the Menadnoc also, a high mountain ; in Grafton the Mooschillock.

Q. What is the climate of New-Hampshire ?

A. It is healthy, cold in winter, and hot in the summer, as other parts of New-England.

Q. What are the soil and productions of New-Hampshire ?

A. The soil is very fruitful producing Indian corn, grain, and excellent mowing and pasturage. A considerable part of the state is still covered with large timber, pine, oak, fir, cedar, chesnut, walnut, &c. of which the people make a profitable use in their commerce, and home consumption.

O 2

Q. What is the state of manufactures in New-Hampshire ?

A. They are chiefly domestic ; ship building is the employment of a number of the inhabitants, for which the forests furnish the materials in abundance.

Q. What is the state of trade in New-Hampshire ?

A. In 1810, the amount of exports was 234,650 dollars.

Q. What number* of inhabitants are there in New-Hampshire ?

A. In the year 1800, there was 183,858, and in 1810, 214,460.

Q. What is the military strength ?

A. The militia is composed of 18,201 infantry, 1776 cavalry, and 710 artillery : aggregate 24,405.

Q. What is the government of New-Hampshire ?

A. It has three branches in its legislature. The governor, the senate, and the house of representatives. The governor and council are the executive.

Q. Are there any universities in New-Hampshire ?

A. At Hanover, in the western part of the state, is an university called Dartmouth College, which is well endowed, and flourishing.

OF VERMONT.

Q. What are the situation and extent of Vermont ?

A. It is situated between 42° 44' and 45o north latitude, and between 71° 33' and 73° 26' west longitude. It is 157 miles long, and 65 broad, containing 10,237 square miles.

Q. How is Vermont bounded ?

A. It is bounded on the north by Lower Canada ; on the east by Connecticut river; on the south by Massachusetts, and on the west by the state of New-York and Lake Champlain.

Q. What are the civil divisions of Vermont ?

A. It is divided into the 12 following counties, viz. Bennington, Windham, Rutland, Windsor, Orange, Addison, Chittenden, Caledonia, Franklin, Grand Isle, Orleans, Essex. These counties are subdivided into 246 townships.

Q. What rivers are there in Vermont ?

A. On the east side of the mountain are White and Black rivers, and on the west side are Onion river, Otter creek, and Lamoilla.

Q. What mountains are there in Vermont ?

A. About the middle of the state is a chain of high mountains, running from north to south through the whole length of the state, and giving name to the state : Vermont being in English, Green Mountain.

* The number of inhabitants in all the states mentioned in this compend is according to the return made to the Secretary's office in 1800 and 1810.

Q. What is the face of this state ?

A. It is hilly and often mountainous.

Q. What are the soil and productions of Vermont ?

A. The soil is generally very good, and where cultivated, produces grass, wheat, rye, oats, barley, &c.

Q. What is the climate of Vermont ?

A. It is very healthy.

Q. What number of inhabitants are there in Vermont ?

A. Eighty-five thousand. In 1800 there were 154,465. In 1810 it had 217,896.

Q. What is the number of militia ?

A. In 1809 it was 15,543 infantry, 1035 cavalry, and 303 artillery : aggregate 20,273.

Q. What is the character of the people ?

A. They are generally emigrants from Connecticut and Massachusetts, and in their manners, customs and religion, resemble those of the aforementioned states.

Q. What is the government of Vermont ?

A. It is like that of Connecticut.

Q. What are the principal towns in Vermont ?

A. Montpelier is the seat of government. Bennington, Windsor, Rutland and Middlebury are the largest towns.

———oxo———

OF MASSACHUSETTS.

Q. What are the situation and extent of Massachusetts ?

A. It is 150 miles long and 90 broad. It is between 41° 23′ and 43° 52′ north latitude, and between 69° 50′ and 73° 10′ of west longitude.

Q. How is it bounded ?

A. On the north by Vermont, New-Hampshire, and the Atlantic : on the east by the Atlantic : on the south by the Atlantic, Rhode-Island and Connecticut ; and on the west by Rhode-Island and New-York.

Q. What are the rivers of Massachusetts ?

A. Connecticut, Merrimack, Charles, Taunton, Concord, Mistic, Westfield, Chickapee, and Deerfield rivers ; beside innumerable mill streams.

Q. What capes are there in this state ?

A. Cape Ann on the north, and Cape Cod on the south side of Massachusetts bay.

A. What islands are there on the coast of Massachusetts ?

A. Nantucket, Martha's Vineyard, Elizabeth's Islands, and Plumb Islands.

Q. What is the religion of Massachusetts ?

A. The congregationalists are much the most numerous.

Q. Into how many counties is Massachusetts divided.

A. Massachusetts is divided into 14 counties.

Q What are their names?

A. Their names are Suffolk, Essex, Middlesex, Hampshire, Franklin, Hampden, Plymouth, Bristol, Barnstable, Duke's, Nantucket, Worcester, Berkshire and Norfolk.

Q. What number of inhabitants are there in Massachusetts?

A. In 1790 there were 374,785; in 1800, 422,845; in 1810, 472,040. Of these last 6737 were blacks.

Q. Are there any slaves?   A. None.

Q. What is the military strength?

A. In 1812 it consisted of 55,158 infantry, 2169 cavalry, and 2564 artillery, in all, including officers, 70,550.

Q. Are there any universities in Massachusetts?

A. There are two, besides several academies. Harvard College is the best endowed of any in New-England, and is very flourishing. Williams' College is an infant institution.

Q. What is the capital of Massachusetts?

A. Boston, which is also the principal town in N. England.

Q. Give a description of Boston?

A. It stands on a peninsula, and is almost enclosed by water. In 1810 it contained 33,250 inhabitants. There are 20 houses for public worship. The public buildings in Boston are the state-house, court-house, Faneuil-hall, a theatre, an alms-house and an gaol. Boston harbor is safe, and large enough to contain 500 ships. In Boston there are seven free schools, besides many others; the education of children being well regulated.

Q. What other towns of importance are there in Massachusetts?

A. Salem is the next after Boston, is 15 miles east of it, and is a place of considerable trade. In 1810 it contained 12,613 inhabitants. It has seven houses for public worship. Forty-five miles east of Boston is Newburyport, which stands on Merrimac river, about two miles from the sea. It contains about 780 dwelling houses, and 7634 inhabitants. Marblehead, Gloucester, Worcester, Charlestown, Springfield and Northampton are flourishing.

Q. What is the constitution of Massachusetts?

A. It is a republic, the legislature has three branches, viz. the governor, senate, and the house of representatives. The executive is a governor and council.

Q. What is the state of commerce in Massachusetts?

A. The exports in 1810 amounted to 13,013,048 dollars.

Q. What is the state of manufactures in Massachusetts?

A. In 1810, the amount of manufactures was 18,595,323 dollars. The manufactures of pot and pearl-ashes; linseed oil, bar and cast iron, cannon, cordage, spermaceti oil and candles, duck, nails, glass, wool cards, and many other articles are considerably advanced, and improving constantly.

Q. What are the mineral productions of Massachusetts?

A. Iron, copper and lead.

OF RHODE-ISLAND.

Q. What are the situation and extent of Rhode-Island?

A. It is situated between 41° 17' and 42° degrees of N. latitude, and between 71° 6' and 71° 52' W. longitude. It is 49 miles long and 29 broad; containing 1580 square miles.

Q. How is Rhode-Island bounded?

A. It is bounded by Massachusetts on the north and east; by the Atlantic Ocean on the south; and by Connecticut on the west.

Q. What are the civil divisions of Rhode-Island?

A. It is divided into the five following counties: Newport, Washington, Kent, Providence, and Bristol, which are subdivided into thirty-one townships.

Q. Are there any bays in Rhode-Island?

A. Narraganset bay is the only one, which contains several fruitful islands, the largest of which is Rhode-Island, which gives name to the state. Block-Island is forty three miles southwest of Newport.

Q. What are the rivers of Rhode-Island?

A. Providence, Patucket and Patuxent rivers are the only considerable ones. Providence river is navigable to the town of Providence, thirty miles from the sea.

Q. What is the climate of Rhode-Island?

A. It is very healthy. The winters are milder and the summers not so hot as in many parts of New-England.

Q. What is the soil of Rhode-Island?

A. It is very fruitful.

Q. What are its productions?

A. It is one of the finest grazing states in New-England; and it produces corn, rye, oats, barley, flax, and many other vegetables in plenty.

Q. What is the state of commerce in Rhode-Island?

A. The amount of exports in 1810 was 1,331,576 dollars.

Q. What are the capital towns of Rhode-Island?

A. Newport and Providence. Newport in 1810 contained 7987 inhabitants. The houses are chiefly built of wood. It has one of the finest harbors in the world.

Q. Give a description of Providence?

A. It is situated about thirty miles northwest of Newport, on both sides of Providence river; it contains 10,071 inhabitants. It is a very flourishing town, and carries on an extensive foreign commerce.

Q. What is the religion of Rhode-Island?

A. The Baptists are the most numerous class of Christians.

Q. What is the state of literature in Rhode-Island?

A. Though there are men of science in all parts of the state, yet there is not that general diffusion of knowledge which is found in other parts of New-England.

Q. Are there any colleges in Rhode-Island?

A. There is one at Providence, which is well endowed and in a flourishing state. There is also a flourishing academy at Newport.

Q. Are there any curiosities in Rhode-Island?

A. Patucket falls may be esteemed a curiosity, the water falls about 50 feet, not perpendicularly, but in a manner uncommonly pleasing, and is conveyed to various mills.

Q. What number of inhabitants are there in R. Island?

A. In 1790 it contained 58,825. In 1800 there was 69,122. In 1810 it had 76,931.

Q. What is the number of militia?

A. In 1811 it was 3204 infantry; 80 cavalry; and 30 artillery aggregate 4211.

Q. What is the government of Rhode-Island?

A. The representatives, are chosen twice in a year; and the legislature sits also twice in a year. They did not change their constitution during the late revolution.

OF CONNECTICUT.

Q. What are the situation and extent of Connecticut?

A. It is situated between 41 and 42 deg. and 2 minutes north latitude, and between 71 deg. 29 min. and 73 deg. 24 minutes of west longitude. It is 90 miles long and 72 broad, containing 7380 square miles.

Q. How is Connecticut bounded?

A. On the north by Massachusetts; on the east by Rhode-Island; on the south by Long-Island Sound; and on the west by New-York.

Q. What rivers are there in Connecticut?

A. Connecticut river, the Housatonic and the Thames; with many others which are smaller. The Housatonic rises in Berkshire, Massachusetts, and empties into Long-Island Sound between Stratford and Milford. It is navigable to Derby, about 12 miles from the mouth. The Thames runs by Norwich, and empties into Long-Island Sound at New-London. It is navigable to the city of Norwich, about 14 miles.

Q. What are the most important harbors of Connecticut?

A. New-London and New-Haven. Beside these there are convenient harbours for small vessels at the distance of a few miles from each other through the whole length of the coast.

Q. What is the climate of Connecticut?

A. It is subject to the extremes of heat and cold, yet is very healthy.

Q. What do you observe of the soil of Connecticut?

A. It is a very fruitful soil, better adapted to grass than to ploughing, though in many parts of the state it produces great crops of wheat, rye, flax, oats, barley, hemp, Indian corn, &c. The gardens are excellent.

Q. What is the face of the state?

A. It is in general uneven ground. The whole country is agreeably diversified with hills and valleys, plains, woods and waters.

Q. What is the state of trade in Connecticut?

A. It is flourishing, being carried on in their own vessels, and is chiefly of the produce and manufactures of the state. The people of Connecticut trade principally with the West Indies. The exports in 1810 were $768,643.

Q. What is the state of manufactures in Connecticut?

A. The manufactures are very flourishing.

Q. What are the civil divisions of Connecticut?

A. It is divided into 8 counties, viz. Hartford, New-Haven, New-London, Windham, Fairfield, Litchfield, Middlesex and Tolland, all of which except Middlesex, have shire towns of the same name with the county. The shire town of Middlesex is Middletown.

Q. What is the population of this state?

A. It is more populous than any other state in the union, and contained in 1790, 237,496 inhabitants, being upwards of 50 to a square mile. In 1800 it contained 251,002. In 1810 it had 261,942.

Q. What is the number of militia?

A. In 1812 it was 16,097 infantry, 6061 cavalry, and 565 artillery: aggregate 21,666.

Q. What are the customs and manners of the inhabitants?

A. They are much like those of the other states of New-England.

Q. What is the religion of Connecticut?

A. The congregationalists are about 200,000, the Episcopalians and Baptists each about 20,000, and the Methodists and Sandemanians 2000.

Q. What are the chief towns in Connecticut?

A. Hartford, New-Haven, (which are the seats of government) New-London, Norwich and Middletown, all of which are incorporated cities.

Q. Give a description of Hartford?

A. It stands on the west side of Connecticut river, fifty miles from its mouth, at the head of ship navigation. It contains a state-house, 4 churches and 6003 inhabitants.

Q. Give a description of New-Haven?

A. It is on a large bay which extends about 4 miles from the shore. It contains 14 houses for public worship, 2 colleges and a state house. The houses are generally built of wood. The streets cross each other at right angles. In 1810 it contained 6967 inhabitants.

Q. Describe New-London?

A. It stands on the west side of the river Thames, near the mouth, and contains 4 churches and 3238 inhabitants. It has the best harbor in Connecticut, and is well fortified by forts Trumbull and Griswold.

Q. Describe the city of Norwich?

A. It stands on the Thames, fourteen miles north of New-London. It contains 2976 inhabitants.

Q. Describe the city of Middletown?

A. It stands about fifteen miles south of Hartford, on the west bank of Connecticut river; contains 5382 inhabitants, and carries on a considerable trade to the West Indies.

Q. What literary institutions are there in Connecticut?

A. In the city of New-Haven is an university, called Yale College; it has produced many characters who have made a conspicuous figure in the literary world.

Q. Are there any medicinal waters in Connecticut?

A. At Stafford are springs which are found beneficial in various diseases.

Q. What is the government of Connecticut?

A. The governor, lieutenant-governor, and members of the council, are chosen annually; and the representatives are chosen in spring and autumn. This state did not change its constitution in consequence of the American revolution.

OF NEW-YORK.

Q. What are the situation and extent of New-York?

A. It is situated between 40° 40' and 45 degrees of north latitude, and between 73 and 79, 55' of west longitude. It is 340 miles long and 300 broad, containing 45,000 square miles

Q. How is it bounded?

A. It is bounded on the N. W. by Upper Canada; N. by Lower-Canada; east by Vermont, Massachusetts and Connecticut; south by Long Island Sound, New-Jersey and Pennsylvania; and west by Pennsylvania.

Q. What are the rivers in New-York?

A. The Hudson, St. Lawrence, Onondago, Mohawk, Delaware, Susquehannah, Tioga, Seneca, Tennessee and the northeast branch of the Allegany river are the principal, and are all considerable rivers. The river Hudson is one of the finest in the United States. Its course is about 250 miles in a southern direction.

Q. What bay is there in New-York?

A. The bay of New-York, which is formed by the confluence of the east and north rivers.

Q. Are there any lakes in this state?

A. Champlain, Oneida, Seneca, Cayuga, Otsego, and Caniaderago lakes.

Q. What is the face of the country?

A. It is generally an uneven country, and the hills run chiefly in a northeastern direction, between which are many fruitful vallies.

Q. What are the productions of the soil?

A. They are much the same as in New-England. From the rock maple large quantities of sugar are made annually.

Q. How many counties are there in New-York?

A. In New-York there are forty-three counties, and 452 towns.

Q. What number of inhabitants is there in New-York?

A. In 1790 there was 340,120. In 1800, 586,050. In 1810, 959,049; and in 1814, 1,050,000.

Q. What is the number of militia?

A. In 1812 it was 75,876 infantry, 3191 cavalry and 3251 artillery: aggregate 98,606.

Q. What is the character of the inhabitants?

A. The inhabitants are of various origin, but principally composed of English and Dutch. Though the Dutch manners and customs still exist in some parts of the state, yet the manners of the New-Englanders are prevailing throughout the state. The English and Dutch languages are both spoken, but the English is increasing while the Dutch is decreasing.

Q. What is the capital city of this state?

A. The city of New-York.

Q. Give a description of it?

A. It stands on a point of land which is formed by the junction of the north and east rivers, in the finest situation for commerce in the United States. There are 51 houses for public worship in New-York. The city-hall is an elegant building, and there are several other public buildings. The city in 1810 contained 96,373 inhabitants. Its streets are not regular, but they are generally well paved, and it is a place of extensive commerce.

P.

Q. What other cities are there in the state?

A. Albany and Hudson, [also Schenectady and Troy.] Albany is inhabited extensively by descendants from the Dutch, contains 9350 inhabitants, is a place of considerable commerce, and stands on the west side of the river Hudson, about 160 miles above New-York. Hudson stands on the east side of the same river, about 130 miles from New-York.

Q. What is the state of agriculture and manufactures in this state?

A. In agriculture, the people of this state are far behind their neighbours in improvement. In 1810 the amount of manufactures was 12,109,536 dollars.

Q. What is the state of commerce in New-York?

A. It is very flourishing and extended over the world; and the inhabitanss are distinguished by their industrious attention to business. The amount of exports in 1810 was 17,242,230 dollars.

Q. What mountains are there in this state?

A. At the place called Catskill, begin the Allegany mountains, which are there called the Catskill mountains. They run in various branches through this state in a southwest direction.

Q. Are there any mineral springs in this state?

A. There are three which are celebrated, viz. those of Saratoga, Ballstown and New-Lebanon.

Q. What minerals are there in this state?

A. Iron, lead, copper, crystals, isinglass, and asbestus, are found in various parts of the state in plenty.

Q. What is the state of literature in this state?

A. Literature in this state is less assiduously cultivated than in some of the New-England states.

Q. What colleges and academies are there in New-York?

A. In the city of New-York is Columbia college, which is well endowed. Union college in Schenectady is flourishing, [also Hamilton college, at Paris, in Oneida county.] Academies are found at Flatbush and East-Hampton, on Long-Island; in the city of New-York, at Albany, at Goshen, and at Kingston.

Q. What is the religion of New-York?

A. All religions are alike protected and privileged as in Connecticut, but the Presbyterians are the most numerous, though the Dutch Reformed, the Lutherans, the Baptists, the Episcopalians, the Methodists and Quakers are numerous.

Q. What is the government of this state?

A. The legislature of this state is composed of two houses, a senate and assembly. The first is never to exceed thirty-two in number, and the latter one hundred and fifty. The executive power is lodged in a governor. He is chosen once in three years.

OF NEW-JERSEY.

Q. What are the situation and extent of New-Jersey ?

A. It is situated between 39 and 41° and 45' of north latitude, and between 74 and 75° 29' of west longitude. It is 160 miles long and 52 broad ; containing 8320 square miles.

Q. How is New-Jersey bounded ?.

A. It is bounded north by New-York ; east by Hudson's river and the Atlantic ocean ; south by the ocean, and west by the bay and river of Delaware.

Q. What rivers are there in New-Jersey ?

A. They are small but numerous. Hackinsack, Raritan, and Pasaic rivers are the principal.

Q. What are the civil divisions of New-Jersey ?

A. It is divided into the 13 following counties, viz. Cape May, Cumberland, Salem, Gloucester, Burlington, Hunterdon, Sussex, Bergen, Essex, Middlesex, Monmouth, Somerset and Morris.

Q. What is the number of inhabitants in New-Jersey.

A. In 1790, there was 184,189. In 1800, 211,149. In 1810, 245,562.

Q. What is the number of militia ?

A. In 1811 it was 28,095 infantry, 1350 cavalry, and 668 artillery and 40 riflemen ; aggregate 33,891.

Q. What is the face of the country ?

A. In the north it is mountainous, in the middle it is variegated with vallies and rising grounds, and on the seacoast it is flat, level and sandy.

Q. What is the soil of New-Jersey ?

A. It is various ; a considerable proportion of it is barren. In passing from the southeast and south to the northwest and north, a traveller progresses through every degree of soil, from barren sand to the highest degree of fertility.

Q. What are the productions ?

A. The productions of this state, both animal and vegetable, are much like those of New-York. The cider made in some parts of the state, particularly in Newark, is remarkably fine.

Q. What is the state of commerce in New-Jersey ?

A. It is principally carried on through New-York and Philadelphia. In 1810 the exports amounted to $430,267.

Q. What is the state of manufactures and agriculture in New-Jersey ?

A. The manufactures are improving, particularly those of iron ware, nails and leather. The agriculture is also in some parts improving.

Q. What mines does this state produce ?

A. It furnishes great quantities of iron, and there are several copper mines in different parts of the state.

Q. What is the character of the inhabitants of N. Jersey?

A. They are frugal and industrious, though many of them discover very little taste for learning.

Q. What is the religion of this state?

A. The Presbyterians and the Friends are both numerous, and there are some of almost every other class of Christians in New-Jersey.

Q. What seminaries of learning are there in New-Jersey?

A. There are two colleges, one at Princeton and another at Brunswick. There are several academies and grammar schools.

Q. What is the capital of New-Jersey?

A. Trenton. It is handsomely built, and contained in 1810, 3002 inhabitants; but Newark is much larger, containing in the same year, 8008 inhabitants. New-Brunswick and Morristown, are both larger than Trenton, and Elizabethtown is about the same population.

Q. What is the government of New-Jersey?

A. It is vested in a governor, legislative council, and house of representatives. The governor is chosen annually by the council and assembly; the council is chosen annually by the people, and consists of one member from each county; the house of assembly is chosen in like manner, and consists of three members from each county.

OF PENNSYLVANIA.

Q. What are the situation and extent of Pennsylvania?

A. It is situated between 39 deg. 43 minutes and 42 deg. of north latitude, and between 74 and 84 deg. of west longitude. It is 307 miles long, and 160 broad, containing 36,373 square miles and 86 acres; or 23,278,806 acres.

Q. How is Pennsylvania bounded?

A. It is bounded on the north by New-York; east by the Delaware river; south by Delaware, Maryland and Virginia, and west by Virginia and Ohio.

Q. What are the mineral productions of the state?

A. In the eastern part of the state, iron mines, and in the western, coal mines. Lead is also found.

Q. How many counties are there in Pennsylvania?

A. In 1810 there was 43 counties and 644 towns in Pennsylvania.

Q. What are the principal rivers of this state?

A. The Delaware, the Schyulkill, the Susquehannah, the Yohtogany, the Monongahela, and Allegany.

Q. What mountains are there in Pennsylvania?

A. About one third part of the state is mountainous. The names of the principal ridges are Kittatinny, Allegany, Laurel and Chesnut ridges.

Q. What is the face of the country?

A. That part of the state which is occupied by the mountains already mentioned, which run obliquely through the state, covering a breadth of from twenty to fifty miles in width, is uneven, the rest is a level country.

Q. What is the soil of the state?

A. The soil is various but a large proportion of it is very good, and many of the mountains will admit of cultivation almost to the top.

Q. What are the productions of the soil?

A. These as well as the animal productions are generally the same with those of New-York and New-Jersey—Wheat is the staple commodity of the state, of which large quantities are raised.

Q. What is the climate of this state?

A. It is much the same as in Connecticut, only that the seasons are more uniform. West of the Allegany, the seasons are more regular than in the east.

Q. What is the number of inhabitants in Pennsylvania?

A. In 1790 there was 484,372. In 1800 they had increased to 602,545. In 1810 to 810,091.

Q. What is the number of militia?

A. In 1812 it was 94,723 infantry, 1759 cavalry, 846 artillery, and 2086 riflemen: in all 99,414.

Q. What is the character of the Pennsylvanians?

A. The Germans, Quakers, English, Episcopalians, and Scotch and Irish Presbyterians, are the most numerous classes. They are of very different characters, but generally agree in being temperate, plain, industrious and frugal. Many of the yeomanry, in some parts of this state, are impatient of good government, order and regularity.

Q. What is the religion of Pennsylvania?

A. Quakers are the most numerous. Then Presbyterians and Lutherans.

Q. Are there any colleges in Pennsylvania?

A. There are three, viz. The college at Philadelphia, Dickinson college at Carlisle, and Franklin college at Lancaster.

Q. What academies are there in Pennsylvania?

A. In Philadelphia are four: at Yorktown one: at Germantown one: at Pittsburgh one, and one at Washington. At Bethlehem is the celebrated Moravian school for young ladies.

Q. What is the capital city of Pennsylvania?

A. Philadelphia.

Q. Give a description of Philadelphia?

A It stands on the west bank of the Delaware, on a level

situation, about 110 miles from the sea. It is a regular city, all the streets crossing each other at right angles. It contains 35 churches. Philadelphia extends three miles along the banks of the Delaware, and two miles in width. In 1810 it contained 92,866 inhabitants.

Q. Are there any other important towns in Pennsylvania?

A. Lancaster, on Connestogo creek, 66 miles from Philadelphia, contains a handsome court house, a number of churches, and 5405 inhabitants. Carlisle is 120 miles west of Philadelphia. It contains 2491 inhabitants. Pittsburgh on the Allegany river, contains 4768 inhabitants.

Q. What is the state of commerce in Pennsylvania?

A. It is very flourishing and extensive. It is formed chiefly of the produce and manufactures of the state. The exports in 1810 amounted to $10,993,398.

Q. What is the state of agriculture in Pennsylvania?

A. It is in a flourishing state. Above two thirds of the inhabitants are husbandmen.

Q. What is the government of Pennsylvania?

A. It is republican. The executive power is vested in a governor, who is chosen for three years, but cannot hold his office more than nine years in twelve. The legislative power is committed to the senate and the house of representatives. The senators are chosen for four years, the representatives for one.

Q. Are there any crimes punishable with death?

A. Murder, arson, and a few others are, but hard labor for a term, or for life, is the punishment for most of the crimes which in other states are punished with death.

Q. Where is the seat of government?

A. At Harrisburgh.

OF OHIO.

Q. What are the situation and extent of Ohio?

A. It is situated between 38° 10′ and 42° north latitude, and between 80° 30′ and 85° 45′ west longitude. It is about 200 miles long, and 200 wide.

Q. How is it bounded?

A. By Pennsylvania on the east; by the Ohio river on the south; by the Indiana territory on the west; and by Michigan territory, and Lake Erie on the north.

Q. What are the principal rivers in Ohio?

A. The Ohio in the south is much the largest and most important. The Muskingum, Hockhocking, Sciota and Little Miami. all run southerly and empty into the Ohio: and all except the last, afford batteau navigation from the country down to the Ohio. The Cayahaga, Sandusky and Miami, all run northerly, and empty into Lake Erie, and thus furnish a water carriage by the lake to Upper Canada.

Q. What are the soil and climate of Ohio?

A. The soil is rich and productive. The climate, though subject to intermitting and remitting fevers, like other new uncleared countries, is pleasant and healthy, and less severe than in the same parallels on the Atlantic.

Q. What are the natural productions of the soil in Ohio?

A. They are sugar-maple, sycamore, black and white mulberry, black and white walnut, butternut, chesnut ; white black, spanish and chesnut oaks ; hickory, cherry tree, gum tree, iron wood, ash, aspin, sassafras, crab-apple, custard-apple, and several kinds of plum trees.

Q. What are the animal productions of Ohio?

A. Deer, wild cattle, bears, wolves, catamounts, and foxes, turkeys, geese, ducks, swans, teal, pheasants and partridges. Many of the rivers furnish a plentiful supply of fish.

Q. What is the face of the state?

A. It is not mountainous, but variegated with hills, vallies and intervale. There is very little waste land in this state.

Q. How many counties are there in Ohio?

A. In Ohio there are 26 counties, and 320 towns.

Q. What is the number of militia?

A. In 1811, it was 27,104 infantry, 793 cavalry, 70 artillery, and 2336 riflemen : aggregate 35,277.

Q. What is the number of inhabitants in Ohio?

A. By the census which was taken in 1800, it was found to contain 45,365. It 1810, it had 230,760, of whom 1899 were blacks.

OF THE MICHIGAN TERRITORY.

Q. What is the situation of the Michigan territory?

A. It lies N. of Ohio, between Lake Michigan on the W. and Lakes Huron and St. Clair and Detroit river on the E. ; including also the peninsula between Lakes Michigan and Superior. It is 500 miles long and 800 broad.

Q. What are the divisions?

A. It is divided into four districts : Erie, Detroit, Huron and Michilimackinac.

Q. What is the climate?

A. It is cold and healthy.

Q. What is the face of the country?

A. It is a mere flat. The soil is fertile and produces apples, maize, wheat, oats, barley, buckwheat and potatoes.

Q. What are the rivers?

A. St. Mary's, St. Clair, Detroit, Raisin, Huron and St. Joseph.

Q. What lakes border this territory?

A. Michigan, Superior, Huron and St. Clair.
Q. What is the natural growth?
A. The trees and wild fruits of New-England.
Q. What island belongs to this territory?
A. The island of Michilimackinac, in the straits of the same name, on which is a fort.
Q. What is the population?
A. In 1810, it was 4762, besides a considerable number of Indians.
Q. What are the religious denominations?
A. Catholics and Methodists.
Q. What is the government?
A. It is under the government of congress.
Q. What is the capital?
A. Detroit. It had in 1810, 80 houses, and 770 inhabitants.

OF THE ILLINOIS TERRITORY.

Q. What is the situation of the Illinois Territory?
A. It is the N. W. region of the United States, lying between 37° and 49° 37' N.; and between 85° 45' and 96° 6' W.
Q. What are the boundaries?
A. On the N. Lake Superior and the N. W. boundary of the United States; on the E. Lake Michigan; on the S. E. the river Illinois; on the S. W. and W. the Missisippi; and on the N. W. the United States' boundary.
Q. What are the divisions?
A. It is divided into 2 counties; St. Clair and Randolph: and into 12 townships.
Q. What are the rivers?
A. The Missisippi, Winnipec, Pidgeon, Quiscosin, Illinois, Fox and St. Louis.
Q. What are the lakes?
A. Superior, Michigan, Rainy Lake, Lake of the Woods, White Bear and Pepin.
Q. What are the natural productions?
A. The forest trees and wild fruit trees are similar to those in New England.
Q. What are the metals?
A. Copper and lead in vast abundance.
Q. What is the population?
A. In 1810 it was 12,282, of whom 781 were blacks.

OF INDIANA TERRITORY.

Q. What is the situation of Indiana Territory?
A. It is between 37° and 42° 10' N.; and between 82° 40' and 85° 45' W. It is 350 miles long, and in its greatest breadth 300 broad. It is now a state.

Q. What are its boundaries?

A. On the N. Lake Michigan and Michigan Territory; on the E. Ohio; on the S. the river Ohio, dividing it from Kentucky; on the W. the Missisippi; and on the northwest the Illinois.

Q. How is it divided?

A. Into 4 counties; Dearborn, Clark, Harrison and Knox.

Q. What is the soil?

A. The soil is excellent, yielding corn, wheat, rye, oats, cotton, hemp, flax and tobacco.

Q. What are the rivers?

A. The Missisippi is a frontier river for 204 miles; the Illinois for its whole length; and the Ohio for 525 miles. In the interior the Wabash, Kaskaskias, Blue River and Great Miami are among the largest.

Q. What is the population?

A. In 1810 it was 24,520, besides numerous Indians.

OF DELAWARE.

Q. What are the situation and extent of the state of Delaware?

A. It is 96 miles long and 23 broad. It is situated between 38° 29′ and 39° 54′ of north latitude, and between 74° and 56′ and 75° 40′ of west longitude. It contains 2120 square miles.

Q. How is Delaware bounded?

A. North by Pennsylvania, east by Delaware river and bay; south and west by Maryland.

Q. What is the climate of Delaware?

A. In many places unhealthy. The land being flat, the waters stagnate and produce intermittent fevers.

Q. What are the civil divisions of Delaware?

A. It is divided into three counties; Newcastle, Kent and Sussex; and into 25 towns.

Q. What are the shire towns of the counties?

A. Of Newcastle, Newcastle; of Kent, Dover; of Sussex, Lewistown.

Q. What rivers are there in Delaware?

A. Choptank, Nanticock and Pocomoke all fall into Chesapeake bay. The Delaware is the eastern boundary.

Q. What is the soil of Delaware?

A. The southern part of the state is flat, and some of it is barren. Some of it produces Indian corn in large quantities. The northern part is fertile, and yields wheat and other grain. A large part of the state is covered with forests of pine and cedar, which are very profitable to the inhabitants. Wheat is the staple commodity of this state.

Q. What is the capital town?

A. Dover, the seat of government, stands on Jone's creek, and contains 100 houses

Q. What is the situation of New-Castle ?

A. It stands on the west bank of the Delaware, 40 miles below Philadelphia, contains about 60 houses, and was first settled by the Swedes.

Q. What is the situation of Wilmington ?

A. It stands on Christiana creek, 28 miles southward of Philadelphia. It is the largest town in the state, containing about 500 houses. In 1810 it contained 4200 inhabitants. It is built on a rising ground, and contains an academy.

Q. What is the state of trade in Delaware ?

A. The trade is principally confined to Philadelphia. The trade of Wilmington extends to Europe ; but its situation will never admit of extensive commerce.

Q. What is the religion of Delaware ?

A. Presbyterians are the most numerous.

Q. What is the number of inhabitants in Delaware ?

A. In 1790 there was 59,094. In 1800 they had increased to 64,272. In 1810 it had 72,674, of whom 17,313 were blacks.

Q. What is the number of militia ?

A. In 1810, 6475 infantry, 116 cavalry and 81 artillery, and 32 riflemen : aggregate 7451.

Q. What is the character of the inhabitants ?

A. Like the Pennsylvanians.

Q. What is the government of Delaware ?

A. A general assembly, consisting of a senate and house of representatives. The senators are chosen for three years, and the representatives annually. The governor holds his office for three years, and is elected by the people.

OF MARYLAND.

Q. What are the situation and extent of Maryland ?

A. It is situated between 38 and 39° 44' north latitude, and between 75° 10' and 79° 20' west longitude. It is 196 miles long and 120 broad and contains 14,000 square miles.

Q. How is Maryland bounded ?

A. It is bounded on the N. by Pennsylvania ; on the E. by the Ocean and Delaware state; S. by the Potomac and Virginia; and W. by Virginia.

Q. What are the civil divisions of Maryland ?

A. Maryland is divided into 19 counties. Eight are on the east, and 11 on the west side of the Chesapeake.

Q. What is the climate of Maryland ?

A. Near the sea it is unhealthy, in the interior healthy and pleasant.

Q. Are there any bays in Maryland ?

A. Chesapeake bay divides this state into what are called the Eastern and Western Shores.

Q. What are the rivers in Maryland ?

A. The Potomack and Susquehannah, the Pocomoke, Choptank, Chester, Elk, Patapsko, Severn, and Petuxent.

Q. What is the face of the country ?

A. East of the mountains the land is flat and sandy, but westward it is hilly.

Q. What is the soil of this state ?

A. Wheat and tobacco are the staple commodities of Maryland. Swine are left here to run wild in the woods, and after they have become fat, the inhabitants hunt them as other wild game.

Q. What number of inhabitants are there in Maryland ?

A. In 1790 there was 319,721. In 1800 they had increased to 349,692. In 1810 to 380,546, of whom 145,429 were blacks.

Q. What is the number of militia ?

A. In 1811, 28,123 infantry, 1135 cavalry, and 403 artillery ; aggregate 29,661.

Q. What is the character of the inhabitants ?

A. The country people are generally planters, holding large numbers of slaves. An almost necessary consequence of slave-keeping is to render the slave-holder haughty and imperious ; but the people of Maryland are hospitable to strangers.

Q. What is the capital town of Maryland ?

A. Annapolis is the seat of government, but Baltimore is much the largest town.

Q. What is the situation of Annapolis ?

A. It stands 30 miles south from Baltimore, on the Severn, and contains 260 houses.

Q. Give a description of Baltimore ?

A. It lies on the north side of Patapsko river, and is divided by a creek into the town and Fell's point. It has a good harbor, an extensive commerce, and has had the most rapid growth of any town in America. In 1810 it contained 46,555 inhabitants.

Q. What other towns of note are there in Maryland ?

A. Fredericktown is an inland town, containing about 300 houses, and 4 houses for public worship. Hagarstown is nearly as large.

Q. What are the mineral productions of Maryland ?

A. Iron is the only one ; and the working of that is the only manufacture in the state, except the making of flour.

Q. What is the state of commerce in Maryland ?

A. It is flourishing, and is principally carried on at Baltimore with Europe and the West-Indies. It is formed in a great measure of tobacco and wheat.

Q. What is the religion of Maryland?

A. All the different religious sects of Christians inhabit Maryland. The Roman Catholics form a numerous class.

Q. What seminaries of learning are there in Maryland?

A. There are 4 colleges and 1 academy, viz. at Charlestown, Washington college; at Annapolis, St. Johns' college; at Georgetown, a Roman Catholic college; at Abington, a Methodist college, called Cocksbury college; and in Summerset county is Washington academy. Few private schools are established in Maryland.

Q. What is the government of Maryland?

A. The legislature is composed of two branches, a senate and house of delegates. The senators are chosen once in five years, the delegates annually. The governor is chosen annually by the joint ballot of the two houses. He has an executive council also chosen by the legislature.

OF THE DISTRICT OF COLUMBIA.

Q. What is the situation of the District of Columbia?

A. It is a tract of 10 miles square, or 100 square miles, ceded by Maryland and Virginia to the Union, lying on both sides of the Potomac, 120 miles from its mouth, in 38° 53' N. and 77° 45' W.

Q. How is it divided?

A. Into 2 counties; Washington on the N. E. side of the Potomac; and Alexandria on the S. W. The district is under the immediate government of congress.

Q. What is the population?

A. In 1800, it was 8124; and in 1810, 24,023; of whom 16,088 were whites and 7935 blacks.

Q. What is the religion?

A. It is at a very low ebb. Presbyterians and Episcopalians are the most numerous sects.

Q. What are the towns?

A. Washington and Georgetown on the E. side of the Potomac; and Alexandria on the W.

Q. Describe the city of Washington?

A. It is built on a point of land between the Potomac and the East Branch, which forms a commodious harbour; and consists of 5 little clusters of houses, scattered over an extensive tract of waste land. Its population in 1810 was 5904 whites and 2304 blacks; in all 8205. The buildings are about half of wood, and the rest of brick and stone. The public buildings, before they were destroyed in August 1815, were remarkably elegant.

Q. Describe Georgetown?

A. It is on the E. side of the Potomac, 4 miles above Washington, has 4 churches, a catholic college, and 4948 inhabitants, and is a place of some trade.

Q. Describe Alexandria?

A. It is on the W. side of the Potomac, near the S. angle of the district, is well built, has 2 churches and a population of 5071; and is an important commercial town.

Q. What is the trade of the district?

A. In 1810 the exports amounted to $1,038,103; and the tonnage in 1807, to 13,431.

OF VIRGINIA.

Q. What are the situation and extent of Virginia?

A. It is 440 miles long, and 290 broad. It is between 36° 30' and 40° 40' north latitude, and between 75° 25' and 83° 40' west longitude. It contains 70,000 square miles.

Q. How is Virginia bounded?

A. It is bounded on the north by Pennsylvania; on the east by the Atlantic: south by North-Carolina; west by Kentucky; and N. W. by Ohio.

Q. How many counties are there in Virginia?

A. In Virginia there are 98 counties.

Q. What are the rivers of Virginia?

A. They are the Roanoke, James, York, Elizabeth, Chickahominy, Appamatox, Rivanna, Rappahanok, Potomac, Shenandoah, and the great and little Kanhaway, and Ohio.

Q. What are the mountains of Virginia?

A. The Allegany mountains run through Virginia; the ridges on the eastern side of them are Blue ridge, the North mountain and Jackson's mountain; on the western side is the Laurel ridge.

Q. What natural curiosities are there in Virginia?

A. In Rockbridge county is a natural bridge over Cedar-creek, in the form of an arch, from the middle of which to the bottom of the channel is at least 205 feet.

Q. What are the mineral and fossil productions of Virginia?

A. Lead, iron, black lead, copper, coal, and marble, are found in various parts of the state, and some of them in great quantities.

Q. Are there any mineral springs in Virginia?

A. There are several, but the most celebrated and efficacious are two in Augusta, called the "hot springs," and the "warm spring."

Q. What is the population of Virginia?

A. In 1790 there was 747,610, but a great part of these are slaves. In 1800, they had increased to 886,149. In 1810 it had 974,622, of whom 423,088 were blacks.

Q. What is the number of militia?

A. In 1811, it was 60,248 infantry, 4194 cavalry, 1720 artillery: aggregate 75,780.

Q. What is the character of the Virginians?

A. They are sociable and hospitable, attached strongly to pleasure and dissipation, and highly jealous of personal independence. The holders of slaves have the same character in all countries.

Q. What is the climate of Virginia?

A. It is not uniform, though agreeable. The summers are hot, but the winters are mild. It is much colder in summer and winter near the Allegany, than either on the seacoast, or on the Missisippi.

Q. What is the capital town of Virginia?

A. Richmond is the seat of government. Richmond and Norfolk are nearly of equal population. In 1810, Richmond contained 9735, and Norfolk 9193 inhabitants. There are properly no townships in Virginia; the state is divided into counties and plantations. Norfolk stands on James river, and on the same river stands Williamsburgh, Petersburgh and Richmond.

Q. Are there any colleges in Virginia?

A. The college of William and Mary, at Williamsburgh, is the only one. There are academies in Prince Edward county, at Alexandria, at Norfolk and at Hanover.

Q. What is the religion of Virginia?

A. Like Maryland it contains some of almost every sect; but the Presbyterians and Episcopalians are the most numerous. The Methodists are increasing.

Q. What is the government of Virginia?

A. The legislature consists of a house of delegates and a senate. The former consists of two members from each county, chosen annually; the latter of 24 members, for the choice of which, once in four years, the state is divided into 24 districts. The executive consists of a governor chosen annually, and a council of 8 members. The governor may not hold his office more than 3 years in seven.

OF KENTUCKY.

Q. What are the situation and extent of Kentucky?

A. It is situated between 36° 30' and 39° 10' of north latitude, and between 82° 50' and 89° 20' west longitude. It is

300 miles long, and 180 broad, containing 50,000 square miles.

Q. How is Kentucky bounded?

A. It is bounded on the north by Ohio; west by the Mississippi; south by North-Carolina, and east by Virginia.

Q. How many counties are there in Kentucky?

A. In Kentucky there are 54 counties.

Q. What are the rivers of Kentucky?

A. The most considerable are the Ohio, Sandy, Licking, Kentucky, Salt, Green and Cumberland rivers.

Q. What is the climate of Kentucky?

A. The climate is healthy, the summers being neither very hot, nor the winters very cold.

Q. What is the face of the state?

A. Great part of it is covered with large timber; and is uneven, though not mountainous. A bed of lime-stone, lying six or eight feet below the surface, extends all over Kentucky.

Q. What is the soil of Kentucky?

A. It is of various kinds, and generally very fruitful in all those productions which are found in Virginia.

Q. What is the chief town in Kentucky?

A. Frankfort, situate in Franklin county, on the north bank of Kentucky river. It has a state house built of stone, and contains many good houses.

Q. What other towns are there of consequence?

A. Lexington on Elk river, 24 miles east of Frankfort, in 1810 contained 4326 inhabitants. Louisville, on the Ohio, at the falls, is a fine stand for trade.

Q. What is the number of inhabitants in Kentucky?

A. By the census in 1790, they were estimated at 73,677. In 1800 there was 220,959. In 1810 it had 406,511, of whom 82,274 were blacks.

Q. What is the number of militia?

A. In 1811 it was 35,483 infantry, 539 cavalry, and 53 artillery: aggregate 44,422.

Q. What is the character of the inhabitants?

A. This state is settled principally by people from different parts of Europe and America, and they retain the manners, customs, habits and religions of the parts from which they originally came. The Baptists are the most numerous sect in Kentucky.

Q. What is the state of literature in Kentucky?

A. Schools are established in various parts of the state, and are much attended to. Provision is made for a college in Kentucky.

Q. What is the government of Kentucky?

A. Similar to that of Virginia.

Q. What are the situation and extent of North-Carolina?

A. It is situated between 33° 50' and 36° 30' north latitude, and between 73° 45' and 84° west longitude. It is 430 miles long, and 180 broad.

Q. How is it bounded?

A. It is bounded on the north by Virginia; east by the Atlantic; south by South-Carolina; and west by Tennesee.

Q. What are the rivers of North-Carolina?

A. Chowan, Roanoke, Pamlico, Neus, Trent, Cape-Fear, and Holston.

Q. What are the remarkable capes of North-Carolina?

A. Cape Hatteras, Cape Lookout, and Cape Fear.

Q. What are the civil divisions of North-Carolina?

A. It is divided into 62 counties.

Q. What is the capital town of North-Carolina?

A. Newbern, the largest town, contains about 400 houses, and stands between the Neus and Trent, on a low sandy foundation. It is principally built of wood. Edenton stands on the north side of Albemarle sound, indifferently built, containing about 150 houses of wood. Wilmington stands on Cape Fear river, about 34 miles from the sea. It contains about 180 houses. This state, like Virginia, is divided into plantations.

Q. What is the face of the country?

A. From the seashore about 60 miles the land is flat, and a large proportion of it is covered with pine and cedar swamps. From about sixty miles the rising ground extends a few miles, and then begins a champaign country.

Q. What is the soil of North-Carolina?

A. In the flat land towards the sea it is very sandy. The state, where it is cultivated, produces corn, wheat, rye, barley, oats, flax, cotton, rice, tobacco, sweet potatoes and ground pease. The timber is very large.

Q. What do you observe of the commerce of N. Carolina?

A. It consists of tobacco, lumber, furs, hides and skins; cotton, Indian corn, wheat, rye, &c. and is principally confined to the northern states and the West-Indies. It is flourishing. The exports in 1810, amounted to $403,949.

Q. What is the climate of North-Carolina?

A. Towards the sea it is unhealthy, but in the interior more temperate and healthy. The summers are very hot and the winters mild.

Q. What is the religion of this state?

A. It contains people of all denominations, but the Methodists are the most numerous class.

Q. What is the number of inhabitants in North-Carolina ?

A. In 1790 there was 393,751. In 1800 they had increased to 478,103. In 1810 to 555,500 ; of whom 179,090 were blacks.

Q. What is the number of militia ?

A. In 1812 it was 42,944 infantry, 1150 cavalry and 120 artillery : aggregate 50,992.

Q. What is the character of the North-Carolinians ?

A. The people in this state live scattered in their plantations : in character they are much like the Virginians.

Q. What is the government of North-Carolina ?

A. The senate consists of a member from each county, chosen annually by ballot : the house of commons consists of two from each county, with representatives from each of the towns of Edenton, Newbern, Wilmington, Salisbury, Halifax and Hillsborough. The two houses choose the governor for one year. He has a council of 7 persons chosen for one year.

OF TENNESSEE.

Q. What is the situation of Tennessee ?

A. It lies between 35° and 36° 30' north latitude, and is 400 miles in length and 104 in breadth.

Q. What are the boundaries of Tennessee ?

A. It is bounded on the north by Kentucky ; on the east by North-Carolina ; on the south by Georgia and the Missisippi Territory, and on the W. by the Missisippi.

Q. What are the civil divisions of Tennessee ?

A. Five districts and 38 counties.

Q. What rivers does it contain ?

A. The Missisippi, Tennessee, Cumberland, Holston, Clinch, Wolf and Hatchee.

Q. What mountains does it contain ?

A. The Unaka mountains separate it from North-Carolina. Clinch mountain divides the waters of Holston and Clinch rivers, and Cumberland mountain separates the western part of the territory from the eastern part.

Q. What are the principal towns ?

A. Knoxville, the seat of government, on the north side of Holston river. Nashville, on the south bank of Cumberland river. Jonesborough in the district of Washington.

Q. What is the number of inhabitants ?

A. In 1791 the number was 35,691. In 1800 it contained 105,602. In 1810 it had 261,727.

Q. What is the number of militia ?

A. In 1812 it was 25,910 infantry, and 357 cavalry : aggregate 29,183.

Q 2

Q. What is its government ?

A. It has a form of government similar to those of the other states.

Q. What are the vegetable productions of this territory ?

A. Majestic red cedars, oak, hickory, black and white walnut, sycamore, locusts, elm, hornbeam, mulberry, cherry and sugar maple. Wheat is cultivated to great advantage.

Q. What animals are found here ?

A. The buffalo, deer, elk, bear, beaver, otter, panther, wild-cat, muskrat, raccoon, fox, wolf and squirrel, patridges, quails, pigeons, wild turkeys, ducks, geese and swans. The rivers are stored with trout, perch, cat fish, buffalo fish, red horse, eels, &c.

Q. What mineral productions have been discovered ?

A. Iron and lead mines. Copperas, allum and nitre have been found in caves. Salt springs are very frequent, and there is limestone in great plenty.

Q. What is the climate ?

A. Temperate and healthy ; on the western side of Cumberland mountain the summer is hotter than on the eastern side. Northeast storms never reach this country.

Q. What is the state of manufactures ?

A. Iron and salt are manufactured, and there is a cotton manufactory established under the direction of workmen from Europe.

OF SOUTH-CAROLINA.

Q. What are the situation and extent of South-Carolina ?

A. It is situated between 32 and 35° 8' north latitude, and between 78° 24' and 83° 30' west longitude. It is 200 miles long and 125 broad and contains 24,080 square miles.

Q. How is South-Carolina bounded ?

A. It is bounded on the north by North-Carolina ; east by the Atlantic ; south and west by Georgia.

Q. What is the climate of South-Carolina ?

A. It is similar to the climate of North-Carolina, except that it is a little hotter in summer.

Q. What are the rivers in South-Carolina ?

A. The largest are the Santee and Pedee and Savannah rivers, and the smaller ones are Conbahee, Wakkamaw, Ashley, Cooper and Black rivers.

Q. What are the mountains in South-Carolina ?

A. Tyron and Hogback mountains lie 220 miles northwest from Charleston, and are 3840 feet high ; and the mountains which lie west and northwest rise much higher.

Q. What are the civil divisions of South-Carolina ?

A. The state is divided into 28 districts.

Q. What is the chief town in South-Carolina ?

A. Charleston, which stands between Ashley and Cooper rivers, about 7 miles from the sea, in latitude 33 degrees 45 minutes north. Its situation is flat and low, and the water is brackish. Most of the streets are narrow, but the houses in general are well built, and some of them are elegant. In 1810 it contained 24,711 inhabitants. Its public buildings are an exchange, state-house, armory, poor house, 12 churches and a synagogue for Jews.

Q. What other towns are there in South-Carolina ?

A. There are none very large, as the people live chiefly on plantations. Beaufort and Georgetown are each the capitals of the districts whose names they bear. Beaufort stands on a small island called Port Royal, containing 60 or 80 houses; Georgetown has 150.

Q. What is the face of the country ?

A. From the coast about 80 miles the land is low and flat. Thence about 60 miles the land is very sandy, though uneven; then begin the highlands, or the ridge ; and beyond that a tract of land resembling the northern states. The first tract produces rice, the second very little but corn and sweet potatoes ; the third good pasturage, and the fourth every kind of vegetable which is found in the same climate, and all in the highest perfection.

Q. What is the state of manufactures and agriculture in South-Carolina.

A. In this state, as well as in North-Carolina and Georgia, these articles are in a state of infancy.

Q. What is the state of literature in South Carolina ?

A. It is at low ebb, though there is more attention paid to it within a few years than formerly. There are a few academies in this state, but none are very flourishing.

Q. What is the religion of this state ?

A. It is much like North-Carolina in this respect.

Q. What is the number of inhabitants in South-Carolina ?

A. In 1790 there was 240,000. In 1800 they had increased to 345,591. In 1810 to 415,115; of whom 200,919 blacks.

Q. What is the number of militia ?

A. In 1811, it was 25,194 infantry, 1587 cavalry, artillery, and 3154 riflemen : aggregate 32,72...

Q. What is the character of the inhabitant...

A. It is similar to that of their neighbou... olina, except that they are generally more

Q. What is the state of commerce in S...

A. This is flourishing.

Q. What is their constitution ?

A. The senate and house of represen

once in two years. The legislature choose the governor and lieutenant governor by ballot ; also a privy council, to consist of the lieutenant governor and eight other persons.

OF GEORGIA.

Q. What are the situation and extent of Georgia ?

A. It is between 30° 42' and 35° of north latitude, and between 80° 20' and 85° 54' of west longitude. It is 270 miles long, and 250 broad, containing 62,000 square miles.

Q. How is Georgia bounded?

A. On the north by South-Carolina and Tennessee ; east by the Atlantic Ocean ; south by Florida, and west by the Missisippi Territory.

Q. What are the civil divisions of Georgia ?

A. Georgia is divided into 38 counties.

Q. What are the rivers in Georgia ?

A. The Savannah, Ogechee and Altamaha, Turtle river, Great and Little Sitilla, Crooked river and St. Mary's, all empty into the Atlantic ; and the Apalachicola, which empties into the Gulf of Mexico.

Q. What is the capital town of Georgia ?

A. The present seat of government is Augusta, on the Savannah river, about 134 miles from the sea, and about 120 northwest from Savannah. It contained in 1810, 2476 inhabitants.

Q. What other towns of consequence are there in Georgia ?

A. Savannah, the largest town in the state, in 1810 contained 5215 inhabitants. It stands on the river of that name, about 17 miles from the sea. It contains an Episcopal church, a German Lutheran church, a Presbyterian church, a Jewish synagogue, a court house, and 240 dwelling houses. The number of white inhabitants is 8490.

Q. What is the climate of Georgia ?

A. Much like that of South-Carolina.

Q. What is the face of the state ?

A. Similar to that of South-Carolina.

Q. What is the soil of Georgia ?

A. The fruitful in rice, indigo and cotton, towards the sea, rivers, and the corn and pasturage further in the country.— ly of the state is yet under cultivation.

Q. What are any mineral springs in Georgia ?

A. Tyron and town of Washington is a remarkable spring, from Charleston a hollow tree, emits a nitrous substance, useful in many diseases.

Q. What are there in Georgia ?

A. The state is miles from the sea is a large bank of oysters.

Q. What is the in three distinct ridges, which run parallel with the seacoast, and the shells are uncommonly large.

Q. What is the state of commerce in Georgia ?

A. It is principally carried on from the port of Savannah. Its manufactures are small and imperfect, but they, as well as the agriculture of the state, are improving.

Q. What is the number of inhabitants in Georgia ?

A. In 1790 there was 82,548. In 1800 they had increased to 162,682. In 1810 to 215,433, of whom 108,820 were blacks.

Q. What is the number of militia ?

A. In 1810, it had 21,070 infantry, 625 cavalry, and 117 artillery : aggregate 25,729.

Q. What is the character of the inhabitants ?

A. No material difference is discoverable between the Georgians and Carolinians ; the slaves do the labor, and the soil is very productive. The inhabitants are chiefly emigrants from Europe and the middle states.

Q. What is the religion of Georgia ?

A. There are Christians of every denomination, but the Baptists and Methodists are the most numerous.

Q. What is the government of the state ?

A. The constitution of Georgia has been lately revised, and very much resembles that of the United States.

OF THE MISSISIPPI TERRITORY.

Q. What is the situation of the Missisippi Territory ?

A. It is in the S. W. corner of the United States Proper, between 31 and 35° N. and between 84° 45' and 91° 25' W. It is 330 miles long, and 278 broad containing 95,000 square miles.

Q. How is it divided ?

A. Into 11 counties.

Q. What is the climate ?

A. It is warm and unhealthy. The soil is remarkably fertile, and the face of the country chiefly a level.

Q. What are the rivers ?

A. The Missisippi on the W. frontier ; the Apilachicola on the E. ; also the Alibama, Tombigbee, Tennessee, Yazoo, Pearl and Pascagoula.

Q. What are the productions ?

A. Live oak, and all the other varieties of oak, cypress, hickory, black walnut, white ash, poplar, plum, cherry and the vine.

Q. What is the population ?

A. In 1810, it was 40,352, including 23,024 whites and 17,238 blacks, of whom 17,088 were slaves. This territory also contains four tribes of Indians : the Cherokees, the Creeks, the Chickasaws and the Choctaws. They are quite numerous.

Q. What is the government ?

A. The governor and judges are appointed by congress and hold their offices during pleasure.

Q. What towns are there ?

A. Natchez, in the S. W. is on the Missisippi, and has 1511 inhabitants. Washington has 524 inhabitants.

OT THE COUNTRY OF LOUISIANA.

Q. What is the situation of Louisiana ?

A. It lies W. of the United States Proper. The Gulf of Mexico bounds it on the S. Its other limits are not defined with precision.

Q. What is its eastern limit ?

A. The Missisippi as far S. as lat. 31. Below that latitude the United States claim that it reaches eastward to the river Perdido, E. of Mobile, in long. 87° 35' W. Spain on the contrary claims that it reaches no farther E. than the outlet of Lake Ponchartrain, 140 miles W. of the Perdido.

Q. What is its south western limit ?

A. The United States claim that it reaches W. on the Gulf to the river Bravo, in lon. 97° 30' and up that river to its source. Spain claims that it reaches no farther W. than the Mexicano in 93° 12' W. and 600 miles N. E. of the Bravo. The true boundary on the Gulf is believed to be the river Colorado in 97° 10' W. and 300 miles, N. N. E. of the Bravo.

Q. What is the western limit ?

A. One of these three rivers is unquestionably the true boundary to its source ; N. of which it extends westward to the Pacific Ocean.

Q. What is the south limit ?

A. The Gulf of Mexico, on the coast ; and in the S. W. Mexico will be the S. boundary.

Q. What is the north limit ?

A. The British will probably claim the continent W. of their present possessions. By the same rule those W. of the United States will belong to us. On this supposition the N. boundary of Louisiana will be a line drawn from the N. W. corner of the Lake of the Woods in lat. 49° 37' to the head of the river Missouri, in lat. 50° and thence westward to the ocean. The extent within these limits must be not far from three million square miles.

OF LOUISIANA STATE.

Q. What is the situation of the state of Louisiana ?

A. It is the southern division of the country of Louisiana, including all the territory S. of lat. 33.

Q. What is the extent?

A. On the coast the distance between the Perdido and Bravo is 1020 miles; but between the Perdido and Colorado only 720. The width from the Gulf to lat. 33? is about 250 miles.

Q. What districts does the state of Louisiana comprehend?

A. The natural divisions of the territory are three : The country S. of the Missisippi territory: The Island of Orleans: and the country W. of the Missisippi and S. of lat. 33.

Q. What is the climate?

A. In winter it is pleasant. In summer it is hot, sultry, and unhealthy.

Q. What is the face of the country?

A. The country S. of the Missisippi territory is a mere flat, and chiefly sandy. The Island of Orleans is so low that an embankment of earth 6 feet high, called the levee, has been raised on the west frontier of the island from its N. end down to Fort Placquemine, a distance of 164 miles, to prevent the Missisippi from overflowing the island in the spring. S. of Fort Placquemine, for want of such an embankment, it is annually overflowed. The country W. of the Missisippi, for a width of 40 miles, is overflowed every spring. The whole coast is a mere flat and sandy. The country N. and W. of the flat marshy region, is an extensive prairie, covered with rank high grass.

Q. What are the rivers?

A. The Missisippi runs through this state. The rivers E. of it are the Perdido, Mobille, Pascagoula and Pearl. The Ibberville is a mere bayau letting the waters of the Missisippi into Lake Ponchartrain. Red River, 1200 miles long, falls into the Missisippi in lat. 31° 5'. The rivers W. of the Missisippi are the Mexicano or Mermentas, Trinity, Colorado, and (if the state reach so far) the Bravo.

Q. What are the divisions of this state?

A. It is divided into 5 districts.

Q. What is the population?

A. In 1810 it contained 76,556 inhabitants, of whom 34,311 were whites, and 42,245 blacks.

Q. What is the government?

A. It is a republic like that of the other states of the Union.

Q. What is the religion?

A. The majority of the inhabitants are of French and Spanish extract, and are Catholics. Of the remainder, religion is scarcely predicable.

Q. What is the character of the people?

A. This part of the Union is distinguished for loose manners and morals.

Q. What is the capital?

A. New-Orleans. It is on the W. side of the island of Orleans, and the E. bank of the Missisippi, 87 miles from its mouth, and 121 below the Ibberville, in lat. 29° 57' long. 89° 58' W. It is regularly laid out, and the houses are chiefly of brick. The population in 1810, was 8001 whites, and 16,551 blacks: in all 24,552. The morals of the place are deplorably licentious. Its commerce is very great.

Q. Describe Mobile?

A. It stands on the W. side of the head of Mobile bay, 30 miles from the Gulf of Mexico, in 30° 36' N. and 88° 4' W.

OF THE MISSOURI TERRITORY.

Q. What is the situation of the Missouri Territory?

A. It lies W. of the United States Proper and N. of Louisiana state, comprising the whole country of Louisiana N. of latitude 33.

Q. What is the extent?

A. The breadth from lat 33° N. to lat. 50° is about 1200 miles. The length from the Missisippi to the Pacific is not less than 1600 miles. In lat. 33° the distance from the Missisippi to the Colorado is not more than 500 miles, and to the Bravo is about 800.

Q. What are the divisions?

A. The settled territory is divided into 5 districts; St. Charles, St. Louis, St. Genevieve, Cape Girandeau, and New Madrid. Almost the whole country however is unsettled.

Q. What is the face of the country?

A. The W. bank of the Missisippi below the Missouri, for 40 miles westward, is almost universally low and overflown in the spring. Farther W. the country rises a little and continues a prairie, covered with long rank grass, for hundreds of miles westward. N. of the Missouri it is said to be more uneven.

Q. What is the population?

A. In 1810 it was 20,895; of whom 17,277 were whites and 3,618 blacks. It contains many large tribes of Indians.

Q. What are the settlements?

A. St. Louis is a village of 200 houses, on the W. bank of the Missisippi, 14 miles below the Missouri. St. Genevieve is 73 miles S. of St. Louis, and New Madrid 254 miles.

OF SPANISH AMERICA.

Q. What territories does Spain possess in America?

A. In North America, Florida, Mexico, and Gautemala ; of the West-India islands, Cuba, and Porto Rico; in South America, New Granada, Venezuela, Peru, Chili, and Buenos Ayres.

Q. What is the religion of the Spanish provinces ?

A. The Roman Catholic.

Q. What is the government?

A. Spanish America is placed under the control of a council in Madrid, called the council of the Indies. Each province is committed to a viceroy or captain-general and a royal audience. There are 13 such audiences.

Q. Who compose the population of Spanish America ?

A. Whites, Indians and negroes, and a mixt progeny of each.

Q. What is the amount of money annually coined in Spanish America ?

A. In 1796, the amount was $38,200,000.

Q. What is the state of commerce ?

A. In the year 1788, the exports from Spanish South America to Spain amounted to 22,667,320l. sterling : and from Spain to Spanish South America, to 7,492,934l. sterling.

————

OF FLORIDA.

Q. What is the situation of Florida ?

A. It lies between 81 and 87° 35′ W. ; and between 25 and 31° N. lat. The breadth in the north is 370 miles. The length from Cape Sable to the St. Mary's, is 420. It consists of a large peninsula, and a narrow tract west of it, on the north shore of the gulf.

Q. What are the boundaries ?

A. Georgia and the Missisippi territory lie on the north ; the Atlantic east ; the Florida channel and the Gulf of Mexico south ; and the Gulf of Mexico and the Perdido, which divide it from the state of Louisiana, west.

Q. What is the face of the country ?

A. The coasts of the peninsula are flat. A chain of low hills runs through the centre from north to south. The tract north of the gulf is a flat country.

Q. What is the soil ?

A. Some parts of the peninsula are very fertile. Generally it is indifferent. The laurel, magnolia and cypress are among the productions.

Q. What are the rivers ?

A. St. John's in the peninsula, St. Mary's in the north, and the Apalachicola, and Perdido, in the northwest.

Q. What bays are there on the coast ?

R

A. Apalachy bay in the N. E. angle of the gulf, and Pensacola bay farther west.

Q. What is the population?

A. It is conjectured to be about 20,000, exclusive of the Seminoles or wandering Creeks, a numerous tribe of Indians.

Q. What are the towns?

A. St. Augustine is on the E. coast, in lat. 29° 45′, is fortified, and has about 3000 inhabitants. Pensacola, on the N. shore of the gulf, is in 87° 17′ W. and 30° 18′ north.

OF MEXICO.

Q. What is the situation of Mexico?

A. It lies between 37° 48′ and 16° 12′ north latitude, and contains 418,933 square miles.

Q. How is it bounded?

A. On the north and northeast by Louisiana; on the east by the Gulf of Mexico; on the southeast by Guatemala; and on the southwest and west by the Pacific.

Q. What are the divisions?

A. Mexico is divided into 15 provinces, viz: on the Pacific, New-California, Old California, Sonora, Guadalaxara, Valladolid, Mexico, Puebla, and Oaxaca; in the interior, New-Mexico, Durango, Zacatecas, and Guanaxuato; and, on the gulf, San Luis, Potosi, Vera Cruz, and Merida.

Q. What is the climate?

A. It is delightful. The extremes of heat and cold are never known. The rainy season lasts from the middle of June to the middle of October, and the dry season the rest of the year.

Q. What is the face of the country?

A. The coast, on each ocean, is low and level for a few miles, and then rises suddenly into a high table land; constituting the great mass of the country, and usually about 7000 feet above the level of the ocean.

Q. What is the soil?

A. It is excellent, yielding on an average 150 fold, and in the best lands 800. Maize is the customary crop. The annual produce of the whole country is estimated at about 35,000,000 bushels. Wheat, rye, barley, the banana, the juca, onions, and other vegetables, and the fruits of temperate and tropical climates, are common.

Q. What are the rivers?

A. The Bravo in the N. E. is 1800 miles long. The Colorado of California, in the N. W. runs about 1000 miles, and empties into the Gulf of California. The Gila, its tributary, runs about 600 miles. The Santiago runs about 650 miles, and falls into the Pacific S. of Acapulco.

Q. What lakes are there ?

A. Lake Chapala W. of Mexico is 90 miles long and 20 broad.

Q. What is the population ?

A. In 1793, it was 4,483,529 ; and in 1803, by calculations made from births and deaths, 5,840,000.

Q. What is the religion ?

A. The Catholic. The clergy are about 10,000 in number, and their revenues and possessions are very great.

Q. What is the government ?

A. Mexico is a viceroyalty. The viceroy governs the whole country. There are two audiences. Each province is committed to an attendant.

Q. How many languages are spoken here ?

A. More than 20 ; of which 14 have regular grammars.— The Aztec is most generally diffused.

Q. What is the capital ?

A. Mexico. It is in the valley of Mexico, in 19° 26' 9" N. ; and 99° 5' W. The streets cross at right angles, and are wide and clean. The population in 1790 was 112,926, and in 1803 was estimated at 137,000.

Q. What are the seaports ?

A. Vera Cruz on the gulf, in 19° 12' N. has 16,000 inhabitants ; and Acapulco, on the Pacific, in 16° 50! N. has 4000.

Q. What are the other towns ?
of,800; Zacatecas, with 33,000 ; and Oaxaca, with 24,000.

Q. What is the trade ?

A. The exports are gold, silver, precious stones, cochineal, cocoa, silk, and cotton. Formerly Acapulco had a valuable trade with the Philippines.

OF GUATEMALA.

Q. What is the situation of Guatemala ?

A. It is the southernmost country of N. America ; reaching from Mexico to the Isthmus. Its length is 750 miles, and the greatest breadth about 350.

Q. How is it bounded ?

A. N. W. by Mexico ; N. E. by the bay of Honduras and the Gulf of Darien ; S. E. by New-Granada ; and S. W. by the Pacific.

Q. How is it divided ?

A. Into 6 provinces : Chiapa, Vera Pas, Guatemala, Honduras, Nicaragua, and Costa-Rica.

Q. What are the productions ?

A. Chocolate, cochineal, cotton, indigo, honey, balsam; woad and logwood.

Q. What are the lakes ?

A. Nicaragua lake which is united to lake Leon. Both are about 600 miles in circuit. Their waters flow into the Gulf of Mexico.

Q. What is the face of the country ?

A. It is a high table land like Mexico. The country is very fertile.

Q. What is the population ?

A. Humboldt says it is the most populous of the Spanish provinces, but the amount is not known. The English have a settlement on the Bay of Honduras.

Q. What is the government ?

A. A captain-general and royal audience reside at Guatemala.

Q. What are the towns ?

A. Guatemala, the capital, is a large populous town in 13° 40' north, and 90° 30' west. Leon and Ciudad Real are also large towns. Chiapa is inhabited by the native Indians to the number of 20,000.

OF THE WEST-INDIES.

Q. What is the situation of the West-Indies ?

A. They are a chain of Islands stretching from Florida southeastward to the coast of Venezuela; between 9 and 28° N. lat. and between 59 and 95o W. lon.

hamas, the Greater Antilles, the Caribbees, and the Lesser Antilles.

OF THE BAHAMAS.

Q. What is the situation of the Bahamas ?

A. They stretch from S. E. to N. W. between 20 and 27° N. lat.; and between 69 and 80° W. long. The new Bahama Channel separates them on the N. E. from Florida; and the old Bahama Channel on the S. W. from Cuba and Hispaniola.

Q. What is the number of their islands ?

A. There are 16 islands that are habitable: Grand Turk, Salt Key, Caicos, Inaguas, Mayaguana, Crooked Island, Long Island, Exuma, Watling's Island, Guanahami, Elenthera, Harbor Island, New Providence, Andros, Abaco, and Bahama: and about 700 Keys or sand Islands.

Q. What is the climate ?

A. The weather is very inconstant. Hurricanes rarely occur.

Q. What is the general face of these islands ?

A. They are level masses of shells and limestone, covered

with a thin vegetable mould. The soil yields luxuriantly; but is thin and soon exhausted.

Q. What are the trees?

A. The buttonwood, palmetto, wild fig, pimento, mahogany, brazil-wood, mastic, lignumvitæ, iron-wood, bullet wood, and cabbage tree.

Q. What is the population?

A. It is estimated at 15,000.

Q. What is the government?

A. They all placed under a governor-general appointed by the British crown; and a legislature composed of a council of 12 members, and a house of representatives of 26.

Q. Which is the most important of these islands?

A. New Providence. It is 35 miles long and 27 broad. Nassau the capital of all the Bahamas is on the N. side. In 1801, this town contained 6212 inhabitants of whom 4613 were blacks. Its commerce is extensive.

Q. What is the most important product of these islands?

A. Salt. This article is derived chiefly from Turk's Island and Salt Key in the S. E. The salt is raked out of salt ponds which are here numerous.

Q. To whom do the Bahamas belong?

A. To the British.

OF THE GREATER ANTILLES.

Q. What is the situation of the Greater Antilles?

A. They are four large islands: Cuba, Hispaniola, Porto-Rico, and Jamaica; lying S. of the Bahamas, between 17° 30′ and 23° N. and between 65° 30′ and 85° W.

OF CUBA.

Q. What is the situation of Cuba?

A. It is the northwesternmost of this group, about 120 miles S. of Florida and 180 E. of False Cape in Yucatan; lying between 74 and 85° W.; and is 700 miles long and 150 broad, containing about 54,000 square miles.

Q. What is the face of the country?

A. A chain of mountains runs from E. to W. The shores are level.

Q. What are the productions?

A. Sugar is the capital article, cocoa, tobacco, coffee, ginger, long pepper, cotton, mastic, amonia, aloes, and honey.

Q. What is the population?

A. It is estimated at 350,000. The religion is the Roman Catholic. The government is in the hands of a captain general and royal audience. The regular troops are about 10,000.

Q. What are the large towns ?

A. The Havanna on the N. shore, has 11 churches, and 70,000 inhabitants. St. Jago de Cuba, in the S. E. has a population of 35,000.

OF HAYTI.

Q. What is the situation of Hayti or St. Domingo ?

A. Hayti lies 40 miles E. of Cuba, between 17° 40' and 20° N. and between 68° 30' and 74° 30' W. It is 430 miles long from E. to W. and 160 broad.

Q. What is the face of the country ?

A. The east is a plain ; the centre mountainous, and the shores level. The soil is remarkably fertile and well watered.

Q. What bays are there ?

A. The Bite of Leogane in the west ; and Samana Bay in the N. E.

Q. What is the population ?

A. In 1790, that of the western part was 534,831 ; and in 1800 was estimated at 686,000. The population of the eastern part is less numerous.

Q. To whom does the island belong ?

A. The eastern division belongs to Spain. The N. side of the W. division to Christophe, a negro, who has proclaimed himself Emperor of Hayti. The south side to Petion, a man of colour, who has the title of President. The former has 60,000 troops ; the latter 20,000.

Q. What are the towns ?

A. Cape Francois on the N. side, belonging to Christophe, has about 20,000 inhabitants. Port-au-Prince on the Bite, has about 15,000, and belongs to Petion. St. Domingo is the Spanish capital.

Q. What is the trade ?

A. Formerly the exports from this island in sugar, coffee, cotton, indigo, cocoa, molasses, and leather, amounted to about 30 millions of dollars. The present state of its commerce is not known.

OF JAMAICA.

Q. What is the situation of Jamaica ?

A. It lies 90 miles S. of Cuba and 120 W. of Hayti : between 17° 40' and 18° 30' S. and between 76° 18' and 79° 57' W. It is 170 miles long and 60 broad ; containing 6000 square miles. It is divided into 3 counties, 6 townships, and 20 parishes.

Q. What is the face of the country ?

A. The northern shore is a plain. The interior and south are mountainous. The soil is generally fertile.

Q. What is the population?

A. It is estimated at 390,000; of whom 40,000 are whites. The church of England is the established religion. Each parish has a rector. The government is committed to a governor and council of 12, appointed by the crown, and an assembly of 43, chosen by the people.

Q. What are the towns?

A. Kingston in the N. has about 30,000 inhabitants; and St. Jago in the S. about 5000.

OF PORTO RICO.

Q. What is the situation of Porto Rico?

A. It is the easternmost of the Great Antilles; lying between 65° 30' and 67° 8' W. long; and in 18° N. lat. It is 115 miles long, and 36 broad.

Q. What are the productions?

A. Sugar, cotton, rice, maize, tobacco and molasses. The soil is fertile, and the country laid into plantations.

Q. What is the population?

A. It has been estimated at 200,000. St. John the capital on the N. shore, has a fine harbour, and a population of about 30,000. Maraguand is another port in the W. of about 6000 inhabitants.

OF THE CARIBBEAN ISLANDS.

Q. What is the situation of the Caribbean Islands?

A. They stretch in a curve from Porto Rico E. and S. to the coast of Venezuela; lying between 9° 30' and 18° 45' N. lat. and between 59° and 66° W. lon.

Q. How are they divided?

A. Into Leeward Islands and Windward Islands. The former lie N. of lat. 15° and the latter S. of that latitude.

Q. Which are the Leeward Islands?

A. St. Thomas, St. John, Virgin Gorda, Tortola, St. Croix, Anguilla, St. Martin's, St. Bartholomew, Saba, Barbuda, St. Eustatius, St. Christopher, Nevis, Antigua, Montserrat, Guadaloupe, Deseada, Marigalante and Dominica.

Q. To whom do they belong?

A. St. Thomas, St. John and St. Croix to Denmark; St. Bartholomew to Sweden; St. Eustatius and Saba to Holland; Guadaloupe and Deseada to France; and the rest to England.

Q. Which are the Windward Islands?

A. Martinico, St. Lucia, St. Vincent, Barbadoes, Grenada, Tobago and Trinidad.

Q. To whom do they belong?

A. Martinico and St. Lucia to France, and the rest to England.

OF THE LESSER ANTILLES.

Q. What is the situation of the Lesser Antilles?

A. They stretch from E. to W. along the coast of Venezuela, between 63 and 70° W. longitude.

Q. Which are they?

A. Margarita, Tortuga, Ochilla, Bonair, Curracoa, and Aruba.

OF SOUTH AMERICA.

Q. What is the situation of South America?

A. It lies between 12° N. and 54° S. lat. and between 34° 30' and 81° W. long. It is 4600 miles long and 3250 broad; containing about 6,500,000 square miles.

Q. How is it bounded?

A. On the N. W. by the Isthmus of Darien; on the N. by the Caribbean Sea; on the E. the Atlantic; on the S. by the Straits of Magellan, which separate it from the Island of Terra Del Fuego; and on the W. by the Pacific.

Q. How is it divided?

A. Into the following territories: New Grenada, Venezuela, Guiana, Peru, Brazil, Chili, Buenos Ayres, and Patagonia.

OF NEW-GRENADA, OR TERRA FIRMA.

Q. What is the situation of New-Grenada?

A. It is the N. W. corner of South America; lying between 10° N. and 3° S. lat. and between 72° 30' and 82° 30" W. The river Tumbez in the S. separates it from Peru.

Q. What is its extent?

A. It is 1080 miles long, and about 280 broad from E. to W.

Q. How is it bounded?

A. N. W. by Guatemala; N. by the Caribbean Sea; E. by Venezuela; S. by Peru; and W. by the Pacific.

Q. How is it divided?

A. Into 24 provinces.

Q. What is the climate?

A. On the coast, it is hot and unhealthy; among the mountains it varies with the elevation.

Q. What are the rivers?

A. The Magdelena, the Guayaquil, and Tumbez.

Q. What are the mountains?

A. The Andes. Chimborazo the highest summit in the world is 21,440 feet in height; and Antisani 19,150.

Q. What are the productions?

A. All the tropical fruits and timber in their highest perfection.

Q. What are the minerals ?
A. Gold, silver, copper, lead and emerald.
Q. What is the religion ?
A. The Roman Catholic.
Q. What is the population ?
A. It is estimated at 2,000,000.
Q. What are the towns ?
A. Santa Fe, the capital, has a population of about 30,000 ; Quito, in the S. has about 65,000 ; Carthagena, on the N. coast, has 15,000 inhabitants, and Panama 10,000.

OF VENEZUELA.

Q. What is the situation of Venezuela ?
A. It lies E. of New-Grenada, has the Caribbean and Atlantic N.; the river Essequibo, which separates it from Guiana, E. ; and New-Grenada south.
Q. What is the extent ?
A. About 1000 miles on the coast, and from 300 to 600 in the interior.
Q. What is the climate ?
A. The year is divided into the rainy and dry seasons. The former lasts from April to November.
Q. What is the face of the country ?
A. The northern part is mountainous. On the Oronoco and E. of it, the country is a mere level.
Q. What is the soil ? ── ── ── ──── ── ─ sugar, and tobacco.
Q. What are the rivers ?
A. The Oronoko and its branches.
Q. What are the lakes ?
A. Lake Maracayho in the N. W. 150 miles long and 90 broad, and lake Valencia, 40 miles by 12.
Q. What is the population ?
A. About 728,000. The religion is the Catholic. The government is committed to a captain-general, and royal audience.
Q. What is the revenue ?
A. It usually amounts to about $1,350,000. A regular force of about 13,000 men is kept up.
Q. What is the character of the people ?
A. They are distributed into Whites, Indians and Negroes. The inhabitants are exceedingly licentious in their morals.
Q. What are the towns ?
A. Caraccas, the capital, before its destruction by the great earthquake of 1812, had about 42,000 inhabitants. Cumana,

farther east, has 24,000 ; and Maracaibo, in the west, 22,000.

Q. What is the state of its commerce ?

A. The exports and imports amount each to about 4 millions of dollars.

OF GUIANA.

Q. What is the situation of Guiana ?

A. It lies between the Essequibo on the west and the Arowary on the east ; and bounds south on Portuguese Guiana or the northern province of Brazil. Its length along the coast is about 700 miles ; and it reaches into the interior from 200 to 300 miles.

Q. How is it divided ?

A. Into Demerara, Berbice, Surinam and Cayenne.

Q. What is the climate ?

A. It is hot and unhealthy. The country is a mere flat. The soil is remarkably fertile. Sugar, coffee, cotton, cocoa, indigo, maize, and Cayenne pepper are cultivated.

Q. What are the rivers ?

A. The Essequibo, Maroni, Surinam, Demerara, Berbice, and Oyapoc.

Q. What is the population ?

A. Probably about 300,000, principally slaves. There are also numerous Indians. This country is a colony belonging to England.

A. Paramaribo has a population of 20,000 ; Stabroek of 8000 ; and Cayenne is about as large. Cayenne, the eastern division of this country, has been lately ceded to France.

OF PERU.

Q. What is the situation of Peru ?

A. It reaches from the river Tumbez in 3° 25' S. to Port De Loa, in 21° 30' S. In the N. it extends eastward to the Tuyo a branch of the Amazon ; and in the S. to the Ytends.

Q. What is its extent ?

A. It is 1260 miles long from N. to S. and about 400 miles wide.

Q. How is it bounded ?

A. On the N. by New-Grenada ; on the E. by Brazil and Buenos Ayres ; on the S. by Buenos Ayres, and on the W. by the Pacific.

Q. What are the divisions ?

A. It is divided into 8 intendencies.

Q. What is the climate ?

A. On and near the coast it is generally unhealthy.

Q. What is the face of the country ?

A. The coast is a plain for a width of 60 miles, bounded by the western chain of the Andes.

Q. What are the rivers ?

A. The head waters of the Amazon and its branches.

Q. What are the productions ?

A. All those of a tropical climate.

Q. What are the minerals ?

A. Peru contains 69 mines of gold, 784 of silver, 4 of Mercury, 4 of copper, and 12 of lead that are wrought. The gold and silver mines in 10 years, from 1780 to 1789 inclusive, yielded metals to the amount of $34,437,979.

Q. What is the religion ?

A. The Catholic. Peru contains one archbishopric and 5 bishoprics.

Q. What is the government ?

A. It is vested in a viceroy, and a royal audience.

Q. What is the population ?

A. It is 1,079,132.

Q. What are the towns ?

A. Lima, the capital, 8 miles from the coast, contains 52,-627 inhabitants. Cusco has 26,000 ; and Arequipa 30,000.

Q. What is the revenue ?

A. About 4,500,000 dollars.

Q. What is the commerce ?

A. Peru exports the precious metals, brandies, wines, maize, rice, flour, cotton, oil, pimento, sugar, and coarse woollens.— The trade is carried on with Spain and the Spanish colonies. The exports amount annually to about 10 millions of dollars; and the imports to ten and a half millions.

OF BRAZIL.

Q. What is the situation of Brazil ?

A. Brazil reaches on the Atlantic, from the mouth of the Arowary in 1° 30' N. to the mouth of the Chuy in 33° 40' S. The length is 2450 miles. The breadth in the N. is about 2000, but in the S. is narrow. According to the line of demarcation between Brazil and the Spanish possessions, it occupies at least one third of S. America or upwards of 2 millions square miles.

Q. What are the boundaries ?

A. On the N. Venezuela, Guiana and the Atlantic ; on the E. and S. E. the Atlantic ; and on the S. W. and W. Buenos Ayres, Peru, and New-Grenada.

Q. What are the divisions ?

A. Brazil is divided into 21 provinces.

Q. What is the soil ?

A. It is fertile. Maize, wheat, rice, sugar, coffee, cocoa, indigo, pepper and tobacco, are the productions.

Q. What is the climate?

A. The seasons are the rainy and the dry. The climate is healthy on the coast, and the heats not distressing.

Q. What are the rivers?

A. The Amazon and its branches, the Maderia, Topayos, and Zingu. The St. Francis and the Tocantin are on the coast; the Parana and Urugnay are branches of the Paraguay.

Q. What are the trees?

A. All the fruit trees and timber trees of tropical climates.

Q. What are the animals?

A. The wild boar, wild cat, porcupine, deer, musk-deer, hare, otter, opossum and armadillo.

Q. What are the minerals?

A. Gold, silver, and diamonds. The gold and silver mines yield about 5 millions sterling annually.

Q. What is the government?

A. The royal family of Portugal removed to Brazil in 1807. It is thought they will soon return.

Q. What is the population?

A. It has been estimated at 2,500,000, exclusive of the wild Indians.

Q. What is the state of literature?

A. Heretofore many of the Brazilians have been educated in Portugal.

Q. What is the capital?

A. Rio Janeiro, in 22° 54' S. The commerce is flourishing and the population 150,000.

Q. Describe St. Salvador or Bahia.

A. It stands on the bay of All Saints, and has about 120,000 inhabitants. Pernambuco has 40,000.

Q. What is the state of Brazilian commerce?

A. Since 1807, it has flourished. The exports are sugar, cotton, cattle, hides, rum, coffee, rice, tobacco, indigo, and brazil-wood.

OF BUENOS AYRES.

Q. How is Buenos Ayres bounded?

A. On the N. by Peru and Brazil; E. by Brazil and the Atlantic; S. by Patagonia; and W. by Chili, the Pacific and Peru.

Q. How is it divided?

A. Into 9 intendencies.

Q. What is the climate?

A. It is generally temperate and healthy.

Q. What is the face of the country?

A. Generally the country is level. The soil is said to be fertile.

Q. What are the rivers?

A. The La Plata and its branches.

Q. What are the lakes?

A. Xarayes, Titicaca, and Iberi.

Q. What are the mountains?

A. In the west the Andes. In lat. 19? south, the Chiquitos runs from the Andes northeast.

Q. What are the vegetable productions?

A. Most of the fruits, vegetables and trees, of both tropical and temperate climates.

Q. What are the animals?

A. The ferocious animals resemble those of the countries farther north. Unnumbered millions of wild cattle and horses roam over the immense plains of this country.

Q. What are the minerals?

A. This province contains 30 mines of gold, 27 of silver, 7 of copper, 2 of tin, and 7 of lead. The silver mine of Potoai is the richest that has ever been wrought. It was discovered accidentally in 1545 by an Indian named Hualpa. In the first 93 years, it had yielded $395,619,000. In 1796 it yielded $3,283,022.

Q. What is the religion?

A. The Catholic. There is one archbishop and 5 bishops.

Q. What is the government?

A. The viceroy resides at Buenos Ayres. There are two audiences, that of Buenos Ayres, and that of La Plata.

Q. What is the population?

A. It is estimated at about 1,250,000; of whom about 1,000,000 are whites.

Q. What is the revenue?

A. It amounts to $4,400,000.

Q. What are the manners?

A. Here, as in all the colonies of South America, the morals of the people are deplorably licentious.

Q. What is the capital?

A. Buenos Ayres, in lat. 34° 37' S. on the S. bank of the La Plata. The houses are of brick, and about 6000 in number. The population is 70,000. Monte Video on the N. shore has a population of 30,000.

Q. Describe the other towns?

A. Potosi in lat. 20° 26' S. and 60 miles W. of the La Plata, is a town of uncommon splendor, and magnificence.— Its population is about 100,000. La Plata and La Pas, are farther north.

S

Q. What is the state of commerce ?

A. The exports in 1789 amounted to $7,500,000 ; of wh ich more than 5 millions consisted of gold and silver. The oth er articles were hides, tallow, beef, horns, wool and copper.— An important overland commerce is carried on between, Buenos Ayres and Lima, through Cordova, Tucuman, Potosi, La Pas and Cusco. The whole distance is 2822 miles ; of which 1566 are passed on mules.

OF CHILI.

Q. What is the situation of Chili ?

A. It is on the western coast, between 25° and 41.° 43′ S. latitude. It is 1150 miles long, and from 140 to 250 broad. It reaches to the eastern chain of the Andes.

Q. How is it bounded ?

A. On the N. the desert of Atacama, an extensive province of Buenos Ayres, separates it from Peru ; on the E. by Buenos Ayres ; on the S. by Patagonia ; and on the W. by the Pacific.

Q. How is it divided ?

A. Into 15 provinces. The southern part of the country beyond 36° 44′ S. belongs to the Araucanians, a powerful nation of Indians, constituting a well regulated aristocracy.

Q. What is the climate ?

A. It is very healthy. The seasons are two: the rainy and the dry.

Q. What is the face of the country.

A. Except on the coast, it is chiefly mountainous. The soil is remarkably fertile.

Q. What are the rivers ?

A. The Maule, Biobio, and Tolten.

Q. What are the mountains ?

A. The Andes occupy a breadth of 140 miles. There are 14 volcanoes. Earthquakes are common.

Q. What are the productions ?

A. Chili is remarkably rich in the number both of its plants and animals.

Q. What are the minerals ?

A. Gold, silver, copper, iron, lead, quicksilver, antimony, sulphur, naphtha, jet, sal ammoniac, salt-petre, and various precious stones. The quantity of gold dug annually is worth about $4,000,000 : that of copper amounts to 1,500,000 quintals.

Q. What is the religion ?

A. The Chilians are Catholics. The Araucanians are heathens.

Q. What is the government?

A. A captain-general and royal audience reside at St. Jago. That of the Araucanians is an aristocracy.

Q. What is the population?

A. In 1778 it consisted of 80,000 whites and 240,000 negroes, but has since greatly increased. The Araucanians are
said to very numerous.

Q. What is the military strength?

A. In 1796 it was 15,856 militia, and several companies of
regular troops.

Q. What is the character of the people?

A. The Chilians resemble the other Spanish colonists. The
Araucanians are a brave, hardy race, whom the Spaniards have
never been able to subdue.

Q. What is the capital?

A. St. Jago, in 33° 31' S. 90 miles from the coast, has a university, and a population of 46,000. Valdivia is nearly as
large. Valparaiso, in 33° 3' S. on the coast, has 13,000 inhabitants.

Q. What is the state of commerce?

A. Chili carries on considerable trade with the other colonies and with Spain. About $1,900,000 in silver and gold is
annually exported.

OF PATAGONIA.

Q. What is the situation of Patagonia?

A. It is at the southern end of America, reaching north-
ward on the Atlantic to Cape Labos in 37° 30' S.; and on the
Pacific to Fort Maullin in 41° 43' S. Its southern extremity
Cape Isidro, is in lat. 54° south.

Q. What is the extent?

A. It is about 1300 miles long from N. to S. and its average breadth 450.

Q. How is it bounded?

A. On the N. W. by Chili; on the N. E. by Buenos Ayres;
on the E. by the Atlantic; on the S. by the Straits of Magellan;
and on the W. by the Pacific.

Q. What are the rivers?

A. The Hueyque, the Colorado and the Negro, all emptying into the Atlantic. The last has a course of 800 miles.

Q. What is the face of the country?

A. The Andes run parallel with the western coast. The
eastern coast is level.

Q. What are the native tribes?

A. The Indians of the Andes and western coast are called
Moluches, and are divided into three powerful tribes. They

are numerous and warlike. The Indians inhabiting all the country E. of the Andes are called Puelches, and are divided into 4 tribes : viz. the Taluhets, in the N. the Diuihets S. W. of them; the Chechehets, farther S. and the Tehuelhets or Patagons, in the S. These last are a remarkably athletic race ; and, for Indians, of a fair complexion.

Q. What islands are there in these seas ?

A. Terra del Fuego, Diego, Statenland, Falkland islands, and Isle of Georgia and in the Pacific, Madre de Dios, and St. Francis.

Q. Describe Terra del Fuego ?

A. It is a large island, separated from the continent by the Straits of Magellan, about 500 miles long from E. to W. and upwards of 200 broad. The country is dreary and inhospitable. The inhabitants are of a fair complexion, middle stature, uncivilized and ferocious. The Straits of Magellan are 350 miles long, and from half a league to 8 or 10 leagues broad.

Q. Where are Diego and Statenland ?

A. Diego, about 40 miles by 20, is S. of Terra del Fuego, and separated by a narrow Strait. Its southern cape is called Cape Horn. Statenland, of about the same size, is separated from the E. point of Terra del Fuego by the narrow Straits of Le Maire.

Q. Where are the Falkland Islands ?

A. They are two large islands in lat. 52° S. and long. 60° W. The English have a colony at Port Egmont. They are rude and inhospitable, and of no value except as a watering place.

Q. Where is the Isle of Georgia ?

A. In lat. 54° S. and long. 37° W. and 360 leagues E. of Terra del Fuego. It is a well known resort in sealing voyages.

Q. Where are Madre de Dios and St. Francis ?

A. They are large islands close to the W. coast of Patagonia.

ADVANTAGES AND IMPROVEMENTS

OF

GEOGRAPHY.

——◦◦——

Q. What are the advantages attending the study of Geography?

A. Geography is a science highly entertaining and important. It opens to our view much of the wisdom and goodness of the Creator, in making various and bountiful provision for his creatures, in appointing them their residence in different parts of the globe, and suiting their capacities to their respective circumstances. It teaches us that mankind are one great family, though different in their complexions, situations and habits. It promotes social intercourse and mutual happiness.

Q. Is Geography a science capable of improvement?

A. It has been greatly improved, especially of late years, by the discoveries and observations of voyagers and travellers, and is capable of much greater improvement by the same means.

Q. What ideas had the ancients of Geography?

A. The Phœnicians and Carthagenians knew more of it than any other nation, but they kept their knowledge concealed, through mercantile jealousy. The Greeks and Romans knew less, but were more communicative. Several of their philosophers wrote on the subject, and their works are still preserved.

Q. To how great a part of the globe did their knowledge extend?

A. They were well acquainted with the temperate regions of Europe and Asia, and the northern parts of Africa, and they had some knowledge of India.

Q. What false opinions had they of the globe?

A. They imagined the torrid and the frigid zones to be uninhabitable, and that it was impossible to pass from one of the temperate zones to the other.

Q. What was the state of navigation among them?

A. Their vessels were small and without decks;—they were fit only for coasting voyages in temperate climates and favourable seasons, and were generally laid up at the approach of winter. They never ventured far out of sight of land, because in cloudy weather they had nothing by which they could direct their course, though in clear weather they could steer by the sun or stars.

Q. By what means was navigation improved?

A. By the discovery of the magnetic needle, or the power of the magnet in pointing to the poles of the earth.

Q. When was this discovery made?

A. It was first known in Europe in the 13th century; but the Chinese claim the honor of a prior discovery.

Q. What were the consequences of this discovery?

A. It gave the mariner courage to venture farther into the ocean, and make longer voyages, by which means new islands were discovered.

Q. What was the boldest adventure of this kind?

A. The discovery of America by Columbus in the fifteenth century.

Q. When was the first circumnavigation of the globe performed?

A. In the sixteenth century, about thirty years after the discovery of America. It was undertaken by Ferdinanda Magellan, who died on the passage, but the ship returned to Europe.

Q. Who was the first English circumnavigator?

A. Sir Francis Drake, in the reign of Queen Elizabeth.

Q. Who was the most remarkable of all the circumnavigators?

A. Capt. James Cook, who, after having passed round the globe twice and discovered the eternal boundaries of navigation towards the north and south poles, was killed when on his third voyage, by the natives of Owhyhee, in 1779.

Q. Have circumnavigatory voyages been more frequent since his death?

A. Yes, they are much more frequent, and are grown familiar to seamen.

Q. For what reasons?

A. Partly by reason of the lucrative trade between the northwest coast of America and China, which his last voyage opened, and partly because methods were successfully practised by him to preserve the lives and health of seamen, which were not in use before.

FINIS.

For Sale at Websters and Skinners' Bookstore, Albany,

The Youth's Companion,

OR AN

HISTORICAL DICTIONARY;

Consisting of Articles selected chiefly from Natural and Civil History, Geography, Astronomy, Zoology, Botany and Mineralogy; arranged in Alphabetical order. By EZRA SAMPSON, author of the selection, entitled "Beauties of the Bible."— From the Hudson edition, with sundry emendations, retrenchments, and enlargements. *Price* $1.

Reccommendations of the Work.

The Rev. DAVID PORTER, D. D. of Catskill, has favored us with his opinion, as follows :

" I have examined the Historical Dictionary with some care, and think it contains as rich a compendium of facts, concisely and elegantly expressed, as any work of its size within the compass of my knowledge. It is a book, in my opinion, admirably adapted to youth ; and such is its real merit that I am convinced that it needs only to be known to entitle it to the universal patronage of schools and academies throughout our country.

" The book contains an epitome of science, chaste, moral and beautifully descriptive ; and it cannot fail both to entertain and instruct.   DAVID PORTER."

The Rev. JOHN CHESTER, of Hudson, transmits to us the following remarks :

" The 'Historical Dictionary,' in the opinion of the subscriber, is a most important and valuable acquisition to the schools of our country. Its learned and judicious author has manifested uncommon discrimination and ability in his work. The Dictionary is extremely interesting and instructive to the scholar, who, as he learns to read, stores his mind with facts which are always useful. It is a kind of Text Book, the usefulness of which outlives the period of pupilage, and may be retained with advantage among the number of those works which will always amuse and instruct the person of mature age. It is, in my opinion, one of the best school books with which I am acquainted, and has a fair claim to esteem and patronage.   JOHN CHESTER."

Mr. ASHBEL STRONG, well known for many years as an instructor in several academies in this state, and who has had the best opportunity of becoming acquainted with the merits of this book, has favored us with his remarks :

" Sampson's Historical Dictionary is, in my opinion, one of the best school books ever published. It contains in the compass of a

few hundred pages a great variety of important historical, geographical and philosophical facts, ranged in alphabetical order, and expressed in a neat, concise and perspicuous manner. The book is well adapted to the capacities of youth, and extremely well suited to engage their attention. I have kept it in constant use among my pupils ever since its first publication, and think it needs only to be generally known to gain the fullest credit and currency in our academies and schools.
ASHBEL STRONG."

The following remarks on the Historical Dictionary, were made by the learned SAMUEL WILLIAMS, L. L. D. author of the History of Vermont, in a letter to a friend.—" I thank you cordially for the *Historical Dictionary*, and must request you to tender my thanks and best regards to its author. The work is so well adapted, although on a novel plan, that I feel myself bound to acknowledge how much I am indebted for the acquisition. Already have my sons with their classes gone eagerly through it two or three times. I shall take a great deal of pleasure in introducing it among my friends, and do most devoutly hope it may become extensively known. As a little compend of useful knowledge in Natural History, I regard it as the best work of the size that I have ever seen in our language. The references to authorities from which this valuable miniature is drawn will be found very serviceable.

The Rev. TIMOTHY CLOWES, minister of the episcopal church in the city of Albany, has politely furnished us with the following recommendation:
Albany, May 24, 1813.

Messrs. WEBSTERS & SKINNERS,
At your request I have examined Mr. Sampson's Historical Dictionary, and have no hesitation in stating it as my opinion, that the plan and execution of the work are alike excellent.— Compilations of this kind are of more use than is generally imagined.—The young and the ignorant need them ; the better informed have frequent occasion to be reminded of what they formerly learned. Much is contained in this book which every child ought to know, and with which he has few opportunities of being acquainted in the course of a common school education. What is here comprised will have a beneficial tendency to excite curiosity in youth, and direct their attention to works of more established credit and greater pretensions. Were it to be introduced into schools as a class book, it would advance the pupils in the art of reading as rapidly as any other, while at the same time it would impart to their minds a store of useful and interesting knowledge.
-Yours, TIMOTHY CLOWES.

Select Lives of Plutarch, containing the most illustrious Characters of Antiquity, abridged for the use of Schools—by William Mavor, Esq. *Price* $1,25.
Lemprier's Classical Dictionary.
Melmoth's Pliny—Ashley's Xenophen.
Middleton's Cicero, and most other classical school books.

corner of State and Pearl-Streets,

\ (By the gross, dozen or single)

THE EASY INSTRUCTOR,

Or, A NEW METHOD OF TEACHING

SACRED HARMONY;

Containing the Rudiments of Music on an improved Plan, wherein the naming and timing the Notes are familiarized to the weakest capacity.—With a choice Collection of Psalm Tunes and Anthems from the most celebrated Authors, with a Number composed in Europe and America, entirely new; suited to all the Metres sung in the different Churches in the United States.

Published for the Use of Singing Societies in general, but more particularly for those who have not the advantage of an Instructor. By WILLIAM LITTLE and WILLIAM SMITH.

ADVERTISEMENT.—As the Authors are well aware, that whatever has the appearance of novelty is, from this very circumstance, in danger of meeting with an unfavorable reception; they request nothing more than an impartial examination of the method proposed, being willing to submit the merit of the performance to the determination of the candid and judicious. As the introduction of the four singing syllables, by characters, shewing, at sight the names of the notes, may perhaps be considered as subjecting those who are taught in this manner to difficulty in understanding other books, without this assistance; the authors would just observe, that if pupils are made acquainted with the principles here laid down, the objection will be found, by experience, more specious than solid.—To this it might be added, that in the old way, there are not less than seven different ways of applying the four singing syllables to the lines and spaces, which is attended with great difficulty: But this difficulty is entirely removed, upon the present plan; and we know of no objection to this plan, unless that it is not in use; which objection is no objection at all, or at least, cannot be decisive, as this would give currency to the entire rejection and exclusion of all improvements whatever. And as the novelty of a singing book rendered so easy, from its improvements, that any person of a tolerable voice might actually learn the art of psalmody without an instructor, if they could but obtain the sounds of the eight notes, which has led its advocates to request a publication of the same. We have, therefore, the pleasure to inform the public, that since subscriptions have been in circulation, for this book, we have been honored with upwards of three thousand subscribers: In consequence of which, we flatter ourselves, that this book will meet with a kind reception.

WILLIAM LITTLE,
WILLIAM SMITH.

Philadelphia, August 15th, 1798.

For sale as above, Writing and Letter Paper, Writing and Cyphering Books, Copy Slips, Lead and Slate Pencils, Slates, Quills, Ink-powder, Ink-Stands, Penknives, Pocket-Books, &c. &c.

THE CLERK's MAGAZINE,

Containing the most Useful and Necessary Forms of Writings, which commonly occur between Man and Man, under the names of Acquittances, Assignments, Agreements, Awards, Bargains, Bills, Bonds, Conveyances, Covenants, Deeds, Declarations, Exchanges, Gifts and Grants, Indentures, Leases, Letters of Attorney, Livery and Seisin, Mortgages, Notes, Petitions, Pleas, Receipts, Releases, Sales, Surrenders, Wills, Writs, &c. and other Instruments, calculated for the use of the Citizens of the United States—Also, various Forms of Indictments and Inquisitions. To which are added, the Constitution of the United States, and of the State of New-York, with amendments to each ; an Act of Congress prescribing the mode in which the Public Acts, Records and Judicial Proceedings of each State shall be authenticated, so as to take effect in every State ; an Act respecting the Election of a President and Vice-President of the United States ; an Act respecting the Money of Account of the State of New-York—Together, with Schedules of the whole Number of Inhabitants in each of the United States, in the years 1790, 1800 and 1810 ; and in the several Counties in the State of New-York, in the years 1771, 1786, 1790, 1800 and 1810. To which is also added, Forms of Proceedings under the Insolvent Law—the Poor Law, and the Law relative to Bastardy.

The Life of George Washington ;

With curious Anecdotes, equally honorable to himself and exemplary to his young countrymen.

A life how useful to his country led !
How lov'd, while living !—how rever'd, now dead !
Lisp ! lisp ! his name, ye children yet unborn !
And with like deeds your own great names adorn.

Tenth Edition—greatly improved. Embellished with eight engravings. By M. L. WEEMS, formerly rector of Mount Vernon Parish.

Bibles from one to 20 dollars ; Testaments ; Common Prayer Books ; Heidlebergh, Hellenbrook, and Alberthoma Catechisms ; Shorter, Episcopal, and Roman Catholic Catechisms ; Dutch Church Psalms ; David's Psalms ; Watts and Dwight's Psalms and Hymns ; Jenk's Devotion ; Henry on Prayer ; Gospel Sonnets ; Beauties of the Bible ; Bible Stories ; Cases of Conscience ; Dickinson's Five Points ; Boston's four fold State ; Confession of Faith of the Presbyterian Church ; Holy War ; Pilgrim's Progress ; Olney Hymns—Goldsmith's Rome ; do. Greece ; do. England ; Carver's Travels ; Boyle's Voyages ; Æsop's Fables ; Cooper's History of North America, 8s. several Books on Cookery, from 3s. to 24s. Latin, Greek and English Grammars ; Dictionaries and Arithmetics of various kinds ; Steuben's Exercise ; Stevens' Exercise for the Artillery ; Van Horne's Instructions for the Cavalry ; Lord's Military Catechism ; Revised and Session Laws of New-York ; New-York Justice ; Town and County Officer ; Blackstone's Commentaries ; Militia Act ; Ten Pound Act ; Road Act and Fee Bill.

www.ingramcontent.com/pod-product-compliance
Lightning Source LLC
LaVergne TN
LVHW050151060326
832904LV00003B/115